Starting Strong

EARLY CHILDHOOD EDUCATION AND CARE

OECD

ORGANISATION FOR ECONOMIC CO-OPERATION AND DEVELOPMENT

ORGANISATION FOR ECONOMIC CO-OPERATION AND DEVELOPMENT

Pursuant to Article 1 of the Convention signed in Paris on 14th December 1960, and which came into force on 30th September 1961, the Organisation for Economic Co-operation and Development (OECD) shall promote policies designed:

- to achieve the highest sustainable economic growth and employment and a rising standard of living in Member countries, while maintaining financial stability, and thus to contribute to the development of the world economy;

- to contribute to sound economic expansion in Member as well as non-member countries in the process of economic development; and

- to contribute to the expansion of world trade on a multilateral, non-discriminatory basis in accordance with international obligations.

The original Member countries of the OECD are Austria, Belgium, Canada, Denmark, France, Germany, Greece, Iceland, Ireland, Italy, Luxembourg, the Netherlands, Norway, Portugal, Spain, Sweden, Switzerland, Turkey, the United Kingdom and the United States. The following countries became Members subsequently through accession at the dates indicated hereafter: Japan (28th April 1964), Finland (28th January 1969), Australia (7th June 1971), New Zealand (29th May 1973), Mexico (18th May 1994), the Czech Republic (21st December 1995), Hungary (7th May 1996), Poland (22nd November 1996), Korea (12th December 1996) and the Slovak Republic (14th December 2000). The Commission of the European Communities takes part in the work of the OECD (Article 13 of the OECD Convention).

Publié en français sous le titre :
PETITE ENFANCE, GRANDS DÉFIS
Éducation et structures d'accueil

Foreword

In 1998, OECD's Education Committee launched a *Thematic Review of Early Childhood Education and Care Policy*, with the goal of providing cross-national information and analysis to improve policy making in early childhood education and care in all OECD countries. Twelve countries volunteered to participate in the project: Australia, Belgium (Flemish and French Communities), the Czech Republic, Denmark, Finland, Italy, the Netherlands, Norway, Portugal, Sweden, the United Kingdom, and the United States. The main impetus for the project was the 1996 Education Ministerial meeting on *Making Lifelong Learning a Reality for All*. In their communiqué, the Ministers assigned a high priority to the aim of improving access to, and quality of, early childhood education in partnership with families. It was significant that the Ministers recognised the importance of strengthening the foundations of lifelong learning starting in the early childhood years, for it paved the way for this ground-breaking project. This is the most extensive cross-national study of early childhood education and care conducted within the Organisation. The focus on early childhood as a policy priority was reinforced at the 2001 Educational Ministerial meeting on *Investing in Competencies for All*.

The Thematic Review has taken a broad and holistic approach to studying children's early development and learning. Within a lifelong learning framework, the study has been concerned with all educational and care arrangements for children under compulsory school age, regardless of setting, funding, opening hours, or programme content. In addition, the review has examined links with family support, health, employment, and social integration policy domains. Recognising the growing consensus in the field, the review has treated care and education as inseparable and necessary parts of quality provision. The use of the term "early childhood education and care" supports this integrated and coherent approach to the field. Over the past two years, the project has documented the range of policy approaches to early childhood education and care, analysed major policy issues and concerns, proposed feasible policy suggestions suited to different contexts, and highlighted particularly innovative policies and practices. In addition, it has identified the types of data and instruments needed to support policy making and development. These cross-national analyses have informed decision makers of the various policy options for improving quality and access to early childhood education and care.

The review has produced several outputs in addition to this comparative volume. Guided by a common framework, each of the participating countries produced a national Background Report which provides an overview of the country context, early childhood policy and provision, and key policy concerns. After studying the Background Report, a team of OECD Secretariat members and international experts conducted a country visit to meet with major stakeholder groups and to observe a range of early childhood provision. The team visits formed the basis of Country Notes summarising the reviewers' impressions and policy suggestions. Both sets of reports have been published on the OECD Internet site and have contributed to national and international policy discussions. This comparative report draws on the Background Reports, Country Notes, as well as commissioned papers, and other materials collected during review visits. It provides an analysis of the major trends and policy issues in the 12 countries participating in the project, and suggests policy recommendations that can be adapted to different country contexts.

This report represents the final product of the Thematic Review and the culmination of more than three years of work. Throughout the review process, many individuals have dedicated their time and energy toward making this project a success. This work would not have been possible without the ongoing commitment and support of the OECD Education Committee, and in particular the governments of the 12 participating countries, who made the national reviews and overall comparative study a reality. The organisation of the review team visits, as well as the preparation of the Background Reports, were made possible by National Co-ordinators and Steering Committees in each of the participating countries. The National Co-ordinators also helped guide the project, contributing their expertise and enthusiasm throughout the process. The high calibre of experts involved in the review teams must be acknowledged as a vital element in the study's success. The Secretariat would like to recognise, in particular, the Rapporteurs for their contributions to the preparation of the Country Notes. The Secretariat also would like to thank the many government officials and early childhood experts who took the time to provide feedback on earlier drafts of this report. While these individuals are not mentioned by name in the report, their assistance is greatly appreciated.

Within the OECD Secretariat, Michelle Neuman and John Bennett were responsible for the study and the preparation of the comparative report. The authors would like to dedicate this report to those who work with and for children on a daily basis. It is hoped that this study will strengthen their efforts on behalf of the world's youngest citizens. The project was carried out by the Education and Training Division under the supervision of Abrar Hasan. Administrative support for the project was provided by Deborah Fernandez and Sabrina Leonarduzzi. The report is published under the responsibility of the Secretary-General of the OECD.

Table of Contents

Executive Summary

1. Introduction

Early childhood education and care has experienced a surge of policy attention in OECD countries over the past decade. Policy makers have recognised that equitable access to quality early childhood education and care can strengthen the foundations of lifelong learning for all children and support the broad educational and social needs of families. There is a need to strengthen knowledge of the range of approaches adopted by different countries, along with the successes and challenges encountered. Recognising that this cross-national information and analysis can contribute to the improvement of policy development, the OECD Education Committee launched the Thematic Review of Early Childhood Education and Care Policy in 1998.

Twelve countries volunteered to participate in the review: Australia, Belgium (Flemish and French Communities), the Czech Republic, Denmark, Finland, Italy, the Netherlands, Norway, Portugal, Sweden, the United Kingdom and the United States. The review has taken a broad and holistic approach that considers how policies, services, families, and communities can support young children's early development and learning. The term *early childhood education and care* (ECEC) includes all arrangements providing care and education for children under compulsory school age, regardless of setting, funding, opening hours, or programme content. The methodology of the study has consisted of four elements: 1) preparation by participating countries of the background report; 2) review team visits to participating countries; 3) preparation of the country note; and 4) preparation of the comparative report.

2. Contextual issues shaping ECEC policy

The first part of this chapter reviews the main contextual trends and developments that have shaped ECEC policy and provision. The second part of the chapter explores how these contextual issues have shaped different views of early childhood, the roles of families, and the purposes of ECEC, and in turn, how these views have shaped policy and practice.

2.1. *Demographic, economic, and social trends*

- Ageing populations, declining fertility rates, and a greater proportion of children living in lone-parent families are part of the changing demographic landscape. Countries with the highest female employment rates are those with higher competed fertility rates, which suggests that female employment and childrearing are complementary activities.

- The sharp rise in dual-earner households, spurred by increased female employment, makes ECEC and parental leave policies more important for the well-being of families. Women are more likely than men to work in non-standard employment which carries lower economic and social status.

– Paid and job protected maternity and family leave policies are widely accepted in almost all participating countries as an essential strategy to help working parents reconcile work and family life and to promote gender equity. The length, flexibility, level of payment and take-up by men and women vary across countries.

– While taxes and transfers can help redistribute income to families with young children, in a few countries more than 20% of children still live in relative poverty. Income support, measures to improve parent employability and targeted early interventions may improve children's life-course chances and promote social cohesion.

2.2. Recognising diverse views of children and the purposes of ECEC

– The reasons for investing in ECEC policy and provision are embedded in cultural and social beliefs about young children, the roles of families and government, and the purposes of ECEC in within and across countries.

– In many countries, the education and care of young children is shifting from the private to the public domain, with much attention to the complementary roles of families and ECEC institutions in young children's early development and learning.

– Many countries are seeking to balance views of childhood in the "here and now" with views of childhood as an investment with the future adult in mind. These diverse views have important implications for the organisation of policy and provision in different countries.

3. Main policy developments and issues

Drawing on the background reports, country notes, and other materials collected during the review process, this chapter explores seven current cross-national policy trends: 1) expanding provision toward universal access; 2) raising the quality of provision; 3) promoting coherence and co-ordination of policy and services; 4) exploring strategies to ensure adequate investment in the system; 5) improving staff training and work conditions; 6) developing appropriate pedagogical frameworks for young children; and 7) engaging parents, families and communities.

3.1. Expanding provision toward universal access

– The age at which children typically make the transition to primary education ranges from 4 to 7. School starting age influences the duration and nature of children's ECEC experiences.

– In several countries, access to ECEC is a statutory right from age 3 (or even younger). The trend in all countries is toward full coverage of the 3- to 6-year-old age group, aiming to give all children at least two years of free publicly-funded provision before beginning compulsory schooling.

– Out-of-school provision for children of working parents has not been a policy priority in most countries in the review. Yet, demand is high, which suggests the need for attention to the concept, organisation, funding, and staffing of this form of provision.

– Policy for the under 3s is closely linked with the nature of available parental leave arrangements and social views about caring. While there have been government efforts toward expanding provision and increasing the educational focus, there is still differential access and quality for this age group.

– Countries are trying to develop a) more flexible and diverse arrangements while addressing the regional and local variation in access and b) strategies to include children in need of special support (i.e., children from low-income families, children with special educational needs, children from ethnic, cultural, and linguistic minorities).

3.2. Raising the quality of provision

–   Definitions of quality differ considerably among stakeholder groups and across countries. Although national quality guidelines are necessary, they need to be broad enough to allow individual settings to respond to the developmental needs and learning capacities of children.

–   Many common elements in definitions of quality exist, especially for provision for children from the age of 3. Most countries focus on similar structural aspects of quality (*e.g.*, staff-child ratios, group size, facility conditions, staff training), which tend to be weaker for infant/toddler provision.

–   To measure quality, some countries use standardised observation scales and child assessment measures. Other countries favour co-constructing the programme aims and objectives at local level, engaging a range of stakeholders in the process.

–   The responsibility for quality assurance tends to be shared by external inspectors, pedagogical advisors, staff, and parents (and occasionally children). There is a trend toward externally-validated self-evaluation to promote ongoing reflection and quality improvement.

–   Major quality concerns that emerged during the review include: lack of coherence and co-ordination of ECEC policy and provision; the low status and training of staff in the social welfare sector; the lower standards of provision for children under 3; and the tendency for children from low-income families to receive inferior services.

–   Governments promote quality improvement through: framework documents and goals-led steering; voluntary standards and accreditation; dissemination of research and information; judicious use of special funding; technical support to local management; raising the training and status of staff; encouraging self-evaluation and action-practitioner research; and establishing a system of democratic checks and balances which includes parents.

3.3. Promoting coherence and co-ordination of policy and services

–   Unified administrative auspices can help promote coherence for children, as can co-ordination mechanisms across departments and sectors. In particular, there is increasing trend toward co-ordination with the educational sector to facilitate children's transition from ECEC to primary school.

–   The trend toward decentralisation of responsibility for ECEC has brought diversification of services to meet local needs and preferences. The challenge is for central government to balance local decisionmaking with the need to limit variation in access and quality.

–   At the local level, many countries have recognised the importance of integrating services to meet the needs of children and families in a holistic manner. Services integration has taken many forms, including teamwork among staff with different professional backgrounds.

3.4. Exploring strategies to ensure adequate investment in the system

–   In almost all countries in the review, governments pay the largest share of costs, with parents covering about 25%-30%. The two or three years of ECEC prior to compulsory schooling are often free.

–   Direct provision through services and schools makes up the bulk of government assistance in most countries. Even when the mix of public and private providers is great, a high percentage of services receive direct or indirect public funding.

–   Countries have adopted a range of financing mechanisms to improve affordability including: direct funding, fee subsidies, tax relief, and employer contributions. Affordability remains a barrier to equitable access, particularly in systems where the cost burden falls on parents.

–   While most countries seek to expand supply and raise quality through direct subsidies to providers, a few countries favour indirect demand-driven subsidies – fee subsidies and tax relief to parents. In both cases, there are equity concerns about access to and quality of provision.

–   Regardless of the financing strategy adopted, it is clear that substantial *public* investment is necessary for the development of an equitable and well-resourced *system* of quality ECEC.

3.5. Improving staff training and work conditions

- Countries have adopted two main approaches to staffing: a split regime with a group of teachers working with children over 3 and lower-trained workers in other services; or a pedagogue working with children from birth to 6, and sometimes older in a range of settings. There is a cross-national trend toward at least a three-year tertiary degree for ECEC staff with the main responsibility for pre-school children.

- While the degree of early childhood specialisation and the balance between theory and practice vary across countries, there appear to be common training gaps in the following areas: work with parents, work with infants and toddlers, bilingual/multi-cultural and special education, and research and evaluation.

- Opportunities to participate in in-service training and professional development are uneven. Staff with the lowest levels of initial training tend to have the least access.

- Low pay, status, poor working conditions, limited access to in-service training and limited career mobility are a concern, particularly for staff working with young children in infant-toddler, out-of-school, and family day care settings.

- As ECEC provision expands, recruitment and retention are major challenges for the field. Many countries are seeking to attract a diverse workforce to reflect the diversity of children in ECEC. Another major issue is whether a more gender-mixed workforce is desirable, and if so how it can be achieved.

3.6. Developing appropriate pedagogical frameworks for young children

- Most countries in the review have developed national pedagogical frameworks to promote an even level of quality across age groups and provision, help guide and support professional staff in their practice, and facilitate communication between staff, parents, and children.

- There is a trend toward frameworks which cover a broad age span and diverse forms of settings to support continuity in children's learning.

- For the most part, these frameworks focus broadly on children's holistic development and well-being, rather than on narrow literacy and numeracy objectives.

- Flexible curricula developed in co-operation with staff, parents, and children, allow practitioners to experiment with different methodological and pedagogical approaches and adapt overall goals for ECEC to local needs and circumstances.

- Successful implementation of frameworks requires investment for staff support, including in-service training and pedagogical guidance, as well as favourable structural conditions (e.g., ratios, group size, etc.).

3.7. Engaging parents, families and communities

- Parent engagement seeks to: a) build on parents' unique knowledge about their children, fostering continuity with learning in the home; b) promote positive attitudes and behaviour toward children's learning; c) provide parents with information and referrals to other services; d) support parent and community empowerment.

- Patterns of parent, family, and community engagement in ECEC differ from country to country. Several formal and informal mechanisms may be used to foster full participatory and managerial engagement.

- Some of the challenges to active engagement of parents include, cultural, attitudinal, linguistic, and logistical barriers (i.e., lack of time). It is particularly difficult to ensure equitable representation and participation across families from diverse backgrounds.

4. Policy lessons from the thematic review

The report identifies eight key elements of policy that are likely to promote equitable access to quality ECEC. The elements presented are intended to be broad and inclusive so that they can be considered in the light of diverse country contexts and circumstances, values and beliefs. They should form a part of a wider multi-stakeholder effort to reduce child poverty, promote gender equity, improve education systems, value diversity, and increase the quality of life for parents and children. The eight key elements are:

– A *systemic and integrated approach to policy development and implementation* calls for a clear vision for children, from birth to 8, underlying ECEC policy, and co-ordinated policy frameworks at centralised and decentralised levels. A lead ministry that works in co-operation with other departments and sectors can foster coherent and participatory policy development to cater for the needs of diverse children and families. Strong links across services, professionals, and parents also promote coherence for children.

– A *strong and equal partnership with the education system* supports a lifelong learning approach from birth, encourages smooth transitions for children, and recognises ECEC as an important part of the education process. Strong partnerships with the education system provide the opportunity to bring together the diverse perspectives and methods of both ECEC and schools, focusing on the strengths of both approaches.

– A *universal approach to access, with particular attention to children in need of special support*: while access to ECEC is close to universal for children from age 3, more attention to policy (including parental leave) and provision for infants and toddlers is necessary. It is important to ensure equitable access, such that all children have equal opportunities to attend quality ECEC, regardless of family income, parental employment status, special educational needs or ethnic/language background.

– *Substantial public investment in services and the infrastructure*: while ECEC may be funded by a combination of sources, there is a need for substantial government investment to support a sustainable system of quality, accessible services. Governments need to develop clear and consistent strategies for efficiently allocating scarce resources, including investment in an infrastructure for long-term planning and quality enhancement efforts.

– A *participatory approach to quality improvement and assurance*: defining, ensuring, and monitoring quality should be a participatory and democratic process that engages staff, parents, and children. There is a need for regulatory standards for all forms of provision supported by co-ordinated investment. Pedagogical frameworks focusing on children's holistic development across the age group can support quality practice.

– *Appropriate training and working conditions for staff in all forms of provision*: quality ECEC depends on strong staff training and fair working conditions across the sector. Initial and in-service training might be broadened to take into account the growing educational and social responsibilities of the profession. There is a critical need to develop strategies to recruit and retain a qualified and diverse, mixed-gender workforce and to ensure that a career in ECEC is satisfying, respected and financially viable.

– *Systematic attention to monitoring and data collection* requires coherent procedures to collect and analyse data on the status of young children, ECEC provision, and the early childhood workforce. International efforts are necessary to identify and address the existing data gaps in the field and the immediate priorities for data collection and monitoring.

– A *stable framework and long-term agenda for research and evaluation*: as part of a continuous improvement process, there needs to be sustained investment to support research on key policy goals. The research agenda also could be expanded to include disciplines and methods that are currently underrepresented. A range of strategies to disseminate research findings to diverse audiences should be explored.

Countries that have adopted some or all of these elements of successful policy share a strong public commitment to young children and their families. In different ways, these countries have made efforts to ensure that access is inclusive of all children, and have initiated special efforts for those in need of special support. Quality is high on the agenda as a means to ensure that children not only have equal opportunities to participate in ECEC but also to benefit from these experiences in ways that promote their development and learning. While remarkable efforts in policy development and implementation have been achieved in all 12 participating countries in recent years, there are still several challenges remaining. It is hoped that this report will contribute to future policy improvement efforts in the field.

Chapter 1

Introduction

1.1 Why are countries interested in a thematic review of early childhood education and care policy?

Early childhood education and care has experienced a surge of policy attention in OECD countries over the past decade. In part, policy interest has been motivated by research showing the importance of quality early experiences to children's short-term cognitive, social, and emotional development, as well as to their long-term success in school and later life. In addition, equity concerns have led policymakers to focus on how access to quality early childhood services can mediate some of the negative effects of disadvantage and contribute to social integration. At the same time, most governments have acknowledged the need for affordable and reliable early childhood and child care provision to promote equal opportunities for women and men in the labour market and to facilitate the reconciliation of work and family responsibilities. In sum, policy makers have recognised that equitable access to quality early childhood education and care can strengthen the foundations of lifelong learning for all children and support the broad educational and social needs of families (OECD, 1996).

With strong policy interest in early childhood education and care...

Today, most children living in OECD countries will spend at least two years in early childhood education and care settings before beginning primary school (OECD, 2000*a*). As participation becomes an important part of children's lives internationally, the focus of the debate has shifted from whether governments should be involved in early childhood education and care to how they should organise policy and provision to benefit children and their parents. As decision makers consider various policy options, there is a need to strengthen knowledge of the range of approaches adopted by different countries, along with the successes and challenges encountered. Recognising that such cross-national information and analysis can contribute to the improvement of policy development in the field, the OECD Education Committee launched the *Thematic Review of Early Childhood Education and Care Policy* in 1998. The main purposes of the project are to:

...there is a need for cross-national analysis to inform policy development.

- Document the range of policy approaches to early childhood education and care;
- Analyse major policy issues and concerns;
- Propose feasible policy suggestions suited to different contexts;
- Highlight particularly innovative policies and practices; and
- Identify the types of data and instruments needed to support policy making and development.

Two key policy concerns: quality and access.

Over the past two years, the thematic review has investigated different policy approaches to improving the *quality* of and *access* to early childhood education and care. The review has accorded particular attention to six key areas of policy development: i) governance; ii) regulation; iii) staffing; iv) programme content and implementation; v) family engagement and support; and vi) funding and financing. Using the information collected, the review has analysed why similarities and differences may occur across countries. In particular, the review has explored how the unique contexts of countries have shaped the development of policy approaches and the implementation of such policy approaches at the programme level. The review also has sought to understand how diverse policy approaches relate to diverse views of young children and to the purposes and organisation of early childhood education and care in different societies. Potential implications of this analysis have been articulated to inform and strengthen policy development in all OECD countries.

1.2. What do we mean by *Early Childhood Education and Care*?

A *broad and holistic* scope.

The review has taken a broad and holistic approach that considers how policies, services, families, and communities can support young children's early development and learning. The term *early childhood education and care* (ECEC) includes all arrangements providing care and education for children under compulsory school age, regardless of setting, funding, opening hours, or programme content. The early childhood period is commonly defined as birth to age 8. It was felt, however, that this review could not comprehensively cover both policy and provision for children below school age *and* primary education. While a more limited age range has been covered, attention has been accorded to issues concerning children's transition to compulsory school (which usually occurs at age 6) and out-of-school provision. At the other end of the age spectrum, it was deemed important to include policies – including parental leave arrangements – and provision concerning children under age 3, a group often neglected in discussions in the educational sphere. Brain research and learning sciences suggest that there are valuable opportunities for stimulating development and learning in these early years (Shore, 1997; OECD, 2001*b*). In addition, consideration has been given to links between ECEC and other related domains including family support, health, lifelong learning, employment, and social integration policies.

An *integrated and coherent approach* to "care" and "education".

This framework reflects the growing consensus in OECD countries that "care" and "education" are inseparable concepts and that quality services for children necessarily provide both. Some countries make a distinction between "child care" to look after children while their parents are at work and "early education" to enhance child development and prepare children for formal schooling. In practice, the division is not clear, as there are opportunities to learn in settings labelled "care", and "educational" settings provide care for children. Such terms reinforce a split and incoherent approach to services based on separate systems of "care" and "education" that has led to disjointed policymaking and service delivery in some countries. Alternatively, the use of the term ECEC supports an integrated and coherent approach to policy and provision which is inclusive of *all* children and *all* parents, regardless of their employment or socio-economic status. This approach recognises also that such arrangements may fulfil a wide range of objectives, including care, learning, and social support.

Within this broad scope, the review has focused on organised ECEC provision in centres and in group settings (including schools) and family day care (individuals who provide care to non-related children in the carer's home). The review has concentrated to a lesser extent on carers who work in children's homes and on more informal arrangements involving relatives and friends. These individuals provide important supports for children and families, but there is little available information on them. However, the review has looked at the roles of families and communities in supporting the informal early learning that takes place within the home and through children's interactions with the world around them. In particular, the study has investigated the roles of parental leave policies and flexible, part-time community-based services in fostering children's informal learning.

A focus on organised provision.

1.3. Which countries took part in the thematic review?

Twelve countries volunteered to participate in the review: Australia, Belgium (Flemish and French Communities), the Czech Republic, Denmark, Finland, Italy, the Netherlands, Norway, Portugal, Sweden, the United Kingdom, and the United States.[1] These countries provide a diverse range of social, economic and political contexts, as well as varied policy approaches to the education and care of young children.[2] In addition, the participating countries differ greatly in terms of population size, geographical area, and forms of government. They include large, sparsely populated countries, such as Australia, and small, densely populated countries, such as Belgium and the Netherlands. In addition, three countries have federal systems of government (Australia, Belgium, and the US). The review also benefits from the participation of the Czech Republic as a representative of the economies in transition, many of which have well-established ECEC systems that have experienced recent social and economic pressures to change. This group allows for rich comparisons across very different countries, as well within groups of apparently similar countries. Table A1 (in Appendix 1) summarises some general demographic, economic, and social indicators for the 12 countries.

A wide range of countries from three continents.

While the set of participating countries is rich and varied, the inclusion of five (Denmark, Finland, Norway, Sweden, and the UK) out of 12 countries which have adopted, or are moving toward, integrated early childhood systems under unified administrative auspices overstates the prevalence of this approach. In addition, there are a few countries that could have enriched the analysis had they taken part in the review. For example, although New Zealand and Spain did not participate in the project, their experiences of moving toward an integrated early childhood system under education auspices may be of cross-national interest. France, another country absent from the review, represents a long-established early childhood system that is divided between education and welfare. Finally, the review would have benefited from the participation of Japan and Korea to provide more comprehensive coverage of the range of contexts and policies in OECD Member countries.

1. Switzerland withdrew from the project in September, 1999. A background report was commissioned by the Swiss authorities and submitted to the OECD in June, 2000.

2. It should be noted that these countries are all post-industrial, information societies. The analyses contained herein should not be interpreted as presenting a "global model" of ECEC policies.

15

1.4. How was the thematic review conducted?

Four main elements to the methodology:

In the early stages of the project, representatives of the 12 participating countries reached agreement concerning the framework, scope and process of the review, and identified the major policy issues for investigation (OECD, 1998*b*). The methodology of the study entails the investigation, within a comparative framework, of country-specific issues and policy approaches to ECEC. The review process has consisted of four main elements: 1) preparation by participating countries of the background report; 2) review team visits to participating countries; 3) preparation of the country note; and 4) preparation of the comparative report.[3]

i) Background report

Guided by a common framework and questionnaire (Appendix 3), each participating country has drafted a *background report* that provides a concise overview of the country context, current ECEC policy and provision, major issues and concerns, and available evaluation data. The preparation of the background report was managed by a national co-ordinator and guided by a steering committee. The reports were either written by government officials or by commissioned scholars/policy advisors. By providing a state-of-the-art overview and analysis of policy and provision in each participating country, the background reports have been important outputs of the review process. In several countries, it was the first time that such information had been brought together in one comprehensive document. The main purpose of the background reports has been to brief the expert reviewers prior to conducting the country visit. They also have been used as reference material in parliamentary hearings, university courses, research, and media outlets.

ii) Review team visit

After preparing the background report, each participating country hosted a multi-national team of OECD Secretariat members and three reviewers (including a *Rapporteur*) with diverse policy and analytical backgrounds for 10- to 12-day *review visit*. The visits were organised by government officials, in co-operation with the Secretariat, and consisted of meetings with a wide range of stakeholders, including: senior policy makers and officials in education, employment, health, and social affairs; representatives of training institutions, trade unions, professional associations, and non-governmental organisations; and members of the research community. The teams also observed a range of typical and innovative examples of ECEC provision in both urban and more rural settings, and held discussions with programme administrators, staff, parents, and children. A total of 39 external experts from 16 OECD countries and four members of the Secretariat have taken part in the 12 review visits. This wide range of participants has added a rich set of perspectives with which to analyse countries' experiences, while also facilitating cross-national discussions of policy lessons. For consistency purposes, one member of the Secretariat participated in all 12 visits. The details of the National Co-ordinators and members of the review teams are provided in Appendix 4.

iii) Country note

After each visit, the review team has prepared a *country note* that draws together observations and analyses of country-specific policy issues. The qualitative assessments of the review teams have been supplemented by statistics and documents both supplied by participating countries and from the

---

3. This is the third thematic review conducted by the OECD Education Committee. Its methodology was informed by the successes and challenges of past thematic reviews on tertiary education and on the transition from initial education to working life.

OECD and other sources. Through this process, some of the limitations of the available cross-national data on ECEC have come to light. The *country notes* provide insights into current ECEC policy context, identify the major issues arising from the visit, and propose suggestions to improve policy and practice. In addition, each report highlights examples of innovative approaches with the goal of promoting cross-national exchange of good practice. An extensive consultation process with country authorities has helped to minimise the potential for factual error or misinterpretation in the reports.

As the main output of the project, this publication provides a comparative review and analysis of ECEC policy in all 12 participating countries, with policy lessons for OECD Member countries. Using the information collected in the background reports, country notes, review visits, and expert meetings, this *comparative report* documents the range of existing ECEC policies and provision cross-nationally and draws out common themes and issues for comparative analysis. In order to respect the diversity of policy approaches to ECEC, this report does *not* attempt to compare countries in terms of better or worse, or right or wrong, or to rank countries in a league table. Instead, the report seeks to analyse the nature of and reasons for similarities and differences in policy approaches across participating countries and to identify some of the possible implications of the analysis for policymakers.

iv) Comparative report

The descriptions and analyses included in this publication draw heavily upon the country notes prepared by the review teams, and the national background reports. Although these reports are not individually cited in the text (unless they have been directly quoted), they can be found on the OECD web site.[4] The full reports offer rich contextual material on each of the countries, with the country notes providing the review teams' assessments and policy suggestions.

The comparative methodology has encouraged those charged with making decisions regarding ECEC to reflect upon their own policy approaches and to be informed of successful policy initiatives in other countries. It is a collaborative process that has engaged a wide range of stakeholders in the review and analysis and has encouraged knowledge and data sharing amongst all participants. In particular, the tasks of preparing the background reports and the review visits have given different government departments and ministries with responsibility for young children and families the opportunity to work together and exchange information and perspectives. It also has promoted collaboration and consultation between policy officials and other stakeholders in the field. The Secretariat has worked closely with country authorities during the course of the review in preparing the reports, selecting the members of review teams, and developing the programmes for the review visits.

A collaborative and consultative process.

The decision to cover a large group of countries over a short time-period has called for a balance between breadth and depth. Given the limited time available to visit each country, and the potentially broad range of topics to be reviewed, there has been a risk of providing only a cursory review and analysis of complex issues. However, the intention has not been to provide carefully controlled data for in depth research, but to provide illustrative material and insights into policy issues and trends identified in country reports and other sources. One advantage of adopting a short-time frame has been that sufficient cross-national data can be collected to make useful comparative assessment, allowing lessons from country experiences to be considered

The challenge of studying a dynamic policy context.

---

4. The web site for the review is http://www.oecd.org/els/education/ecec.

before national circumstances have changed. The short time-frame, however, was not sufficient to address rather spectacular policy changes that occurred after the visits in some of the participating countries, particularly those visited toward the beginning of the review process. These major policy changes show the more recent political recognition of the importance of ECEC in some of the participating countries and the possible contribution of the visit of the OECD review team to moving the policy agenda forward. To the extent possible, the Secretariat has worked with participating countries so that these post-visit changes are reflected in this report.

A *focus on issues of current interest to governments and other stakeholders.*

Participating countries had substantial ownership over the process and have tailored the review to their foremost policy concerns. As a result, there has been a trade-off between country-specific perspectives and cross-national consistency. The selection of issues addressed in-depth in the background reports and country notes reflect those of greatest interest to the countries concerned. This has led to some loss of comparability and variation in the degree to which particular issues are covered from country to country. In addition, there have been limitations to the strategy of using open-ended interviews and observations without a structured protocol. On the other hand, the flexibility and informality of the sessions have been conducive to in-depth discussions about the issues and concerns that matter most to country correspondents. Thus, the process has ensured that the review has focused upon issues that are of real current interest to policy makers *and* to those working in the early childhood field.

1.5. The structure of the report

The report begins, in *Chapter* 2, with a discussion of the main demographic, economic, political, and social trends and issues that have shaped the development of current ECEC policy. The chapter examines how these contextual issues have influenced the structure of the early childhood system, as well as how they have shaped the need, demand, and use of ECEC services in participating countries. It also includes a discussion on different views of early childhood and the purposes of early childhood institutions. The following chapter, *Chapter* 3, explores the main policy developments and issues concerning ECEC that have emerged throughout the review and highlights innovative approaches to address policymakers' concerns. Drawing on this comparative analysis, *Chapter* 4 identifies the major policy lessons from the review. It focuses on eight key elements of successful ECEC policy, that is policy which promotes equitable access to quality ECEC. The report concludes with a discussion of key policy challenges and directions for the future. *Appendix* 1 provides an overview of the ECEC systems found in each of the 12 participating countries.

1.6. Terminology and conventions used in the report

Age ranges are mentioned frequently in the report. This report follows the conventions adopted by the EC Childcare Network (1996*b*) as illustrated by the following two examples: "Children aged 0-3 years" covers children from birth up to 36 months, *i.e.* up to their third birthday, but does not include 3-year-olds. "Children aged 3-6" covers children from 36 to 72 months *i.e.* up to their sixth birthday, but does not include 6-year-olds.

As forms of ECEC provision and professional profiles have developed from the specific traditions and contexts of individual countries, similar terms and labels sometimes express quite different concepts from country to country (*e.g.*, kindergarten, day care, pre-school, nursery). Translations often neglect the nuances in the original language that are important to understanding policy. In order to avoid misunderstandings, original language terms referring to specific forms of ECEC services and staff are used in this report. The key terms for provision are found in Table 3.1, and the key terms for staffing are presented in Table 3.5. In addition, we use the following English terms in the report:

- *Centre-based* ECEC: provision for children under 3 (*infant-toddler centre, family and child centres, play-groups*), provision for children from 3- to 6-year-olds (*kindergartens*), and provision for children under compulsory school age (*age-integrated centres*), usually within the social welfare system.

- *School-based* ECEC: provision for children below compulsory school age (*pre-school, nursery school*) within the education system.

- *Pre-primary education* (applies to figures developed using the OECD Education Database): school-based and centre-based settings designed to meet the educational and developmental needs of children at least three years of age, which employ staff who are qualified to provide an educational programme for children.[5]

- *Primary schooling*: school-based provision for children of compulsory school age within the education system.[6]

- *Out-of-school provision*: services outside regular school hours for children in pre-primary and primary schooling, either within the education or social welfare system.

- *Teachers, pedagogues,* or *educators*: individuals who work directly with children in centre-based or school-based settings described above.

- *Staff, workers,* and the *workforce*: terms used generically to refer to those who work in the ECEC field, regardless of their professional role or the setting in which they are employed.

- *Family day care providers*: individuals who provide care for non-related children in the carer's own home. *Organised* family day care refers to providers who are recruited, supported, and in some cases employed, by a public authority or publicly-funded private organisation. Alternatively, family day care providers are self-employed and make private arrangements directly with parents.

Public provision refers to services that are publicly-managed (*e.g.* by a municipality) and publicly-funded, but may charge user fees. *Private provision* includes for-profit and non-profit services that are managed by an individual or private organisation. Private *for-profit* provision includes owner-operators

---

5. See the International Classification of Educational Systems (OECD, 2001*a*) for more information.

6. In 1986, kindergarten (for 4- and 5-year olds) and primary school were integrated into the Dutch *bassischool* which now covers children from age 4 to 12. Since the focus of the review has been children under 6, we refer to the first two years of the *bassischool* as school-based ECEC provision, though we recognise that they form a part of an integrated and continuous educational process.

running a single centre or commercial providers running a number of centres as profit-making businesses. Self-employed family day care providers also may be considered as part of the for-profit sector. Private *non-profit* providers include voluntary or community groups (*e.g.*, parent co-operatives) with the legal status of charities or other non-profit organisations. Private provision may be fully or partly publicly-funded (private, subsidised) or entirely privately-funded (private, non-subsidised). The extent to which the private sector is regulated or allowed to operate within free-market conditions differs across countries. These distinctions in management, funding, and regulation of public and private ECEC are important for understanding issues concerning quality and access in different countries and are explored in the report.

Chapter 2

Contextual Issues Shaping ECEC Policy

Introduction

Over the past two decades, the context for ECEC policy has been shaped by a number of important demographic, economic, and social changes. The most dramatic development over the past twenty years in many countries has been the increase in female labour force participation. Most women are obliged to juggle household and family demands with involvement in paid work structures that, for the most part, are designed to fit male employment patterns. The availability and affordability of ECEC and other work-family provisions – such as temporary withdrawal from the labour market through parental leave – have a great influence on whether mothers are required to make a choice between labour market participation and childrearing (OECD, 1999a). In recent years, more government attention and expenditure have been given to increasing ECEC opportunities. Some countries have shown increasing policy sophistication in the way they deal with the work-family interface – moving beyond the debate over parental vs. non-parental care – while others just are beginning to address the issue. There also have been widespread demographic, economic, and social changes in OECD countries that have influenced child and family well-being. The first part of this chapter reviews the main contextual trends and developments that have shaped ECEC policy and provision. The second part of the chapter explores how these contextual issues have shaped different views of early childhood, the roles of families, and the purposes of ECEC, and in turn, how these views have shaped policy and practice.

2.1. Demographic, economic and social trends

Key points

This section discusses the main demographic, economic, and social trends and developments over the past two decades, which are essential for understanding the context of current ECEC policy. The section examines how these contextual issues have influenced the structure of the early childhood system, as well as how they shape the need, demand, and use of ECEC services:

- Ageing populations, declining fertility rates, and a greater proportion of children living in lone-parent families are part of the changing demographic landscape. Countries with the highest female employment rates are those with higher completed fertility rates, which suggests that female employment and childrearing are complementary activities.

- The sharp rise in dual-earner households, spurred by increased female employment, makes ECEC and parental leave policies more important for the well-being of families. Women are more likely than men to work in non-standard employment which carries lower economic and social status.

- Paid and job protected maternity and family leave policies are widely accepted in almost all participating countries as an essential strategy to help working parents reconcile work and family life and to promote gender equity. The length, flexibility, level of payment and take-up by men and women vary across countries.

- While taxes and transfers can help redistribute income to families with young children, in a few countries more than 20% of children still live in relative poverty. Income support, measures to improve parent employability and targeted early interventions may improve children's life-course chances and promote social cohesion.

Demographic trends: fertility rates, family formation, and diversity

Ageing populations, declining fertility rates, and delayed family formation are cross-national trends.

The demographic landscape for families has changed dramatically in the past two decades (see Table 2.1). Declining fertility rates, combined with longer life expectancies at birth and declining mortality rates, have contributed to the shift in the age structure of the population in OECD countries. As a result, the percentage of children as a proportion of the population (currently between 5-9% in countries participating in the review) has decreased and is expected to decline further in coming decades, while the proportion of the elderly has increased. Within countries, the general ageing of the population is more marked in rural and remote areas as younger workers seeking employment opportunities migrate toward urban areas. Fertility rates have fallen dramatically and are below replacement in all countries in the review, with the exception of the US. At the same time, female labour force participation rates have increased substantially in most countries. Labour market developments appear to strongly influence family formation. Young people are waiting to get married and have children until they have completed more education and when one or both parents are more securely established in their careers (OECD, 1999a). This process is taking longer than in the past, as seen, for example, in the increasing age at first marriage and at first childbirth. The average age of women at first childbirth is above 25 in all participating countries, except for the Czech Republic.

Table 2.1. **Demographic trends**

	Population under 6				Total fertility rates[a]		Number of lone parent families			Age of women at first childbirth	
	1990	As a % of total population, 1990	1999	As a % of total population, 1999	1987	1997	(year) / as a % of all families with dependent children (1990s)		% increase 1983-96	1980	1993
Australia	1 536 473 [b]	8.7 [b]	1 536 498	8.1	1.9	1.8 [c]	1993	17	m	25.3 [d]	28.3
Belgium	708 475	7.1	700 550	6.9	1.5	1.6	1996	15	75	m	26.0 [e]
Czech Republic	760 160 [b]	7.4 [b]	591 961	5.8	1.9	1.2		m	m	22.4	22.3
Denmark	339 752	6.6	413 540	7.8	1.5	1.8	1996	13	m	24.1	26.7
Finland	374 746	7.5	369 870	7.2	1.6	1.8	1996	17	32	m	26.7
Italy	3 379 798	6.0	3 207 866	5.6	1.3	1.2	1996	11	5	24.4	26.9
Netherlands	1 103 910	7.4	1 173 578	7.4	1.6	1.5	1996	11	m	27.5	27.8
Norway	326 451	7.7	362 566	8.2	1.8	1.9	1993	20	m	m	25.5
Portugal	699 710	7.1	663 030	6.6	1.6	1.5	1996	12	m	23.6	25.2
Sweden	636 440	7.5	608 859	6.9	1.8	1.5	1993	18	94	25.0	26.5
United Kingdom	4 551 448	7.9	4 412 519	7.4	1.8	1.7	1996	23	m	24.6	27.5
United States	23 354 000 [b]	9.1 [b]	23 026 004 [f]	8.6 [f]	1.9	2.1		m	m	25.7	26.4
Austria	534 216	6.9	530 973	6.6	1.4	1.4	1996	14	m	m	25.0
Canada	2 376 750 [b]	8.3 [b]	2 308 017 [f]	7.7 [f]	1.6	1.6 [c]	1991	20	48	24.6	26.8
France	4 532 350	8.0	4 294 293	7.3	1.8	1.7	1996	15	m	25.0	27.6
Germany	5 205 315	6.6	4 757 243	5.8	1.4	1.4	1991	16	33	m	m
Greece	674 725	6.7	607 490	5.8	1.5	1.3	1996	7	m	m	25.7
Hungary	738 332	7.1	640 044	6.3	1.8	1.4	1990	24	m	m	m
Iceland	25 213	9.9	26 098	9.5	2.1	2.0	1993	21	m	m	24.3
Ireland	345 991	9.9	309 021	8.3	2.3	1.9	1996	13	100	m	m
Japan	7 551 000 [b]	6.1 [b]	7 164 000 [f]	5.7 [f]	1.7	1.4	1995	13	m	26.4	27.2
Korea (Republic of)	3 939 212 [b]	9.0 [b]	4 292 484	9.2	1.6	1.6 [c]	1995	9	m	24.4	26.3
Luxembourg	27 031	7.1	34 307	8.0	1.4	1.7	1996	11	58	m	m
Mexico	13 346 195	16.1	13 365 611 [f]	13.9 [f]	3.7	2.7 [c]		m	m	m	m
New Zealand	342 800 [b]	9.8 [b]	341 610 [f]	9.0 [f]	2.0	2.0 [c]	1996	26	m	24.9 [d,g]	28.7 [g,h]
Poland	3 303 876	8.6 [b]	2 609 598	6.7	2.2	1.5		m	m	m	m
Spain	2 575 922	6.6	2 296 673	5.8	1.5	1.2	1996	8	m	26.4 [i]	27.1
Switzerland	460 434	6.9	486 798	6.8	1.5	1.5	1991	14	m	m	28.1 [i]
Turkey	7 964 000 [b]	13.5 [b]	7 931 000 [f]	12.4 [f]	3.8	2.7 [j]		m	m	m	m

m: missing data.
a. Average number of children per woman aged 15-49.
b. 1993.
c. 1996.
d. 1981.
e. 1990.
f. 1998.
g. Data relates to live births in current union only.
h. 1995.
i. Married women only.
j. 1994.

Sources: OECD Education Database (2000); OECD *in Figures* (2000); EUROSTAT (1998); OECD (1999*a*).

High female labour force participation is linked to higher completed fertility rates.

In some countries (*e.g.*, Australia, Czech Republic, Italy), declining birth-rates cause concern, while other countries seem to be less affected or are experiencing increasing birth rates (*e.g.*, the Netherlands). Countries with the highest female labour participation rates tend to have higher completed fertility rates – average number of births per woman aged 50 during her past reproductive years. This suggests that childrearing and paid work are *complementary*, rather than *alternative* activities (OECD, 1999*a*). It is not clear whether policies to increase female labour force participation will increase fertility rates, but it is interesting to note that a fall in fertility in Sweden in the 1990s followed a rise in unemployment. Declining fertility rates have wide social, economic, and educational consequences. The likely long-term shrinkage of the population of working age means that the skills of women will be increasingly needed in paid employment to ensure the continued competitiveness of OECD economies. While the demand for services for children is likely to decrease, the demand for care services and professional care staff generally will continue to increase with more and more elderly people living alone (see Section 3.5). On the other hand, smaller family sizes mean that many children are growing up in families with few or no siblings. Informal opportunities for socialisation – in both rural and urban areas – are becoming more rare, leading to greater need for early childhood settings where young children can interact with other children and adults.

Societies are becoming more ethnically, culturally, and linguistically diverse.

The populations of OECD countries also are becoming increasingly heterogeneous as a result of immigration, the arrival of refugees and asylum seekers, and economic migrants seeking work in countries with labour shortages. These minority groups tend to have more children, and earlier in life than the rest of the population. As a result, the share of ethnic minority children is growing more rapidly than the ethnic majority population in countries such as Australia, Belgium (Flemish and French Communities) and the Netherlands, although data in this area are incomplete. The diversification of the population and increasing cultural pluralism of society have an impact on education, including ECEC provision. In several countries (*e.g.*, Belgium, Denmark, Finland, the Netherlands, Norway, Sweden), policies to expand access to early childhood services for immigrant and ethnic minority groups have been pursued in order to expose children and families to the language and traditions of mainstream society, and provide opportunities for parents to establish social contacts and networks. Countries with indigenous populations (Australia, Finland, Norway, Sweden, US) are seeking to preserve traditional languages and cultures, while seeking to empower families within mainstream society. The need for early childhood staff and provision to value and respond to the needs of ethnically, culturally, and linguistically diverse families remains a challenge in many countries (see Section 3.1).

Lone-parents carry the dual responsibility for childrearing and income support.

Another trend is the growing population of children living with only one parent, and a growing number of women acting as the only, or main, responsible parent for both childrearing and income support. National rates of lone parenthood vary; for example, children in Sweden, the UK, and the US are much more likely to be in lone-parent families, than those in Italy or Portugal. Table 2.1 shows that the proportion of lone-parent families of total families is 20% or more in many countries. These trends are linked to the increase in divorce and separation and to a lesser extent a rise in births outside of marriage. The number of children born to unmarried mothers has increased substantially in most countries, particularly in the UK and the US. The figures also are high in the Nordic countries, though a substantial proportion of children are born to stable cohabiting couples. The likelihood of lone parenthood is linked to early childbearing, whether in or out of marriage. Lone-parents face many challenges:

Lone mothers must carry the dual responsibility of being the main breadwinner and the main carer wishing to enter the labour market where caring responsibilities may not be recognised, and in the face of social arrangements which often continue to take for granted the flexibility of a mother's time (e.g., the time schedule of schools, the offer of child care services, the opening hours of shops, public offices, etc.) (OECD, 1999a, p. 16).

The consequences for ECEC policy are many. In order for lone mothers to enter and remain in the labour market, there is a need for greater access to affordable ECEC. ECEC services need to be sensitive to the time and financial constraints faced by lone mothers when they conceive of opening hours, fees, and parental engagement objectives. Yet, the labour market also needs to respond with more flexibility so that lone-parents – like other parents – can balance their work and family responsibilities.

Family and work: a delicate balance

In recent years, there have been many significant changes to family arrangements with implications for educational and social policy. Women's desire for greater economic independence and increased household standards, their improved educational levels, and demands from the economy for more labour (particularly due to the growth of the service sector) all have contributed to increasing female labour force participation in paid work (OECD, 1999a). Cross-national variation in labour market participation by women is related to cultural patterns, social and economic behaviour, and available supports, including access to formal and informal ECEC. As the data for mothers with young children under 6 are not reported consistently across countries, it is difficult to make cross-national comparisons. Instead, this section looks at trends in employment rates among 25-34 year olds. Given the fact that average childbearing age at first birth falls within that range, it can be assumed that this age group includes many men and women with young children.

As more and more women enter the labour market...

As Figure 2.1. shows, in all countries participating in the review, except Italy, more than 60% of women are employed. Female labour force participation has increased dramatically since the beginning of the 1980s in Belgium, the Netherlands, Norway and Portugal, and to a lesser extent in Australia, the UK and the US. The economic recession in the early 1990s reduced participation rates in the Czech Republic, Denmark, Finland, and Sweden, but levels remain high. In contrast, male employment rates have fallen in most countries. The increasing precariousness of employment among males and the growing instability of marriage also has encouraged women to participate in the labour market to ensure economic stability for their households. As a result, more women – and also more men – are facing dual and also conflicting employment and family responsibilities. In Finland, for example, over 60% of women with a 3-year-old child are employed (compared with 70% of all women aged 25-34), while in Australia, only 47% of women with a child under 3 work (compared with 64% of all women aged 25-34). Most governments have invested in expanding ECEC services, as well as hours of provision, to meet the increased demand. In some countries, however, limited access to ECEC has been a barrier to female employment.

...women and men face conflicting work and family responsibilities.

Figure 2.1. **Trends in employment rates[1] of 25-34 year-olds, 1980-99**

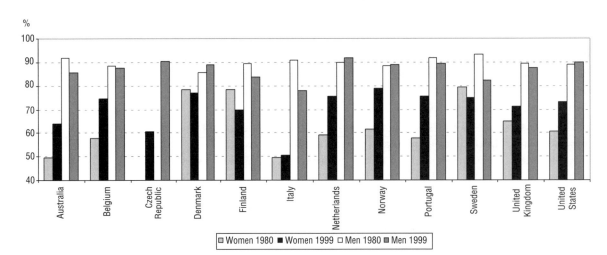

1. Employment/population ratio.
Sources: For all countries except Italy, OECD Labour force statistics database; data for Italy provided by EUROSTAT.

In particular, labour-market participation by *lone mothers* depends to a greater extent than for married women on social policy provisions. Many lone parents still are reliant on social benefits rather than on employment as their main source of income, and they also have the lowest relative incomes of all households. Employment rates are lower for lone mothers in countries, such as Australia, the Netherlands, and the UK, where income assistance policies have allowed lone-parents to care for their children and receive economic support. Recent concern about the growing dependency on welfare benefits (*e.g.*, Australia, the Netherlands, Norway, UK, US) has led to time-limited benefits and the expansion of education and training programmes to help lone-parents enter the labour market. In the US, welfare benefits (Temporary Assistance for Needy Families) are now time-limited and some states require job search activity 14 weeks after giving birth. These policies have led to a surge in demand for affordable, quality ECEC arrangements for very young children, which, to date, has not been met adequately.

Men with young children are working long hours...

In most OECD countries, the working life span is compressed into a relatively short period due to increased time spent in education on the one hand, and early retirement on the other. This means that the critical time for career advancement typically coincides with the period when children are young and the demands of the family are the greatest. At the same time, there are trends for both men and women to work long hours. It is not surprising, however, that mothers with young children tend to work fewer hours than fathers (see Figure 2.2). Average weekly hours worked among mothers with a child under 3 were 32.7 hours across the EU[7] while for fathers it was 42.7 (Moss and Deven, 1999). Women's domestic responsibilities may prevent them from competing equally in the labour market and from pursuing more lucrative and fulfilling career tracks. The long hours worked by fathers and the pressures of their workplace commitments may prevent them for taking part equally in house-

7. Not including Denmark, Luxembourg, and Sweden.

Figure 2.2 **Average hours worked per week by employed women and men with a child under 3 years, selected countries, 1997**

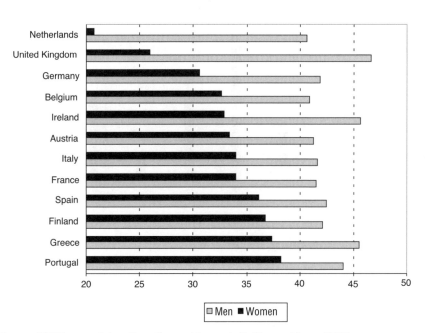

Source : 1997 European Labour Force Survey data reported in Moss and Deven (1999).

hold and care responsibilities within the home. "Real compatibility between family and employment responsibilities depends on enhanced flexibility in both working hours and in the organisation of household and caring tasks, supported by an adapted social infrastructure" (OECD, 1991, p. 11).

While high female labour force participation is becoming more common across OECD countries, the work patterns of men and women continue to differ. Part-time employment has increased in the past decade in most OECD countries, and typically accounts for over 20% of total female employment and around 10% or less for males. As Figure 2.3. shows, the incidence of part-time female employment among employed women 25-34 years old is highest in the Netherlands (54%), followed by Norway (37%) and the UK (36%). In the UK and the US, the part-time workforce consists mostly of married women with children, who have returned to paid part-time work between and after childbearing. There has been a slight upward trend in the incidence of part-time work among men. The highest proportion of male part-time work is also in the Netherlands (9%), followed by Sweden (7.4%) and Norway (7%). In contrast, there are relatively few part-time female workers in Portugal (8%), the Czech Republic (13%) and Finland (14%) and male part-time work is very rare in the Czech Republic (less than 1%), Portugal (2%), and Italy (4%). The incidence of part-time work among mothers with young children is generally higher than among other female employees. These different patterns of part-time and full-time work have implications for the ECEC system, for example, in the Czech Republic where 96% of kindergartens are open full-time to accommodate the working schedules of parents.

...while many women are in part-time work...

A high level of part-time work among women may be a sign of difficulties in combining family life and a career. For many women, flexibility in working

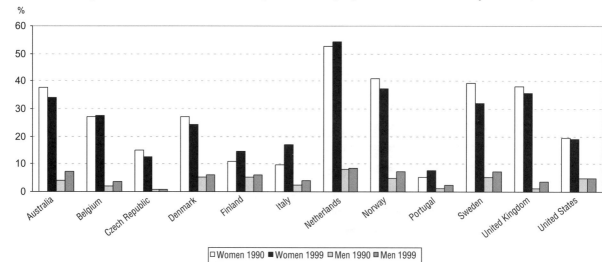

Figure 2.3. **Trends in incidence of part-time employment rates [1] for 25-34 year-olds, 1990-99 [2]**

[1] Part-time employment / total employment.

[2] 1993-99 for Czech Republic; 1990-98 for the Netherlands.

Sources: For all countries except Italy, OECD Labour force statistics database; data for Italy provided by EUROSTAT.

hours usually means adjusting their domestic schedules to take on part-time employment (OECD, 1991). A high level of part-time work may also reflect societal beliefs that it is in the best interest of very young children for parents (usually mothers) to reduce their working hours. Mothers with high educational attainment levels are more likely to work full-time, while the incidence of part-time work is higher for mothers with low and medium levels of educational attainment. In part, this may reflect the lower opportunity cost for women with lower education (and lower earnings) of working part-time or it may reflect the difficulty of mothers with low education to find full-time work. Part-time work not only involves shorter hours, but in may also be associated with lower status, and less favourable conditions of employment. While part-time positions may make employment compatible with meeting family responsibilities, in some cases, workers with part-time jobs do not have control over the hours they work and end up working irregular hours, evening, nights, and weekends.

... and other forms of non-standard employment.

In addition to part-time work, other forms of non-standard employment – sub-contracting, temporary and casual employment, work at home, short-term employment and self-employment – are a growing reality in OECD countries. While these more flexible forms of employment can expand employment opportunities, especially for women, job and income security and conditions of employment are usually inferior, which leads to a risk of labour market marginalisation. In most OECD countries, about 10% of workers are employed with temporary employment contracts which may give rights to lower levels of social protection than full-time permanent contracts. In Australia, for example, about 27% of the workforce is employed on a casual basis, and the vast majority are women. Self-employment has also increased by 3% or more in OECD countries over the past two decades (OECD, 1999a). An increasing number of parents with small children have unstable working conditions, with short and varying employment relationships. Parents often are forced to accept jobs that may be very difficult in terms of working hours, and a relatively large percentage also work shift hours and/or nights and weekends (see Figure 2.4). In Finland, for example, about 9% of all children in ECEC had parents who worked shifts or irregular hours. Across countries, ECEC provision typically has developed to meet the needs of parents working regular office hours. As there are limited formal options for children who need care during atypical hours, many parents have no option but to rely on informal arrangements (see Section 3.1).

Recent employment gains have not been shared equally. The changing needs of the labour market in favour of highly-skilled workers has led to large differences in employment patterns for women (and to a lesser extent men) from different socio-economic groups. Women with young children who have completed higher levels of educational attainment usually have at least twice the level of labour market participation as their counterparts with lower qualifications, and they also are more likely to work full-time (see Figure 2.5).

There are signs of a growing polarisation of the labour market.

Unemployment rates are much higher among those with low educational attainment. There also have been sharp increases in the proportion of households in which there is no employment income of any sort, with large economic and social implications for children (*e.g.*, in the Czech Republic, the unemployment rate of the Romany minority is estimated at 90%). In fact, there has been a simultaneous increase in both workless and fully-employed households in many countries, leading to a growing gap between the work-rich and the work-poor (Förster, 2000). In Europe, a child who lives in a household with no working adult is more than four times as likely to be growing up in poverty than a child in a household with at least one working adult (UNICEF, 2000). Even if low-skilled parents are working, they may not earn enough to support their families. Countries with greater income inequality – measured as the ratio of median earnings to bottom decile earnings – have a higher incidence of low-paid jobs. The incidence of low-pay has increased in Australia, the UK, and the US in line with the increases in earnings inequality in these countries (OECD, 1999*a*).

These labour market changes have large implications for ECEC policy. Not only are more women with young children participating in the labour market, but they are involved in a range of employment types, including permanent full-time or part-time, as well as casual arrangements. Non-standard employment, including self-employment and seasonal work, as well as atypical hours are becoming more common. The need to accommodate the range and complexity of parental working patterns has been a challenge for ECEC policy. In addition, the trend toward the lengthening of the average working week has far-reaching implications for the organisation (*e.g.*, opening hours) of ECEC provision. At the same time, labour market variation and polarisation by socio-economic status is reflected in the trends in overall employment, full-time work and workless families. Services need to respond to the fact that parents of some children will endure short or long periods of unemployment, leading to resource constraints and other challenges. ECEC policy focused on working parents, in fact, may reinforce the increasing economic polarisation of families, with children of working and non-working parents having very different early childhood experiences. Finally, there is a need for the labour market to become more flexible in accommodating the needs of all parents and children, especially given that the more equitable sharing of family and household responsibilities between men and women is a goal in many OECD countries.

Figure 2.4. **Employed men and women engaged in shift, night and Sunday work, 1997**

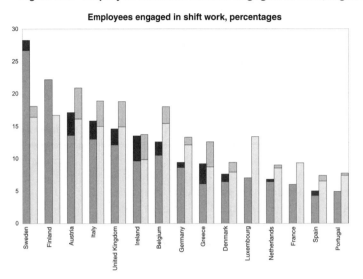

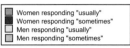

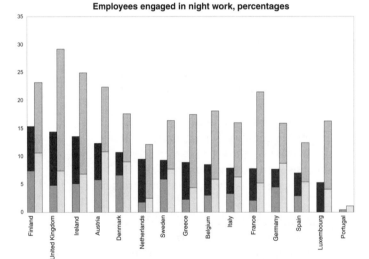

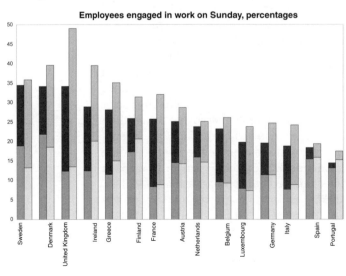

Source : EUROSTAT Labour Force Survey (1997).

Figure 2.5. **Employment status of women with a child aged under 6 years by highest educational qualification, selected countries, 1997 (%)**

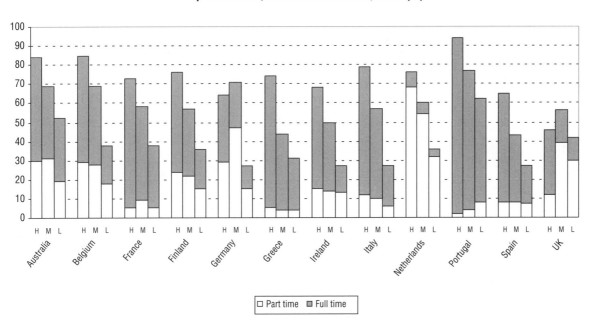

Educational qualifications: H= High; M= Medium; L= Low.

Source: 1997 European Labour Force Survey data reported in Moss and Deven (1999).

Parental leave policies

Parental leave measures are an important part of ECEC systems in participating countries. With the exception of Australia[8] and the US, mandatory job-protected and paid *maternity leave* policies exist for working mothers in all the countries reviewed. Statutory, job-protected *parental leave* – equally available to mothers or fathers and to adoptive as well as biological parents – exists in all 12 countries, though this leave is unpaid in a few countries (see Table 2.2). Such policies are acknowledged as an important contribution to providing care and education for infants and toddlers, and as a means of reconciling work and family responsibilities.[9] In many countries, maternal and parental leave schemes are considered as one of the cornerstones of equality for women. At the same time, opinion surveys in several countries show wide support, among men and women, for a less pronounced division of labour in the everyday lives of families with children.

Parental leave is an important element of most ECEC systems.

Parental leave policies seem to be acceptable to both employers and employees, and are developing in almost all countries. There is some cross-national variation in eligibility, length, flexibility, and benefit levels, and take-up. In European countries, leave policies range from conformity to the

There is variation in existing leave policies.

---

8. In Australia paid maternity leave covers about 17% of working women.

9. The extent to which the nature and availability of family leave policies affects the need and demand for ECEC provision will be explored in Section 3.1.

31

Table 2.2. **Maternity, paternity and parental leave policies**

Country	Duration of maternity leave entitlement[a]	Percentage of wage replaced[a]	Duration of parental leave entitlement	Benefit paid	Supplementary leaves
Australia	[b]		12 months (family-based leave)	unpaid	
Belgium	15 weeks	82% for the 1st month and thereafter at 75%	6 months (3 months for each parent or 6 months part-time)	20 400 FBE monthly flat rate	Paternity, 3 or 4 days paid at 100%. Possibility of a career break at 12 308 FBE monthly (a supplement of 4 450 FBE is paid by the Flemish Community)
Czech Republic	28 weeks	69%	until child's 4th birthday	flat rate	
Denmark	18 weeks	100 % for most mothers	10 weeks for each parent generally paid full-time, plus a further "use or lose" 2 weeks for the father	100% of earnings or 60% of unemployment benefit	Paternity leave entitlement of 2 weeks, generally at 100% earnings. Child Care Leave of 13 (or 26) weeks for each parent at 60% of unemployment benefit
Finland	18 weeks	66%	6 months	66% of earnings	Paternity leave at 18 days (3 weeks). Child Care Leave up to the child's 3rd birthday paid at about 1 500 FM monthly
Italy	21 weeks	80%	10 months	30% of earnings	Parental leave is extended to 11 months if the father takes 3 months leave
Netherlands	16 weeks	100% (with upper limit)	6 months unpaid parental leave for each parent, but they must also work at least 20 hours per week	unpaid	
Norway	included in parental leave		42 or 52 weeks	For 42 weeks, 100% earnings (with upper limit); for 52 weeks, 80% earnings (with upper limit)	Unpaid paternity leave of 2 weeks. 30 days of the paid parental leave is available to the father on a "use or lose" basis
Portugal	18 weeks	100%	6 months for each parent	unpaid	
Sweden	12 weeks	100% (with upper limit)	18 months	80% of earnings (with upper limit) for 1 year; thereafter 60 SEK daily for 6 months.	Paternity leave is 10 working days paid at 80% (with upper limit). 30 days of paid parental leave is available to fathers on a "use or lose" basis, 80% earnings
United Kingdom	18 weeks after 1 year of employment	6 weeks at 90% and 12 weeks at flat rate	22 weeks	unpaid	A further unpaid 4 weeks yearly is available to parents for 3 years until their child reaches 5 years
United States	[c]		12 weeks leave in firms with 50 or more workers[d]	unpaid, job-protected	

a. In almost all countries, benefits are financed as part of social insurance or social security, that is, governments and employers bear the major costs. In some countries, direct employee contributions from part of the financing. With the exception of Finland and Sweden, the total costs of maternity and parental leave shemes do not exceed 1 % of GDP (Kamerman, 2000b).
b. Only 17% mothers receive payment from 6 to 12 weeks at birth (depends on workplace agreement).
c. Some paid maternity leave depending on workplace agreement. Five states provide paid disability leave which, since 1977, is required to cover pregnancy and maternity.
d. Provided by the 1993 Family and Medical Leave Act. At the time of pregnancy, childbirth or illness. Employers can require that employees use their vacation and sick leave before claiming the family leave.

Sources: Country background reports; Moss and Deven (2000).

minimal standards set by the EU Directives[10] to the generous leave schemes available in Denmark, Finland, Norway, and Sweden. Across OECD countries, the average duration of parental leave is 44 weeks (10 months), with paid leave lasting an average of 36 weeks. The latter period typically includes 14-16 weeks of paid maternity leave supplemented by other forms of parental leave (Kamerman, 2000*b*). Benefits are typically funded by a combination of social-insurance funds and general tax revenue, and may be supplemented by employers, either voluntarily or as a result of collective bargaining (Evans, 2001). Take-up is high among women in countries where the leave is paid at an adequate level. Despite some progress, fathers take minimal parental leave in most countries. In Belgium, Denmark, Norway, Portugal and Sweden, paid *paternity leaves* reserved for fathers exist.[11] Increasingly, parental leave schemes also include a father's quota available on a "use-it-or-lose-it" basis.

Several important issues arise around the question of parental leave. First, studies in France suggest that when parental leave is taken predominantly by women, particularly in contexts where unemployment is high, it can reinforce both gender discrimination in the labour market and gender stereotyping of tasks in the home (Fagnani, 1999). Moreover, when wage replacement levels are low, families with young children can experience a considerable reduction in income. Women in Belgium (Flemish and French Communities) and in Italy also expressed concern that the hard-won gains of feminism could be undermined by long parental leaves, which are taken almost exclusively by mothers. Career interruptions – however short – can still have long-term negative effects on earnings, income security, and career advancement in some countries. Similar issues have been raised with regard to *child care* leaves lasting two or more years (*e.g.*, Czech Republic, Denmark, Finland, Norway) which provide subsidies at a low, flat rate to parents who care for their own children. Mothers with lower levels of education, who have worked in less skilled occupations, are most likely to take these low-paid leaves, which may further marginalise them from the labour market. In some cases, children are not allowed to attend public ECEC during the leave period which raises equity concerns. It is not surprising, therefore, that children from low-educated households are often the last to enter formal ECEC provision. In short, some leave policies may undermine equal opportunity and contribute to socio-economic inequality.

Some policies may have negative consequences for equality.

Second, when interviewed about their reluctance to take up parental leave, men generally cite the drop in family income, but go on to speak of other reasons, such as, problems of re-entry to work after leave, the dangers of a break in their professional careers and even, the negative reactions of bosses and colleagues. In many countries, men miss out on the emotional rewards of care and education for young children because they are constrained by the gender-based division of household and labour responsibilities. Public engagement campaigns may help raise awareness and support for fathers to take leave, as can policy incentives such as rights for

"Fathers quotas" may increase leave take-up by men.

---

10. A EU Directive mandating a paid 14 week maternity leave as a health and safety measure was adopted in 1992, and a directive mandating at least three months of job-protected parental leave as an individual entitlement to male and female workers was enacted in 1998.

11. Paid paternity leaves also exist in a few countries not participating in the review: Austria, France, and Spain.

fathers available on a use-it-or-lose-it basis. In Norway, before the introduction of a period of leave reserved for fathers, only 1-2% of fathers took some period of leave. In 1998, however, with the introduction of a four-week non-transferrable father quota, take up among men has increased to 78% of eligible fathers (Statistics Norway, 1998). Parental leave arrangements with a father quota have also been developed in Denmark, Italy, and Sweden to create an incentive for new fathers to play a more active role in childrearing.

Social networks, flexible services and family-friendly workplaces support working parents.

Third, a work/family balance can be supported in a number of other ways. For example, legislation ensures flexible working hours for parents with young children in Denmark, Finland, the Netherlands, and Sweden, and allows parental leave to be taken part-time in Norway. In some countries (Australia, the Netherlands, UK, US), it is common for firms to complement existing legislation with other family-friendly arrangements (*e.g.*, leave from work for family reasons; changes to work arrangements for family reasons; practical help with ECEC; and the provision of training and information) (Evans, 2001). These arrangements can be particularly important to families in countries where national legislation is limited and public ECEC is not well-developed. Yet, this approach raises equity concerns, as higher-skilled employees, and those who work in the public sector and in large firms tend to have more access to these arrangements than other workers (OECD, 2001c). Parents who take leave may be supported by formal or informal parents clubs, family houses, family and child centres, which can help to break the isolation of young mothers and provide opportunities for the early socialisation and stimulation of infants and toddlers. Such centres or meeting points can also be critical for early detection and intervention, if either young parents or their children need special help. In the larger urban neighbourhoods, the traditional social services structures may no longer be adequate. Societies now may need to recreate consciously the social networks that were formerly available through the extended family and traditional community resources.

Well-paid, job-protected leaves seem to be key, though more research is needed on the optimal length.

In sum, countries need to strike a balance between, on the one hand, giving a real choice to parents (through adequate funding of parental leave and job protection) and, on the other, keeping women and men attached to the labour market in an equitable way. Well-paid and job-protected parental leave policies for about a year followed by a guaranteed place for children in ECEC seem to be key, rather than long-term, low-paid leave schemes, which resemble social welfare payments. The latter schemes are generally taken up by poorly educated women, who are effectively excluded from the labour market, and gender stereotyping of care and domestic work is reinforced. More research is needed on the optimal length of parental leave, *from the perspective of the best interest of the young child*. The issue is not simple, as the individual preferences of parents must be taken into account, as well as the presence or absence of social networks, flexible services and family-friendly workplaces – all of which can significantly impact the context of child-rearing. Another question is what are the social and economic costs of prioritising leave schemes over publicly-funded ECEC services for very young children.

Social policies and child well-being

ECEC policies need to be considered as part of a system of wider supports to promote the well-being of children and families. Government benefits for families may include: universal or means-tested income support for families with young children; income support payments for caring for children at home; birth grants; maternity and parental leave benefits; cash benefits for lone parents; and spending on family services (*e.g.*, child protection, counselling, assistance to victims of domestic violence) (OECD, 2000*b*). According to OECD social expenditure data, spending on family benefits is highest in Denmark, Finland, Norway, and Sweden at about 3.5% of GDP, which is considerably above such spending in other OECD countries (about 2% GDP). More than in most other countries, expenditure in the Nordic countries focuses on services, including ECEC provision (OECD, 2000*c*). Countries often supplement these benefits with generous assistance for children with disabled children in the form of cash allowances, additional services, payments to carers, etc. Low-income families usually are eligible for considerable targeted support (*e.g.*, housing and health benefits). The tax system also plays a role in redistributing income toward families in most countries. Cross-national variation in available supports for children and families can be explained in part by wealth, demography, and economic changes, but also reflects differing social values and political priorities (Kamerman and Kahn, 1997).

A major goal of social policy in OECD countries is the reduction of child poverty. Child poverty rates are influenced by a number of factors including lone parenthood, employment and its distribution, wage inequality, and state transfers to the workless and low-paid (UNICEF, 2000). Even though most OECD countries have experienced similar demographic and labour market changes during the past two decades, relative child poverty rates vary dramatically from less than 3% to more than 20% (see Figure 2.6). *Relative poverty* includes households with income below 50% of the national median. This definition is commonly used in most OECD countries and is enshrined in the UN Convention on the Rights of the Child (Article 27) which provides for the right

The negative effects of poverty on the well-being of children and society.

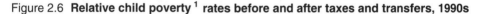

Figure 2.6 **Relative child poverty [1] rates before and after taxes and transfers, 1990s**

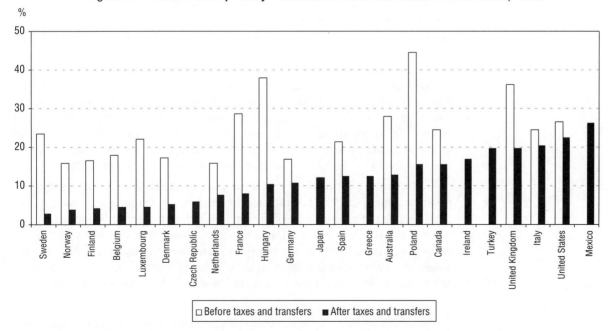

1. Includes households with income below 50% of the national median.
2. Information on taxes and transfers is not provided for the Czech Republic, Greece, Ireland, Japan, Turkey and Mexico.
Source: UNICEF (2000).

35

to "a standard of living adequate for physical, mental, spiritual, moral and social development." The overall well-being of children – in both the short-term and the long-term – is drastically reduced by growing up in poverty (Duncan and Brooks-Gunn, 1997; Gregg *et al.*, 1999). Low-income parents can buy fewer goods and services for their families and are more likely to live in poorer housing in low-income neighbourhoods, with health and safety risks and sub-standard local schools. Children living in poverty have fewer material resources (*e.g.*, shoes and clothing) and fewer opportunities to participate in social and cultural activities. Research shows that poverty saps children's hope and initiative and leads to reduced expectations and ambitions (Kempson, 1996). The long-term effects of child poverty are discouraging as well:

Whether measured by physical and mental development, health and survival rates, educational achievement or job prospects, incomes or life expectancies, those who spend their childhood in poverty of income and expectation are at a marked and measurable disadvantage (UNICEF, 2000, p. 3).

Child poverty threatens the quality of life of all citizens as children who grow up in poverty are more likely to have learning difficulties, to drop out of school, to commit crimes, to be out of work, to become pregnant at too early an age, and to live lives that perpetuate poverty and disadvantage into succeeding generations.

What are the strategies used to keep child poverty low?

The six OECD countries with the lowest relative poverty rates (Sweden, Norway, Finland, Belgium, Luxembourg, and Denmark) all combine a high degree of economic development with a reasonable degree of social and gender equity. Figure 2.3 shows poverty rates before and after taxes and transfers to evaluate the effectiveness of *policies to redistribute resources* to protect the poorest children.[12] State intervention reduces poverty by 20 percentage points in Sweden (and France) and by 16 percentage points in the UK. In Denmark, Finland, and Norway, the reduction exceeds 10 percentage points. Only in Italy and the US do taxes and transfers reduce poverty by less than 5 percentage points; in these two countries, child poverty exceeds 20%. It is notable that in the Czech Republic – despite unemployment, greater wage inequality, and cuts in redistributive spending brought about by economic and social transition – the government has kept child poverty low by maintaining significant redistributive taxes and social transfers. Child poverty rates rose by about 3 percentage points during the first half of the 1990s and remain among the lowest in the OECD area. While the reorganisation of tax and benefits has been able to lift some families out of poverty, a major problem is one of income inequality, and the more limited access to goods and services which children living in low-income households experience (UNICEF, 2000).

Concerns about poverty and its impact on child development suggest a need for a multi-faceted approach to: reduce poverty among lone-parent families; reduce the proportion of children in workless households; reduce severe wage inequalities at the bottom end of the income scale; and prevent too wide a gap from opening up between state benefit payments and average wages. Countries with low rates of child poverty redistribute income to overcome inequality in market income and support female labour force

---

12. Data is not available for the following OECD countries: Austria, Iceland, Korea, New Zealand, Portugal, and Switzerland. Information on taxes and transfers is not provided for the Czech Republic, Greece, Ireland, Japan, Turkey, and Mexico in UNICEF (2000).

participation through generous parental leave policies and publicly-funded ECEC. Another strategy is to improve the economic and social environment in which the child is raised through work and education training programmes for low-skilled parents, which have shown to be successful as long as quality ECEC is available. Research reveals a strong link between high female labour participation and low child poverty, and a corresponding link between comprehensive levels of family policy and high employment among women. A third correlation exists between family policy legislation and low rates of child poverty (UNICEF, 2000). In countries with high child poverty rates, there may also be a need to garner political will to reallocate resources and develop effective policies. Setting poverty reduction targets may stimulate public support and provide a framework for different agencies to work together, as in the UK, where the government has committed to halving poverty in ten years and to eradicating it by the year 2020.

In addition to income redistribution and job training and education for low-skilled parents, *early intervention* programmes have been explored by governments both to mediate some of the negative effects of poverty on children and as a long-term strategy to break the cycle of disadvantage. H*ome-visiting programmes*, for example, can improve parenting skills and prevent low birth weight, which is strongly correlated with lower cognitive ability. These schemes, which generally consist of health-care advice and general social services support are common in Europe, and to a lesser extent in Australia and the US. Research shows that participation in quality, centre-based ECEC *programmes* can have important immediate and short-term impacts on the cognitive and socio-emotional development of disadvantaged children (Barnett, 1995; Boocock, 1995; Jarousse *et al.*, 1992). Some positive effects have been shown to remain, leading to improved levels of social and economic well-being in adolescence and adulthood (Karoly *et al.*, 1998; OECD, 1999*b*). Early intervention may improve children's life chances but it cannot immunise them against their subsequent educational experiences, nor can it substantially address structural poverty (Kagan, 1999). Also, it is difficult for ECEC services to focus on children's development and learning, when their basic health, nutrition, and housing needs are not met. Countries concerned about addressing these needs target resources *and* comprehensive services to poor children and to the communities in which they live.

ECEC policy can contribute to efforts to fight poverty...

Even in countries with lower-levels of child poverty, a widespread and increasing concern in OECD countries regards the *socially excluded*, the growing section of the population that faces extraordinary barriers to full participation in the labour force and society. There is concern that these barriers are likely to lead to dependence on benefits, financial deprivation, poor health status, and limited access to services. Most European countries now have an increasing immigrant and refugee population, who are particularly marginalised. Women and young children tend to be over-represented in such populations. Refugees, in particular, are often traumatised, yet because of their ambivalent status are among the least likely to access benefits and services (Rutter and Hyder, 1998). The Roma communities in Portugal and the Czech Republic, and to a lesser extent in other countries, are another group at great risk for social exclusion. It is of great policy concern that the most vulnerable children are likely either to miss out on ECEC services, or find that the services they use are insensitive to their needs (see Section 3.1).

... and social exclusion.

Countries such as Belgium (Flemish and French Communities), the Netherlands, Portugal, and the UK have developed strategies to combat poverty and social exclusion that incorporate policies for urban regeneration, improved access to social services, and integration of immigrants or ethnic minority groups. Social assistance policy to address social exclusion has taken the form of cash assistance, social help via services (*e.g.*, to address disability, homelessness, addiction), and supports for labour market reinsertion (OECD, 1999*a*). A more recent focus of governments has been on the role of early childhood policy and programmes in promoting social cohesion by providing marginalised families, particularly those from immigrant and ethnic minority communities, an opportunity to develop informal relationships and build social support and networks.

2.2. Recognising diverse views of children and the purposes of ECEC

Key points

- The reasons for investing in ECEC policy and provision are embedded in cultural and social beliefs about young children, the roles of families and government, and the purposes of ECEC in within and across countries.

- In many countries, the education and care of young children is shifting from the private to the public domain, with much attention to the complementary roles of families and ECEC institutions in young children's early development and learning.

- Many countries are seeking to balance views of childhood in the "here and now" with views of childhood as an investment with the future adult in mind. These diverse views have important implications for the organisation of policy and provision in different countries.

Multiple objectives shape ECEC policy.

In most countries, ECEC policy is shaped by a multiplicity of objectives, including:

- facilitating the labour market participation of mothers with young children and the reconciliation of work and family responsibilities;
- supporting children and families "at risk" while promoting equal opportunities to education and lifelong learning;
- supporting environments which foster children's overall development and well-being;
- enhancing school readiness and children's later educational outcomes; and
- maintaining social integration and cohesion.

The relative emphasis on these policy objectives differs across countries and may shift according to the specific political, economic, and social conditions at a given time and place (Cleverley and Phillips, 1986; James *et al.*, 1998; Woodhead, 1999) (see Box 2.1). In many instances, the focus on children themselves is a subset of the broader overarching policy, whether it relates to employment, families, social or educational outcomes.

In addition, the dominant rationale for investing in early childhood education and care is influenced by specific views about young children, about responsibility for young children's care and education, and about the purposes of ECEC institutions (see Dahlberg *et al.*, 1999). ECEC policies reflect

---

Box 2.1 **Social change reflected in new views of children and ECEC in the Czech Republic**

Although the buildings and basic structure of the Czech *mateřská škola* (ECEC for 3 to 6-year-olds) remained intact after 1989, the "velvet revolution" brought with it dramatic socio-political changes that were deeply to influence views of education and early childhood. The conception of education as conformity to accepted knowledge and social norms has given away to a spirit of enquiry and innovation. Great efforts have been made to change the relationships between the education partners, and to lower the pressures put on children in ECEC institutions. There is a fresh appreciation of the child as a subject of rights, and parents as equal partners. Pedagogical approaches and methods of work more suited to the young child's needs and interests have been encouraged, daily routines in kindergartens have been relaxed, age-integrated classes introduced, and individual needs and differences respected. Increasingly, children with special needs are included in kindergartens, which are now more open to the public.

The change in understanding has brought also a wide range of innovative programmes into early education in the Czech Republic. Foreign programmes (Waldorf, Montessori, Step-by-Step) are current, but there are many Czech programmes for young children and their parents reflecting new value orientations and offering a wide range of choice and activities. Immersion in a foreign language, speech therapy, swimming lessons, nature classes, sport activities, art and music clubs are offered in kindergartens in the larger urban centres. Men, too, have been invited into the previously female world of kindergarten teaching: army duty may be replaced by service as assistants in the *mateřská škola* and other institutions, bringing a young male presence – and alternative role models – to young children.

Some of these innovations are trendy and short-lived, and tend to take time from hours that might be more formative for young children. In addition, many parents still look on the *mateřská škola* as a form of care that allows them to take up employment. Indeed, some government ministries may see the *mateřská škola* primarily in this light, as an instrument that serves the labour market. The Ministry of Education is conscious of these views, and wishes to refocus the kindergarten as the first stage in the education cycle, a period in which important skills and personal attitudes are formed. For this reason, it has begun work on the preparation of a framework curriculum for the *mateřská škola*. The new curriculum will be general enough to orient kindergartens to offer systematic and appropriate programmes to young children and flexible to allow innovation and experimentation. The content of education will be worked out in five spheres: biological, psychological, interpersonal, socio-cultural and environmental. The framework will identify general competencies (personal, cognitive and operational) that children should acquire in *mateřská škola*, linked with the behaviours and knowledge expected in the first cycle of primary school.

---

these – mainly implicit – assumptions, which are deeply embedded in how societies are organised and in cultural and social views. This section explores some of the different views of young children and the purposes of ECEC that have been documented during the review.[13] While different views may co-exist within countries, they are rarely made explicit in policy discussions. Recognising these diverse perspectives can help shed light on why countries make certain choices with regard to early childhood policy and provision for example, with regard to governance, staffing, parent engagement, pedagogy, and financing. Our objective is to make these complex political and ethical issues more visible so that they can be subject to critical and democratic discussion.

---

13. Each country note includes a more detailed discussion concerning the dominant views of early childhood and the purposes of ECEC in the country concerned, based on a review of government documents and discussions with policy officials, researchers, practitioners, families, and other stakeholder groups.

Who is responsible for ECEC?

Social views with regard to who is responsible for the education and care of young children are important to understanding policy development in different countries. In other words, what are the implicit or explicit assumptions of the respective responsibilities of mothers, fathers, and other members of society when it comes to the education and care of young children? In the past, the pervading assumption in many countries has been that the education and upbringing of young children is a private affair and not a public responsibility. Early childhood provision therefore has been seen as an issue for parents, usually understood as mothers, not as an issue for people and society, and still less about children's rights to self-fulfilment. When child-rearing is understood as a private affair, there is less public responsibility for very young children – unless the family is deemed "in need". This helps to explain why, historically, many countries have targeted ECEC policies to "at-risk", poor, or abused children, and only more recently have some taken more universal approaches.

A *growing view of* ECEC *as a shared* responsibility.

Government involvement in the rearing of children – particularly infants and toddlers – is still viewed in some societies as interfering with the rights and responsibilities of parents. However, the approach taken by an increasing number of countries in the review suggests that the issue is no longer whether non-parental care is inferior to the care that parents can provide. All countries acknowledge that mothers and fathers have the main responsibility for their children and that the home environment is extremely important to their children's well-being. Increasing attention is also being accorded to the role of fathers in their children's early years. There has been a shift, however, toward a view of children's early care and education as a shared responsibility between the family and the state, and not just for the family alone to bear. As described in the Netherlands background report:

…concepts of childrearing and socialisation are changing. Although the family is still seen as centrally important and primarily responsible for the upbringing of children, there is a trend towards a new view of the socialisation of children being a shared social responsibility, involving many different parties including government. This signifies and exemplifies a new direction in government policy, aimed at creating constructive communities of interest in which citizens, professionals, organisations, and government participate on an equal basis (Ministry of VWS/Ministry of OCenW, 2000, p. 8)

Rather than being viewed as a substitute home, ECEC can be seen as different from, but complementary to, families. In Portugal, for example, the Framework Law defines pre-school education in the *jardim de infância* as:

…the first step in basic education seen as part of life-long education, and complements the education provided by the family, with which it should establish close co-operation, fostering the education and balanced development of the child, with a view to his/her full integration in society as an autonomous, free and co-operative individual (Ministry of Education in Portugal, 1998, p. 24).

According to this perspective, both the home and ECEC provision have very important roles to play in the early years of children's development and learning, and children can benefit from both worlds. Today, most children need some non-parental care and education, most often because their parents are in the labour market or studying. In addition, many children are growing up in small family units, with maybe only one adult and no siblings at home, and few peers in the immediate neighbourhood. Many grow up in urban environments which prohibit freedom of movement. ECEC settings can provide support while parents are working, but also a place for children in their early years to socialise and learn through their relationships with other children and other adults. Most countries recognise that early childhood provision provides an opportunity to identify children with special needs or at-risk and intervene as early as possible in order to prevent or minimise later difficulties. When ECEC is considered as part of the public domain, settings can be viewed as meeting points for the family and community, providing social support, and where both children and adults have an interest and a "voice" in decision-making. For example, in Denmark:

The facilities shall meet a demand for care and provide educational and stimulating environments for the children. The institutions create the framework in co-operation with the children and their parents to further the development, well-being and independence of the children (Ministry of Social Affairs in Denmark, 1997, p. 6).

Whether children are in the home or in organised provision, ECEC policy can support parents in stimulating their children's development and learning. Many countries also have recognised that flexible services for parents, such as drop-in centres and playgroups, can provide important support to families with young children and promote social cohesion.

What are the purposes of ECEC provision?

Societies also differ in the degree to which childhood is regarded as a special time to be cherished in and of itself and the degree to which childhood is regarded as preparation for the future. One common view is that children are in need to be readied to learn or readied for school so that they can eventually take their places as workers in a global economy. In countries where this perspective is particularly prevalent, policies and provision may emphasise the importance of quality early childhood experiences to prepare children to succeed in formal schooling, the labour force, and society. In this framework, there is a need to compensate for the disadvantage experienced by children from home environments that are deemed deficient in some way. Resources may be targeted to children deemed "at-risk" in order to foster their ability to become autonomous and economically self-sufficient individuals, but also to prevent the potential costs to society of welfare dependency, crime, and other social problems. While these are important goals within an overall educational vision, it is important to recognise children's strengths and potential, as well as their vulnerabilities, and to consider in both policies and services, the best interests of the child.

While some countries have targeted programmes to certain groups, other countries have made it a policy priority for all young children to have the right to high quality education from an early age, regardless of socio-economic status or ethnic origin. Universal access to ECEC is sought as a means of promoting equality of educational opportunity and ensuring that all children – and especially those in need of special support or at "at-risk" of school failure – experience the necessary conditions so that they are "ready to learn" when they start primary school. Whether a targeted or more universal approach is taken, there is a similar focus on children as human capital investment which shapes the purposes of ECEC provision. When ECEC focuses primarily on familiarising children with early schooling, there is a risk of downward pressure from a school-based agenda to teach specific skills and knowledge in the early years, especially with regard to literacy and numeracy. This can lead to neglect of other important areas of early learning and devel-

41

opment. Developing communication skills is an essential aspect of ECEC, but the way in which literacy and numeracy concepts are introduced and development is fostered are equally important. With help from the early childhood field, there is growing recognition of the importance of focusing on the "whole child" and fostering children's emerging literacy and numeracy skills within an integrated curriculum (see Section 3.6).

Taking a view of the child as a competent learner.

Another perspective is to view childhood as an important phase of life in its own right. In the words of the *Norwegian Framework Plan*:

...childhood as a life-phase has a high intrinsic value, and children's own free-time, own culture and play are fundamentally important...the need for control and management of the [barnehager] must at all times be weighed against the children's need to be children on their own premises and based on their own interests (Ministry of Children and Family Affairs in Norway, 1996).

Linked to the UN Convention on the Rights of the Child and research on the sociology of childhood (James and Prout, 1990), among other influences, children are seen increasingly as a distinct group in society. As a group, children not only have their own culture, but also their own rights and "voice". ECEC provides opportunities for children to socialise with their peers and with adults and to learn what it means to be a citizen. As young citizens, they are expected to become part of the social and learning communities in ECEC institutions. Again, in accordance with the UN Convention, countries are stressing the rights of children to express their points of view and to participate take part in the choice and planning of activities or to participate according to their maturity in the evaluation of the institutions they attend.

While the main purpose of ECEC is *not* to influence later school or workforce performance, this view of childhood recognises the importance for children to possess the skills and learning strategies they will need in school. As noted in the Sweden background report, the *förskola* for children under 6:

...builds on the view of the child as competent and with great inner resources, capable of formulating [his or her] own theories about the world, discovering and exploring [his or her] immediate surroundings and developing confidence in [his or her] own abilities (Gunnarsson *et al.*, 1999, p. 50).

Children are understood to be competent learners from birth. Since children learn all the time and in *all* aspects of everyday life, divisions between "care" and "education" become meaningless. There is an effort to ensure that all children have access to ECEC, particularly children in need of special support. In particular, participation in ECEC is seen as critical for children from ethnic minority groups to have early exposure to the country's language and traditions so that they can become part of today's society and do not suffer from social exclusion either when they begin school or later in life. Although ECEC settings are viewed as having long-term value for children's learning and well-being, they are not designed specifically to prepare children for the future. In countries that have adopted this view of childhood, quite different teaching and learning traditions have developed in ECEC and schools. Recently, closer collaboration between ECEC and schools has led to cross-influences on pedagogy in both sectors (see Section 3.3).

This discussion does not intend to present a false dichotomy between the present and the future, between the child as "being" and "becoming". In fact, a growing number of countries are seeking a balance between providing opportunities that will enable children to thrive in the next stage of education and adulthood and, at the same time, valuing ECEC institutions as places for children to live out their lives in the "here and now". It seems that if countries choose to adopt a view of the child as full of potential and capable of learning from birth, and a view of childhood as an important stage in its own right, then ECEC provision can be concerned with both the present and the future. This perspective emerges through the New South Wales (Australia) Curriculum Framework for Children's Services:

Children are viewed as current citizens in the community. The investment in children's lives, their learning and development, comes from valuing them in the present, not largely because of the prospect of a pay-off in the future. The experience for a child in a children's service is both life and preparation for life (NSW Department of Community Services, 2000, p. 3).

ECEC institutions adopting this view of the child and of childhood are likely to challenge children and enable them to acquire the abilities that they will need to participate in school, work, and society-at-large. While the main function of early childhood services is not to get them ready for formal schooling, early childhood professionals recognise their responsibility to provide children with a range of appropriate experiences so that they will begin school as a capable learners, confident, flexible, and open to new possibilities and relationships. Early childhood services can give all children a firm foundation so that they are well-equipped to develop fully their potential and play a full and active part in the community and the economy. This view of the child and of childhood asks challenging questions of the school, and how ready it may be for children who are competent learners. Indeed, exploring the relationship between ECEC and school raises issues about both systems, their views of childhood, learning, knowledge, and the need for both to find new views which can form the basis for a relationship of equality. In this sense, the early childhood years are a fundamental part of the continuous process of lifelong learning.

What are the implications for policymakers?

This discussion illustrates the importance of recognising the complex and diverse views of young children, families and the purposes of ECEC that exist within and across societies. Social constructions of children, families, and the purposes of ECEC are reflected in how ECEC systems are envisaged and structured. They can influence whether countries invest in coherent and integrated early childhood systems or accept fragmented arrangements. They have an impact also on the form of services (*e.g.*, centre-based versus home-based; formal versus informal) or whether services are age-split or age-integrated, publicly- or privately-funded. Structural characteristics, in turn, shape the development and implementation of policies and practices for young children. These issues will be explored in the rest of the report.

Chapter 3

Main Policy Developments and Issues

Introduction

At the beginning of the 21st century, the education and care of young children is firmly on the national policy agendas of all 12 countries participating in the thematic review. While in some countries, ECEC has been accorded a high priority for several decades, in others, an unprecedented political focus on young children and families has emerged in the past five years, partly to overcome past neglect. Across countries, we have witnessed and documented strong enthusiasm for improving early childhood policy and practice, at all levels of the system, not least among the dedicated professionals who work directly with young children and their families. Fuelled by major demographic, economic, political, and social changes discussed in the previous chapter, the recent surge in policy attention has fostered several major developments in the field including, rapid expansion of early childhood provision, increased focus on quality improvement, attention to coherence and integration, and higher levels of public investment in the system as a whole.

Given the important changes and developments in recent years, it is timely to take stock of what has been achieved and what remains to be accomplished in the field of ECEC. Drawing on the background reports, country notes, and other materials collected during the review process, the chapter celebrates some of the policy achievements in participating countries, but also raises important issues and concerns for policymakers' consideration. To support and strengthen policy development in the field, particular attention is accorded to strategies to improve quality, access, and coherence of policy and provision. Specifically, this chapter explores seven current cross-national policy trends: 1) expanding provision toward universal access; 2) raising the quality of provision; 3) promoting coherence and co-ordination of policy and services; 4) exploring strategies to ensure adequate investment in the system; 5) improving staff training and work conditions; 6) developing appropriate pedagogical frameworks for young children; and 7) engaging parents, families and communities. Additional information on policy developments in each of the 12 countries can be found in Appendix 1.

It is well recognised that countries have adopted diverse strategies to policy development in this field – strategies which are deeply embedded in particular country contexts, values, and beliefs. Taking this into account, the report does not compare country approaches in terms of better or worse, but raises the possible implications of different policy choices for children, families, and society. In this way, an analysis of different country approaches to ECEC policy may lay out policy options and underscore remaining challenges for policymakers' future attention. From among the many exciting and interesting initiatives underway in all 12 countries, a variety of examples have been selected because of their particular cross-national relevance, not for their potential as models, but as inspiration for reflection and discussion in OECD countries concerning how to improve early childhood policy and provision.[14]

---

14. A wide range of current initiatives in the field of ECEC are described in the background reports and country notes.

Table 3.1. **Terms and organisation of main forms of ECEC provision**

Country	Name of provision	Setting	Ages served	Opening hours#	Administrative auspice (national)	Locus of policy making	Compulsory school age
AUS	Long day care	Centre	0-5	Full-time	Social welfare	Commonwealth	6
	Family day care (FDC)	FDC home	0-5				
	Pre-school	School/centre	4-5	Part-time	Education	State/Territories	
BEL (FL)	Kinderdagverblijf Diensten voor opvanggezin-nen (DOGs)	Centre	0-3	Full-time	Social welfare	Community	6
		FDC home	0-3				
	Kleuterschool	School	2.5-6	Part-time	Education		
BEL (FR)	Crèche	Centre	0-3	Full-time	Social welfare	Community	6
	Gardienne encadrée	FDC home	0-3				
	École maternelle	School	2.5-6	Part-time	Education		
CZE	Creche	Centre	0-3	Full-time	Health/welfare	Local	6
	Mateřská škola	School	3-6	Full-time	Education	National and local	
DNK	Vuggestuer	Centre	0.5-3	Full-time	Social welfare	National and local (primarily)	7
	Aldersintegrerede	Centre	0.5-6+				
	Børnehaver	Centre	3-6				
	Dagplejer	FDC home	0.5-3				
	Børnehaveklasser	School	5/6-7	Part-time	Education		
FIN	Päiväkoti	Centre	0-7	Full-time	Social welfare	National and local	7
	Perhepäivähoito	FDC home	0-7				
	6-vuotiaiden esiopetus	Centre/school	6-7	Part-time	Education		
ITA	Asilo nido	Centre	0-3	Full-time	Health/welfare	Local	6
	Scuola materna	School	3-6	Varies	Education	National	
NLD	Kinderopvang	Centre	0-4	Full-time	Social welfare	National and local (primarily)	5
	Gastouderopvang	FDC home	0-4	Part-time			
	Peuterspeelzaal	Centre	2-4				
	Bassischool	School	4+	Part-time	Education		
NOR	Barnehage	Centre	0-6	Full-time (and part-time)	Children and Family Affairs	National and local	6
	Familiebarnehage	FDC home	0-6				
PRT	Creche	Centre	0-3	Full-time	Social welfare	Regional and local	6
	Creche familiare	FDC home	0-3				
	Jardim de infancia	Centre/school	3-6	Full-time (varies)	Education/ Social welfare	National	
SWE	Förskola	Centre	0-6	Full-time	Education	National and local (primarily)	7
	Familiedaghem	FDC home	0-6	Full-time			
	Förskoleklass	School	6-7	Part-time			
UKM	Day nursery	Centre	0-5	Part-time	Education	National and local	5 in Great Britain and 4 in North-ern Ireland
	Nursery class/school	School	3-5	Part-time			
	Pre-school playgroup	Centre	2-5	Part-time (varies)			
	Childminder	FDC home	0-5	Full-time			
	Reception class (not in Scotland)	School	4-5	Full-time			
USA	Child care centre	Centre	0-5	Full-time	Social welfare	State	5-7 (varies by state)
	Family child care	FDC home	0-5	Full-time		State	
	Head Start	Centre	4-5	Part-time (varies)		National and local	
	Pre-kindergarten	School/centre	4-5	Part-time (varies)	Education	State	
	Kindergarten	School	5-6	Part-time (varies)		State	

Sources: OECD background reports; Meyers and Gornick (2000); Kamerman (2000a); Oberhuemer and Ulich (1997); Rostgaard and Fridberg (1998).
Note: Family day care in many countries accommodates school-age children during before and after-school hours. We do not include other forms of out-of-school provision here.
A full-time place is defined as a minimum of 30 weekly hours (Rostgaard and Fridberg, 1998). Provision covering a full school-day (less than 30 hours/week) is considered as part-time.

Figure 3.1. **Main institutional arrangements for provision of early childhood education and care**

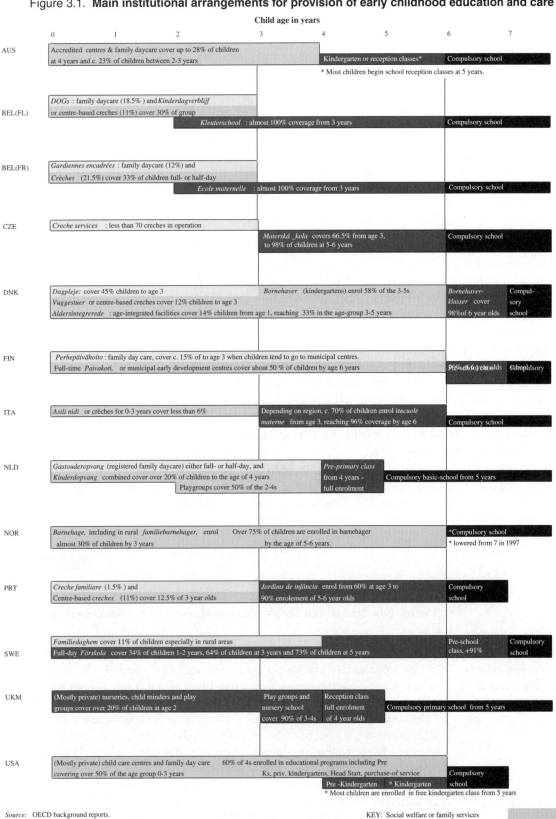

Source: OECD background reports.

KEY: Social welfare or family services
Family daycare
Services under Education Ministry
Free, compulsory primary school

© OECD 2001

3.1. Expanding provision toward universal access

Key points

Improving access – the ease with which children and families can take part in ECEC – is a policy priority in all countries, though with different emphases and approaches. Increasingly, countries are expanding provision toward *universal* access – provision that is available to all children whose parents wish for them to participate. Countries are also striving for *equitable* access, that is quality, affordable ECEC that meets the diverse needs of children and families, especially of children who most need support. Accessibility has a number of dimensions including: availability in all areas (rural and urban), affordability,[15] length of operation during the day and year, flexibility, and availability for different age groups, and for children with special needs. This section presents some of the trends and developments in access to and levels of provision, including:

- The age at which children typically make the transition to primary education ranges from 4 to 7. School starting age influences the duration and nature of children's ECEC experiences.

- In several countries, access to ECEC is a statutory right from age 3 (or even younger). The trend in all countries is toward full coverage of the 3- to 6-year-old age group, aiming to give all children at least two years of free publicly-funded provision before beginning compulsory schooling.

- Out-of-school provision for children of working parents has not been a policy priority in most countries in the review. Yet, demand is high, which suggests the need for attention to the concept, organisation, funding, and staffing of this form of provision.

- Policy for the under-3s is closely linked with the nature of available parental leave arrangements and social views about caring. While there have been government efforts toward expanding provision and increasing the educational focus, there is still differential access and quality for this age group.

- Countries are trying to develop: a) more flexible and diverse arrangements while addressing the regional and local variation in access and b) strategies to include children in need of special support (*i.e.*, children from low- income families, children with special educational needs, children from ethnic, cultural, and linguistic minorities).

The relationship between the starting age of compulsory schooling and ECEC

In several countries, it is common to begin in primary school prior to compulsory school age.

Access to and development of ECEC provision is shaped, in part, by the starting age of compulsory schooling. There is currently some debate concerning the appropriate age for children to start primary school. The statutory age for primary education varies from 4 (Northern Ireland) to 7 (Denmark, Finland, and Sweden), and children in most OECD countries make the transition to compulsory school at the age of 6 (see Table 3.1). Children may begin to attend primary school prior to compulsory school age, particularly in countries where ECEC provision for young children has remained relatively underdeveloped compared to other OECD countries. In the Netherlands and Great

---

15. The relationship between affordability and access will be discussed in greater detail in Section 3.4 on financing.

Britain statutory school age is 5, but it is common practice for almost all young children to enrol in primary school on a voluntary basis at age 4.[16] In Great Britain, there has been some concern about the appropriateness of learning environments for 4-year-olds in reception classes where staff-child ratios may reach 1:30. In Australia and the US, as well, primary schools commonly provide for children under 6 in pre-school or (pre-) kindergarten classes.

In Italy and Portugal, lowering the compulsory school age to 5 has been discussed, and later rejected, as a means of providing access to education for socially disadvantaged children, especially ethnic minority groups. Lowering the school start is also a strategy to provide more places for younger children in ECEC. In Norway, when the 6-year-olds began attending the free public schools, the supply of ECEC for children under 6 increased by 20 000 places, and some of the places for older children were switched to provide for 3- and 4-year-olds. However, in countries that have adopted market approaches to ECEC (*e.g.*, UK, US), there is concern that as 3- and 4-year-olds move into free public education, the unit cost of provision for infants and toddlers will increase and restrict access further for very young children.

The trend is toward compulsory primary schooling at age 6.

In countries where a wide range of ECEC provision is available for children below compulsory school age, children begin school-based provision later, but there are moves toward the European norm of 6 as the age to start formal schooling. After 30 years of debate and experimentation Norway lowered its compulsory school age to 6 in 1997. As part of the joint ECEC and school reform, the pedagogical methods of the first four years of primary school were transformed to provide a gradual transition from early childhood to formal schooling. Denmark and Sweden have kept compulsory school age at 7, but have introduced a free, voluntary kindergarten or pre-school class (*børnehaveklasser*; *förskoleklass*) in the primary schools for 6-year-olds, which provides a bridge from ECEC to formal schooling. In practice, therefore, almost all children enter the school system at age 6. Since August 2000, all 6-year-olds in Finland have the right to attend free part-day pre-school education (*6-vuoti-aiden esiopetus*) either in day care centres or in the primary schools, a policy change which is expected to raise coverage from its present level of 78%.

Trends in provision for 3- to 6-year-olds: moving toward full coverage

Most European countries have recognised the role of government in expanding access toward full coverage of the 3- to 6-year-old age group. Giving children the possibility to benefit from at least two years of high-quality ECEC is viewed as a strategy to promote equality of educational opportunity prior to starting compulsory schooling. To that end, all children have a legal right to attend *free* school-based provision from age 30 months in Belgium (Flemish and French Communities), age 3 in Italy[17], and age 4 in the Netherlands and the UK (see Table 3.2). These education-based programmes are viewed as good for children and are widely accepted by the public. Indeed, over 95% of

Two years of free, part-day education-based ECEC has become standard in most European countries.

---

16. In the Netherlands, the majority of parliament recently agreed to lower compulsory school age to four years, and the government has agreed. The next step toward implementation is to change the current legislation.

17. In Italy, pre-primary education is free only in state-run and municipal schools, not in private schools.

Table 3.2. **Entitlements to ECEC provision**[1]

	Nature of entitlements	Age of children covered	Duration of entitlement[2]	Free or Fee-paying
AUS	– No legal right to services for children aged 0-4 years. Child Care Benefit for families using an approved service. – No legal right to pre-school although most States provide free or almost free pre-school for 4 and 5-year olds.	4-6 years		Free (varies)
BEL (FL and FR)	– No legal right to ECEC for children under 2.5 years, but supervised, subsidised services are broadly available. – Legal right to universal pre-school from 2.5 to 6 years	2.5-6 years	Full school day, with some out-of-school provision	Free
CZE	– No legal right to ECEC for children under 3 years – No legal right to pre-school (3-6 years) but access is generally broad, with priority being given to five year olds.	3-6 years	Full-day	Fee-paying
DNK	– 87% of municipalities guarantee places for all children between 1-5 years. – Legal right to a place in free, kindergarten class in primary schools – Legal right to a place in out-of-school provision	0.5 to 6 years 6-7 years	Full day Half-day Morning/afternoon	Fee-paying Free Fee-paying
FIN	– Legal right to a place in centre-based or home-based ECEC – Legal right to a place in free, pre-school class in centres and primary schools – Legal right to a place in out-of-school provision	0-7 years 6-7 years	Full day Half-day Morning/afternoon	Fee-paying Free Fee-paying
ITA	– No legal right to services for children under-3 years – Legal right to a place in school-based ECEC	3-6 years	School day or Full day	Fee-paying Free in public
NLD	– No legal right to services for children under 4 years, but high investment in subsidies for children 'at risk'. – Legal right to a place in primary school, from 4 years	4-6 years	School day	Free
NOR	– No legal right to services but 80% enrolment has been reached for children over four years, and will be extended progressively to all children.	0-6 years	Full day	Fee-paying
PRT	– No statutory right to services for children under 3 years – Legal right to free *jardim* enrolment from 5 years, to be extended next year to 4-year olds.	5-6 years	5 hours, 5 days/week	Free
SWE	– Legal obligation to provide a place for children of working or studying parents (to be extended to all parents) from 12 months, within 3 months. – Legal right to free pre-school for bilingual children from age 3 – Legal right to a place in free, pre-school class in primary schools, extended progressively in the *förskola* to 5s and 4s	1 to 12 years 3-6 years 6-7 years	Full day 3 hours, 5 days/week 3 hours, 5 days/week	Fee-paying Free Free
UKM	– No legal entitlement for children under 3 years – Legal right to a place in nursery education for all 4-year olds and some 3-year olds. This entitlement will be extended progressively to all 3-year olds	4-5 years	2.5 hours, 5 days a week minimum, often 6,5 hours	Free
USA	– No legal right for children from 0-5 years. – Two States, Georgia and New York, have pledged universal pre-kindergarten to all 4-year olds. Pre-kindergarten for children at-risk in several states. – Most school districts offer free kindergarten class to all 5-year olds as part of primary schooling	4-5 years 5-6 years	Half-day, term-time (varies) Half-day, term-time (varies)	Free Free

1. This table should be read in conjunction with Table 2.2 on maternity and parental leave arrangements in the 12 countries, as well as with Table 3.1 which provides information on the forms of ECEC provision available for children under compulsory school age.
2. Gives minimum duration of legal entitlement. Actual duration of participation may be longer.
Source: OECD background reports.

children attend (see Figure 3.2[18]) regardless of family income or employment status. Most school-based ECEC do not cover the full working day, and many parents work non-standard hours, which raises the issue of out-of-school provision (see below). In countries with near full coverage, there has been little scope for recent development. Other countries have shown remarkable growth in provision. Portugal has rapidly expanded and increased public investment in the pre-school network – public and private providers – over the past five years to overcome long-standing inequities in access, and the government is working toward full enrolment of the 3- to 6-year-olds. Between 1996 and 1999, coverage increased dramatically, from 57 % to 72%. Moreover, to encourage full coverage in the year before compulsory schooling begins, Portugal has introduced a free daily five-hour session for 5-year-olds in the *jardim de infância* (over 90% coverage).

There has been an increase in coverage in Denmark, Finland, Norway, and Sweden as well, in part as a result of recently introduced entitlements to ECEC. Current coverage for 3- to 6-year-olds varies from about 65% in Finland, over 70% in Norway and Sweden, and almost 90% in Denmark. As noted earlier, enrolments rise to almost full coverage by age 6. As early childhood provision has developed with the dual purpose of supporting children's development *and* promoting equal opportunities for men and women to participate in the work force, most services are full-day. Parents pay fees, usually on a sliding-scale according to income. With the exception of Sweden, these services fall under auspices outside the education system at the national level, and take place in centres, and less frequently, family day care homes.[19] Access to ECEC is a right enshrined in legislation and covers a much wider age group than the 3- to 6-year-olds. In Finland, children under 7 have a legal right to attend publicly-funded ECEC[20], and in Denmark, municipalities are expected by law to meet local parental demand. Sweden currently provides an entitlement for all children aged 18 months to 12 years whose parents work or study. There is a new government proposal to extend this right to include a part-time place in the *förskola* or family day care for children whose parents are unemployed or on parental leave (as of 2001-2002). As a sign that the policy orientation is shifting toward a more universal right-to-education approach, a government bill has proposed to provide a *free* half-day pre-school session by 2003 for all 4-and 5-year-olds (many of whom are already attending ECEC). Norway has not instituted a legal right, but it is a political goal to achieve universal access to the *barnehager* for all children under 6 by 2003.

Of the countries participating in the review, only the Czech Republic has experienced a decrease in coverage due to the political, economic, and social changes that have occurred in the past decade (see Box 2.1). Coverage for 3- to 6-year-olds declined from about 96% in 1989 to 86% in 1999. Declining enrol-

In the Nordic countries, full-day ECEC supports children's development and parental employment.

Contextual changes have led to declining enrolments in the Czech Republic.

---

18. These figures should be read with caution as they use a more narrow definition of "pre-primary education" that does not include "non-educational" or more informal forms of ECEC.

19. Specifically, ECEC falls under the Ministry of Social Affairs (Denmark, Finland), the Ministry of Children and Family Affairs (Norway), and the Ministry of Education and Science (Sweden). The impact of administrative auspices on policy and provision is discussed in more detail later in the report.

20. The legal entitlement has been in force since 1990 for under threes and since 1996 for 4- to 7-year-olds.

51

Figure 3.2. **Net enrolment rates by single year of age in pre-primary[1] and primary education, 1999 (%)**

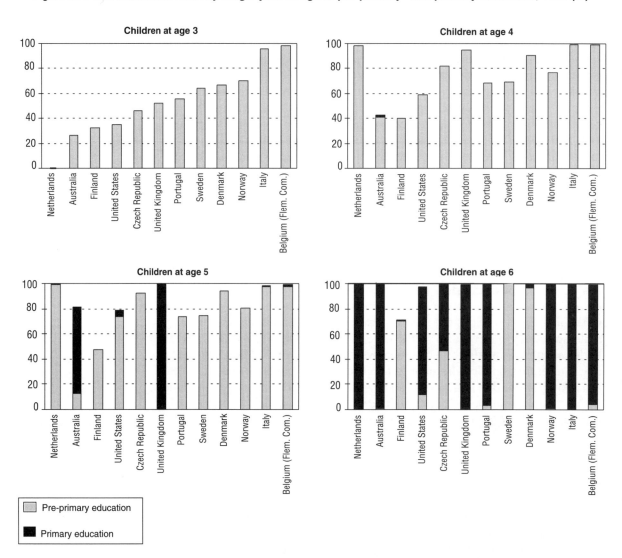

1. The data refer to pre-primary education, which is limited to organised centre-based programmes designed to foster learning and emotional and social development in children for 3 to compulsory school age. Day care, play groups and home-based structured and developmental activities may not be included in these data.

Source: OECD Education Database (2001).

ments have been linked to changing attitudes toward female employment, the extension of maternity leave to four years, and the closing of kindergartens due to decreasing numbers of young children. Yet, coverage remains high (98% at age 5) and is commonly assessed as meeting need except in areas with small and dispersed populations of children. The Ministry of Education has stressed the important role of the *mateřská škola* as part of the education system, and there are signs that attitudes are changing again: more women are entering the labour market and participation in kindergartens is on the increase.

In contrast to most other OECD countries, policy in Australia, the UK, and the US has not been based on the notion of statutory entitlement to a place in ECEC, especially for the younger children. Until recently, for example, access to public provision in the UK and the US has been limited to low-income families or children deemed "at risk."[21] Even for these groups, access is not universal (*e.g.*, Head Start in the US serves about 36% of eligible children), and coverage is often part-day. Parents who can pay the necessary fees or who receive subsidies from their employers are in a position to gain access to quality programmes in the dominant private sector. Many low- and moderate-income working families – who on the one hand do not have the means to pay high fees, but on the other hand earn more than is needed to qualify for publicly-funded services – tend to experience real difficulties of access. The situation in these countries is currently developing, with more generous fee subsidies being made available to enable low- and middle-income families to purchase ECEC in the private market (see Section 3.4). More universal approaches within the education system also are gaining ground to address real or potential inequities.

More universal approaches within the education system are gaining ground in Australia, the UK, and the US.

In the UK, all 4-year-olds since 1998 have an entitlement to a free part-day *nursery education* session. The right will soon be extended to 3-year-olds – starting with areas of disadvantage and moving toward universal provision for all who want it by 2004. In Australia and the US, there also are trends toward universal access to provision for 4-year-olds under education auspices through state-administered initiatives. In Australia, most states and territories aim for the universal provision of a part-time pre-school place for 4-year-olds, and most children begin school in a preparatory year at age 5.[22] In the US, where almost all 5-year-olds attend kindergarten within the formal school system, the number of part-time state-funded *pre-kindergarten* programmes for 3- and 4-year-olds has grown significantly (Schulman *et al.*, 1999). Like Head Start, most of these programmes are targeted at children considered to be at-risk of later school failure. Two states – New York and Georgia – have developed *universal* pre-kindergarten initiatives for all 4-year-olds regardless of family income.

In sum, the trend across countries is to provide at least two years of free provision, often within the educational system. Countries that have not achieved full coverage for this age group see it as a priority, though in Australia and the US, the focus has been mostly on 4-year olds. In the case of the US, expansion has prioritised children deemed "at risk". In some of the Nordic countries, there is a move toward a more universal educational orientation, which also continues to meet the needs of employed parents and children at-risk. There has been some, but less recognition within the education system of the role of provision in supporting parents who work, and most forms of universal provision do not cover the full working day.

Trends in out-of-school provision: *need for improvement and expansion*

With the exception of the Nordic countries and the Czech Republic, where full-day ECEC services are the norm, the opening hours of ECEC or early primary education generally do not cover the full working day. As pre-school or

Out-of-school provision has received limited attention in most countries.

---

21. In Australia, children at risk and children from working families have higher priority for access to care to services approved for the Child Care Benefit.
22. In many jurisdictions pre-schools may also be attended by younger children although a place is not necessarily guaranteed.

school may end in the early afternoon, many young children spend a substantial part of their day in out-of-school provision, usually alongside older school-age children. Also, most school-based ECEC programmes are closed during the summer holidays and other periods when parents are working. Until recently, out-of-school provision has received limited attention in most countries. It is often loosely regulated, and there is a range of varying services with few reliable statistics or sources of information. Out-of-school provision may take place on school premises, in age-integrated centres, or in family day care homes. In most countries, out-of-school provision takes the form of "wrap-around" services on school premises before and after school hours, and sometimes during lunch time. In some countries (*e.g.*, Australia, Belgium, Portugal, UK), for-profit and non-profit (*e.g.*, parent) associations operate programmes outside school hours either in schools or in separate mixed-age facilities. In general, services are fee-paying, and staff tend to be less well-trained than staff in other forms of early childhood provision.

Currently, Sweden and Denmark are the only countries that provide enough places to meet demand, and employ staff trained at university or higher education level. Sweden is the only country where children under 12 have a legal entitlement to this form of provision. However, there are several promising recent national initiatives to expand and improve out-of-school provision. The UK government has encouraged the development of out-of-school provision through the New Opportunities Fund and other funding sources to schools, local authorities and other organisations.[23] In the Netherlands, the government has increased investment to stimulate expansion (current coverage is 5% of 4- to 7-year-olds), and all quality regulations for ECEC in the welfare sector also apply to out-of-school provision, including staff qualifications. Out-of-school provision in Portugal is expanding mainly in social priority areas aimed at improving the integration of marginalised groups. In the US, Head Start is implementing a major initiative to expand full-day/full-year services through partnerships with other early childhood programmes and funding sources.

The relationships between out-of-school provision, schools, and other services need to be explored.

There are debates within countries (*e.g.*, Belgium, Finland) about whether out-of-school provision should take place in schools, in mixed-age centres, or in family day care, though there seems to be a trend toward school-based arrangements for cost and practical reasons. As a newer and less-established form of provision, the role of out-of-school services is often unclear and ambiguous. These services are often in a weak position in terms of funding, staffing, and even access to facilities and materials, which raises issues about the purposes of out-of-school provision and its relationship with schools and other services. There is some concern that out-of-school provision will become an extension of school activities (*e.g.*, reading and math clubs, which may be helpful for some young children), to the neglect of developmental, recreational or leisure-time activities. For these reasons, some countries emphasise the distinctiveness of out-of-school time from education and schooling, while in other countries, new relationships and ways of working are developing among pre-school, school, and out-of-school provision to provide full-day mixed-aged services for young children (see Section 3.3).

---

23. The New Opportunities Fund has awarded start-up grants in the UK totalling £45 million for out-of-school provision. £220 million is available in the UK for 1999-2003. There were 4 400 out-of-school clubs in England in 2000, compared with 350 in 1992.

Trends in provision for children under 3: more than support for working parents

In most countries, there is little national data collected on ECEC for children under 3, in part due to the high levels of private provision and informal arrangements for this age group, and in part due to the regional/local responsibility for these services. Country reports for the thematic review document that the demand for ECEC for children under 3 is significantly higher than the available number of places in most countries, including those providing long parental leaves. Services for infants and toddlers are provided primarily in centres and family day care homes, and all charge parental fees. Figure 3.1 provides available data on provision for under 3s in the countries participating in the thematic review.[24]

Despite the expansion of formal provision for infants and toddlers, it is still common for parents to rely on a combination of organising their working hours and informal arrangements in many countries, including Australia, Belgium, the Netherlands, and the UK. It seems that only in the Nordic countries is formal provision predominant following the period of paid parental leave. While informal arrangements have continuing importance in most countries, their decline has been noted in other countries, including Italy, Portugal, and the US. There also are variations in family use of informal and formal arrangements. Higher socio-economic groups tend to rely more on formal services, than their counterparts from lower socio-economic groups, particularly immigrant and ethnic minority parents. Although informal arrangements have played a significant role in all countries in the past, they are coming under increased pressure as traditional forms of family support – including grandmothers who are often in the workforce themselves – are no longer available to take care of young children· The declining use of informal arrangements in some countries also suggests that when a good system of formal, affordable services exists, preferences for relatives and other informal arrangements may diminish.

Parental care and informal arrangements have predominated, but are under pressure.

The nature and availability of paid and flexible maternity and parental leaves are closely linked to policy and provision for children under 3, and reflect social views about young children and their education and care. There are four different approaches to policy for under 3s:

- In Denmark and Sweden, policy supports parent employment after a comparatively well-paid parental leave of about 6 to 12 months. A guaranteed place in publicly-subsidised ECEC services is provided from the end of parental leave period, on a sliding-scale, fee-paying basis. Few infants attend ECEC settings before the end of this leave period.

- The explicit policy objective in Finland and Norway is parental choice: child care leaves or cash benefit schemes allow one parent, usually the mother, to stay out of the workforce to care for their child until the age of 2 or 3, and provision for children under 3 is publicly-subsidised as well. In Finland, this choice reinforced by a statutory right to ECEC, and declining waiting lists, while in Norway addressing the shortages in provision for under 3s has become a political priority.

ECEC policy is closely related to available leave arrangements and social views about childrearing.

---

24. Parental leave policies have an important role to play in reducing demand for infant provision, so enrolment figures that cover the age group one to three would better reflect enrolment trends.

– Policy in the Czech Republic favours parents (meaning mothers) caring for their child for 3 or more years, with few publicly-supported alternatives.[25] For example, since paid parental leave was extended to four years in the Czech Republic, the number of public *creches* – which covered 20% of children in 1989 – has fallen to 67 settings under the auspices of the Ministry of Health (covering about 1 900 children in 2000).

– Policy supports the belief that care for the under 3s is to be resolved *primarily* by families, with some help from government. There is a period of paid (Italy, Portugal, UK) or unpaid (Australia, US) statutory leave and low levels of publicly-funded services. Both Belgium (Flemish and French Communities)[26] and the Netherlands have combined short paid leaves with moderate levels of publicly-funded provision. However, access to infant-toddler services in these countries is not a right.

Limited access to quality, affordable infant-toddler provision is a concern.

As a result of these different societal views about the role of parents and the needs of very young children, there is significant variation in levels and quality of infant-toddler services. In all countries, coverage is lower than for 3- to 6-year-olds. Subsidised provision for under 3s is the most developed in Denmark, Finland, and Sweden, countries with a long history of supporting publicly-funded ECEC as part of broader gender equity and family policies. Belgium (Flemish and French Communities) provides for about 30% of children under 30 months. In the past five years, the Netherlands, Norway, and, more recently, the UK have significantly expanded publicly-funded provision for infants and toddlers, to increase access to quality ECEC that also supports maternal employment and children at-risk. As a result of recent incentive schemes in the Netherlands, for example, 20% of children under 4 now have a place in ECEC, in addition to the 50% of 2- to- 4-year-olds attending part-day playgroups. In contrast, in countries where publicly-funded provision for under 3s is limited, most working parents must either seek solutions in the private market, where ability to pay determines accessibility, or rely on informal arrangements with family, friends, and neighbours. In the US, lack of paid parental leave and limited public investment in services means that many low- and middle-income parents struggle to find high-quality, affordable arrangements for infants as young as six weeks old. In 2000, almost 60% of American women with children under age 1 were in the labour force (US Department of Labor, Bureau of Labor Statistics, 2000).

Demand for formal provision may increase with growing attention to its wide-ranging objectives.

In most countries, policy for under 3s still emphasises expansion of services as a necessary support for maternal employment in a strong economy rather than as a public service that can benefit both children and parents. As noted in Chapter 2, there are signs that the concept of services for under 3s is broadening from "child care" to support working or disadvantaged parents to include educational, gender equality, social integration, and family support objectives. In Italy, for example, recent government proposals describe the shift in understanding of the *asilo nido* as a service on "individual demand" to "an educational and social service of public interest". In other countries, as well, there is an increasing focus on the educational role of services for very young children, which is supported by research showing that first three years

---

25. This policy aim is also pursued in two countries that did not participate in the review: Austria and Germany.

26. As 85% of children attend pre-primary school from age 30 months in Belgium, infant-toddler provision concerns mostly children below this age.

of life are extremely important in setting attitudes and patterns of thinking (Shore, 1997). In addition, there has been a focus on providing flexible services – full-time, part-time, and drop-in centres, playgroups – to benefit children and support parents, whether they are working or not. This more universal and wide-ranging approach may help bring provision for the under 3s into the public sphere and obtain much-needed policy attention and investment.

Greater diversity and flexibility vs. regional and local variation in access

Access to ECEC is also a function of whether parents, working and non-working, can arrange education and care to meet the individual needs and circumstances of their families. In some countries, there is widespread provision and high levels of coverage, but the services available are uniform and limited in scope, and, therefore they are less likely to be able to accommodate irregular hours of attendance or requests for longer hours. This tends to be the case for services for children based in the school system. In other countries, there is more fragmented provision, but a great deal of local variation and innovation. This diversity may or may not meet family needs. A shift toward a more consumer-oriented approach has led to a greater emphasis on programme flexibility and parental choice in countries, such as Australia, Denmark, Norway, the Netherlands, Sweden, and the US.

Parental choice is a goal in many countries.

In reality, cost, location, age of child and parent working hours may constrain parental choice. For example, family day care is the dominant form of provision for children under 3 in Finland, Denmark, the Flemish Community of Belgium, and the US, and in rural areas in many countries. In part, this may reflect parental preferences for more home-like arrangements, smaller and mixed-age groups, and flexible hours, or it may be a choice determined by cost and affordability considerations. If family day care is to be treated as a real alternative to centre-based provision, attention is needed to the workers who receive lower salaries, training, and benefits than centre staff (Kamerman, 2000a). In addition, there is a shortage of places and a growing need for services that accommodate irregular and/or longer hours of attendance, as many parents (up to 30% in some countries) work evenings, weekends, and shifts. As countries strive for services that are more flexible and accommodating of parent employment schedules, another issue emerges: is the goal to make services meet these longer and irregular working hours or should the focus be on making the labour market more supportive of parents who wish to spend time with their children? In sum, a central question for ECEC policymaking is raised: which approach is in the best interest of young children?

Cost, location, age of child and parent working hours may constrain parental choice.

With the trend toward decentralisation of responsibilities for educational and social services, there is widespread within-country variation in access and levels of provision across municipalities and regions (e.g., Italy, the Netherlands, Norway). This seems to be the case particularly for services for children under 3 and out-of-school provision. These two forms of ECEC are usually the responsibility of local or regional authorities, who may vary in their willingness or ability to fund services (EC Childcare Network, 1996a). These differences also may reflect variability in parent needs and preferences in different geographic regions. Evidence from the reviews of UK and the US suggests that market-driven approaches to expansion have contributed to uneven growth of services. In particular, supporting ECEC provision through demand subsidies has led to shortages in low-income areas, where private and non-profit operators find it difficult to survive. There is also variation in access between rural and urban areas in most countries. Barriers to equitable access in rural areas

In particular, improving access in low-income and rural areas is a common challenge.

include scattered communities, small scale of demand linked to low population density, poor transport, lack of suitable buildings, and difficulty finding qualified staff. Targeted funding to existing services, integrating ECEC services with public school facilities, itinerant teachers, mobile services, and family day care are among the alternatives to operating settings for small groups of children. These strategies have been explored in countries, such as Australia, the Czech Republic, Denmark, Finland, Norway, Portugal, and the UK.

Strategies to promote inclusion

Issues of ethnicity, culture, and disability have received different emphases and attention in different countries, leading to variation in the extent to which policies and programmes are accessible to children and families of diverse backgrounds and needs. For the most part, countries have chosen to welcome all children into mainstream ECEC settings, while according particular attention and resources to those in need of special support within this regular provision. The inclusion of children with special educational needs is an important goal for all the countries in the review. Children may have *special educational needs* related to physical, mental, or sensory disabilities, learning difficulties, or socio-economic, linguistic, or cultural factors. Article 23 of the UN Convention on the Rights of the Child confirms the rights of such children to enjoy a full and decent life, and to actively participate in community life in a normal and self-reliant manner. Country analyses indicate that 15% to 20% of children have special educational needs at some time during their school career, although few countries, with the exception of the Netherlands and the USA, fund special education at these levels at any given moment (OECD, 1999*d*). Early intervention aims to strengthen the sensory-motor, emotional, social and cognitive development of children with special educational needs as early as possible, as preventive intervention is often more effective than rehabilitation measures in later life.

Mainstreaming is the favoured approach for children with special educational needs.

Most countries favour mainstreaming young children with physical, mental, and learning disabilities into ECEC provision, if this is determined to be best for the child. In several countries (*e.g.* Denmark, Finland, Norway, Sweden), there is a conscious policy to ensure that such children have priority in enrolment and additional resources are allocated to reduce child-staff ratios and to provide more individualised attention and specialised staff. Early intervention services focus on: early detection of problems; prevention of disabilities or further difficulties; stimulation of development; aid and support to families. Before the 1980s, these activities were conducted, almost exclusively in many countries, by health services. Today, the education sector is becoming a key agency in tackling disability and learning difficulties. Moreover, in recent years, important progress has been made in all countries in terms of legislation and the right to inclusion (see Box 3.1).

Structural changes to ECEC systems...

However, real challenges remain, as the inclusion of children with special educational needs requires not only better public attitudes toward disability and disadvantage, but also important structural changes in the organisation of ECEC systems. A difficulty in several countries is the difference in *legal and policy frameworks* in public and private ECEC settings, only the former being legally obliged to accept children with disabilities. In Australia, the Commonwealth Disability Discrimination Act of 1992 applies to both private and public sectors and makes it unlawful to discriminate in the provision of goods, services, or facilities against people who have, or may have, a disability. Even with strong policies and legislation, *de facto* discrimination can take place in coun-

---

Box 3.1 Special education in the United States

The United States federal government has been a leader for many years in promoting access and equity issues related to special education. Its role in the education of young children with special educational needs began in the 1960s with support for training teachers of children with speech difficulties. In 1975 services for special needs children were expanded with the Education for All Handicapped Children Act (Public Law 94-142), further revised in 1997 under the Individuals with Disabilities Education Act (IDEA). According to this law, states receive funds from the federal government to assist in the education of those with special needs from age 3 to 21. One of the programmes under the IDEA fund – Grants for Infants and Toddlers – may be used to implement state-wide early intervention services for children under age 3 and their families. Recently, the U.S. Department of Health and Human Services established the Map to Inclusive Child Care programme which will eventually provide support to all 50 states and the District of Columbia as they prepare a state-wide plan for including children with special needs in a variety of ECEC programmes.

In addition, the right of parents to be active participants in decision-making regarding educational services for their children is clearly established. Parents must be included in the development of a child's Individualized Education Plan (IEP), which lays out the goals and objectives for children from 3 through 5 years of age. Families of children from birth through 2 years of age are to have an Individualized Family Services Plan (IFSP), which is designed to build on each family's strengths, and provide the supports required to ensure that each young child being served with special education receives the appropriate supports and services. The legislation also establishes specific programmes for educating parents about their legal rights by establishing a network of parent training and information centres across the US.

Young children with disabilities are assessed by medical services, mental health professionals and by local school district child study teams, and if necessary are referred to the most appropriate services. The law requires placements in the "least restrictive environment", and insists that, in so far as possible, children with disabilities should receive supports and services in natural environments with typical children, and not in segregated settings. Programme staff and family child care providers in most states are encouraged to enrol children with special needs, and most find it beneficial not only to the child but to all the children in the programme. Head Start programmes in particular offer health and mental health services to their children and families, and 13% of children enrolled have disabilities.

---

tries because of the inability of low-income parents with special needs children to either pay for or have access to adequate early childhood services.

To break down the old divisions (and disparity of funding) between special and mainstream education, countries have tried to develop new *funding models*. Decentralisation of educational funding has been seen to be helpful in this regard as municipalities tend, in many countries, to bring educational, social services and health budgets together. In the Netherlands, special per capita grants are provided directly to ECEC centres and schools to cater for enrolled children with special educational needs. Inclusion of children with special educational needs calls for attention to the *organisation and management of ECEC settings*, in particular the adaptation of premises to the needs of children with disabilities and for more flexible organisation of group sizes and rooms to cater for special sessions for children with disabilities. Similarly, inclusion of children with special educational needs requires a special *pedagogical approach and curriculum*: more intensive team planning and team teaching, more flexible programmes, and careful management of activities.

Staff need to adapt constantly to the learning demands presented by individual children. To reach the learning goals that children can realistically achieve, individualised educational plans (IEP) – determined by children, parents and teachers together – are formulated and implemented (*e.g.*, Finland, Flemish Community of Belgium, the US). *Staff ratios* – both teachers and

... and individualised work with children are necessary to support inclusion.

classroom assistants – are by necessity higher for children with special educational needs and *special training* is necessary, a factor that still inhibits moves toward inclusion in some countries. In Finland and Italy, special education staff provide on-the-job training to their mainstream colleagues. *Parental involvement* is desirable in all programmes for very young children, but particularly in programmes involving children with special educational needs. Finally, ECEC centres that welcome children with disabilities or other special educational needs put into place *co-operative agreements and activities with community health and social services agencies*, an activity that demands expertise and much investment of time.

Successful initiatives support inclusion, while respecting ethnic, cultural, and linguistic difference...

As societies become increasingly heterogeneous, there is increasing recognition of the need to promote ethnic and cultural sensitivity, value linguistic diversity and create learning environments that are respectful of the different backgrounds of all children and families. Primary school curricula in most countries reflect the language, values and attitudes of mainstream society, and there are concerns that children from minority ethnic or language groups who do not participate in ECEC provision may be at a disadvantage when they start school. On the other hand, most countries recognise the role of ECEC in increasing the educational opportunities of those at risk of social exclusion, especially children in poverty or from immigrant backgrounds. As a result, many countries give additional subsidies to families or to areas in need of special support to facilitate access to ECEC, including Belgium (Flemish and French Communities), the Netherlands, Portugal, and the UK. In Australia, Denmark, Norway, Sweden, and the UK, "bilingual assistants" work in pre-schools with new immigrant children and parents to help strengthen their home language and develop proficiency in the country language. Other countries, including Belgium (Flemish and French Communities), Denmark, and the Netherlands, favour language immersion and training in the national language.

...though many barriers remain.

Despite these efforts, children from immigrant or ethnic minority backgrounds are often under-represented in regular ECEC provision. In part, lower enrolment may be linked to lower rates of maternal employment among these socio-economic groups. In addition, there may be different childrearing traditions. Many new immigrants do not share the idea that very young children spend most of their day away from home. Research shows that refugees value education and care for their children, but often have limited knowledge of available services and are reluctant to seek information from national and local government sources (Joseph Rowntree Foundation, 1995; Rutter and Hyder, 1998). Limited proficiency in the country language and lack of interpretation services may also be barriers to children accessing ECEC. Curricular approaches that do not acknowledge cultural, ethnic, and linguistic diversity may prevent diverse groups of children from fully benefiting from ECEC. To provide access to appropriate services, it seems that additional resources are needed to develop comprehensive communication strategies (*e.g.*, materials in different languages, interpretation services), outreach work by community workers, multi-cultural and anti-bias approaches to curriculum, additional staff training and employing staff from the community, and long-term language support for both children and their parents.

To address these barriers, some countries (*e.g.*, Denmark, the Netherlands, Norway, Sweden) have piloted half-day programmes focusing on culture and language as an important part of the pedagogical activities, as these are seen not only as important for children's language skills but also for fostering their social and emotional development. These programmes work with parents and network with other community services and institutions, including the schools

---

Box 3.2 **Immigrant children in ECEC in the Flemish Community of Belgium**

In the Flemish Community of Belgium, an innovative programme – *Milestones towards Quality through Equality* (MEQ) – focuses on women and children from ethnic minority communities. The project, based in Leuven, identifies how conventional understandings of quality childcare generally exclude the voice of immigrant or ethnic women. Women from first, second or even third generation immigrant backgrounds are likely to feel excluded from discussions about childcare for a number of reasons. They will often have left school early, are less likely to be employed (except informally), and their children are least likely to attend any subsidised form of childcare. In short, the most vulnerable children and families are likely either to miss out on services, or find that the services they use are insensitive to their needs.

The MEQ project set out to reconceptualise ECEC services in terms of the particular needs, customs or linguistic diversity of ethnic minority children. A programme of training and employment for immigrant women was established. After two years, 25 immigrant women qualified as care workers, 17 of whom have now found permanent positions in day-care centres. Education, training, mentoring and supervision modules were also offered to the participating day-care centres around multicultural and multiethnic issues. This work proved to be complex and challenging. According to the MEQ project leaders: "Working in an intercultural way involves dealing with all sorts of preconceptions, values and norms."

Among the resources that MEQ has made available to the public and the ECEC community is a CD-ROM, *Respect for Diversity in Early Childhood Education*, and a web site on diversity and early childhood education (http://www.decet.org). These resources give many practical and useful examples of how to deal with a range of multiracial issues. The CD-ROM includes a theoretical overview and reference texts; examples of recruitment and selection procedures; how to build a multi-cultural team; and specific case studies of discrimination and how to address them. It also includes examples of multicultural books: a multicultural music guide which includes lullabies, and an introduction to various musical instruments. There are many examples too of multicultural toys and other classroom resources.

---

and health services. They often employ staff from the community in which they work to help build bridges across language and cultural divides (see Box 3.2). Parents tend to seek out services which value and respect their own culture and customs. As an example, the Dutch government is supporting playgroups which co-operate with primary schools for 2- and 3-year-olds from at-risk and ethnic minority families.[27] In Australia, too, there are a number of special services for Aboriginal and Torres Strait Islander (ATSI) people where local ECEC provision is not available or not suitable, *e.g.* the Commonwealth-funded and ATSI-operated Multi-functional Aboriginal Services (MACS) provide flexible services for children including long day care, playgroups, outside school hours care, school holiday care and cultural programmes.

Though the challenges seem formidable, there are very good reasons, other than respect for the basic human rights of children and parents, to support inclusion. According to studies conducted by CERI (OECD, 1999*d*), inclusive settings eventually cost less than maintaining two separate systems, mainstream and special. Apart from the preventive nature of early intervention, the pedagogical consequences of including all children in need of special support are apparent. The inclusion of diverse groups of children reinforces some of the major aims of early childhood programming, namely, to give young children the experience of living together supportively; to focus on the individual needs and learning patterns of each child; and to foster strong parental involvement in the education of their children.

---

27. Dutch research estimates that 90% of Turkish and 56% of Moroccan parents would like their children to participate in playgroups, particularly when they are connected to a primary school.

3.2. Raising the quality of provision

Key points

After access, raising quality in ECEC is at the forefront of policy priorities in OECD countries. Much recent research emphasises that quality is important in the early childhood years. Children who receive high quality care and education in their early years show better cognitive and language abilities than those in lower quality arrangements (Bowman *et al.*, 2000; Cost, Quality, and Child Outcomes [CQCO] Study Team, 1995, 1999; NICHD, 1997). Children in low quality programmes are likely to have difficulties with language, social and behavioural development (Whitebook *et al.*, 1989). While there are elements of quality that are accepted by many countries, quality is often considered a relative and not a universal measure across early childhood systems (Dahlberg *et al.*, 1999). Variations in emphasis across countries are greatly dependent on the views of particular societies about early childhood and on the goals they formulate (or implicitly hold) for young children. Within countries, there may be a wide diversity of criteria and goals for children and child-rearing – between rural and urban populations, across socio-economic or multicultural contexts, between parents and professionals, and even between ministries. The first part of the section discusses how quality is defined, measured, and ensured. Then, quality issues from the review and government strategies to improve the quality of ECEC systems are identified:[28]

- Definitions of quality differ considerably among stakeholder groups and across countries. Although national quality guidelines are necessary, they need to be broad enough to allow individual settings to respond to the developmental needs and learning capacities of children.

- Many common elements in definitions of quality across countries exist, especially for provision for children from the age of 3. Most countries focus on similar structural aspects of quality (*e.g.*, staff-child ratios, group size, facility conditions, staff training), which tend to be weaker for infant/toddler provision.

- To measure programme quality, some countries use standardised observation scales and child assessment measures. Other countries favour co-constructing the programme aims and objectives at local level, engaging a range of stakeholders in the process.

- The responsibility for quality assurance tends to be shared by external inspectors, pedagogical advisors, staff, and parents (and occasionally children). There is a trend toward externally-validated self-evaluation to promote ongoing reflection and quality improvement.

- Major quality concerns that emerged during the review include: lack of coherence and co-ordination of ECEC policy and provision; the low status and training of staff in the social welfare sector; the lower standards of provision for children under 3; and the tendency for children from low-income families to receive inferior services.

- Governments promote quality improvement through: framework documents and goals-led steering; voluntary standards and accreditation; dissemination of research and information; judicious use of special funding; technical support to local management; raising the training and status of staff; encouraging self-evaluation and action-practitioner research; and establishing a system of democratic checks and balances which includes parents.

---

28. The section does not treat the pedagogical quality of programmes, a question that is addressed in Section 3.6 below.

How is quality defined?

Concepts of quality differ across countries and according to the priorities, visions, and perspectives of different stakeholder groups – national and local government authorities, parents, children, employers, and providers. For example, parents will often value aspects of early education and care that do not necessarily coincide with the priority aims of officials, while teachers in primary school and ECEC professionals will sometimes have very different expectations about what ECEC should bring to children. Likewise, children, if asked, will express their views as to what quality is, and at certain ages will place the making of a friend or mastering a childhood skill far above the educational concerns of either parents or teachers.

Concepts of quality differ across countries and across different stakeholder groups...

One current of recent research has analysed quality at a more macro-level, exploring how definitions of quality differ from one milieu, culture or country to another (Moss and Pence, 1994; Dahlberg *et al.*, 1999). A premise of such research is that variations in notions of quality originate in different social constructions and representations of childhood and society. From this perspective, ECEC policy and the quality of services are deeply influenced by underlying assumptions about childhood and education: what does childhood mean in this society? How should young children be reared and educated? What are the purposes of education and care, of early childhood institutions? What are the functions of early childhood staff? As an example, Carlina Rinaldi from Reggio Emilia has stated, "One point appears to us to be fundamental and basic: the image of the children. The cornerstone of our experience, based on practice, theory and research, is the image of children as rich, strong and powerful" (Edwards *et al.*, 1993, p. 102). This understanding stands out against the *tabula rasa* notion of education, in which children are empty vessels who should be filled as soon as possible with knowledge. The contrast reveals the need for policy makers to become aware of national or cultural constructions of childhood, and their impact on the indicators of quality put forward by different stakeholders.

In addition, national definitions of quality are shaped by economic or political factors driving ECEC systems, families' socio-economic status and culture, age of the child, and beliefs about the roles of government and the welfare state (Bush and Phillips, 1996). For these reasons, cross-national investigations of quality require sensitivity to different national and cultural situations, as the assumptions on which family and child polices are based differ widely from country to country. Within countries, sensitivity to context is equally necessary, in particular when defining national quality goals and standards. Broad outcomes allow ECEC settings to respond to the holistic needs of the young children for whom they cater. In contrast, quality objectives that are detailed, academically-oriented and framed with middle-class children in mind may underestimate the variability that is common among very young children, and overlook the developmental needs of children who require special supports, such as children from low-income, ethnic and immigrant groups. A way must be found to allow ECEC provision to pursue quality objectives while responding to the real needs of children, including for children who can easily pursue advanced cognitive competencies and skills.

...and this variability imposes caution and sensitivity to context.

Substantial agreement is found, however, across most of the countries participating in the review in their understanding of quality ECEC for children from 3 or 4 years of age. Australia, Belgium (Flemish and French Communities), Italy, the Netherlands, Portugal, the UK, and the US have developed ECEC for

Common goals for children aged 3-6 are found across most countries...

this age group on an education-based model, including clear policies, approved educational aims and agreed understandings about the role of the pre-school and teaching profession. In Section 3.6 below, the educational goals for this age group are discussed in terms of:

- *general goals or outcomes*, *e.g.* well-being, citizenship, preparation for school;
- *goals in specific developmental areas*, *e.g.* physical and socio-emotional development;
- *subject and learning areas*, *e.g.* communication and language skills, art, emergent literacy, etc.

These general goals are shared especially with respect to children approaching the year of entry into primary school. In addition, educational programmes in Belgium, Italy, UK and the US define skills that children should, in principle, have mastered before entry into primary school. When judged against the goal of achieving readiness for school, quality in the pre-school sector is generally good, as the goal is clear and can be broken down into objectives and indicators to be used for monitoring and evaluation. However, in some situations the cost may be high for young children, as the research of Sylva and Wiltshire (1993) suggests. When begun too early, formal teaching may actually harm the self-concept of young children, leading to anxiety, low self-esteem and mediocre literacy results in primary school, particularly in reading.

Countries with a strong tradition of integrated care and education – Denmark, Finland, Norway, and Sweden – take a wider view of early childhood and do not wish to assimilate the early childhood institution to a school-like model. A central understanding is that the early childhood institution should contribute, alongside the parents, to the individual child's development and well-being, which is generally interpreted as learning to live in society and sharing a society's fundamental values, including respect for autonomy and independence. Quality evaluations tend to place an emphasis on the quality of life in the institution and the social development of the child (*e.g.*, well-being and friendship). More emphasis is placed on what the municipality or provider should offer to young children rather than on benchmarking children's performance. The belief is strong that there is a time for childhood that can never be repeated. However, some difficulties for children making the transition into primary school have been noted. For this reason, greater emphasis in the Nordic countries is being placed in ECEC on providing emergent literacy environments for children and on focused group work.

...but there is less consensus on the goals of quality ECEC for younger children.

For younger children, conceptions of quality are more diverse. In more integrated early childhood systems (*e.g.*, Denmark, Finland, Norway, Sweden), policy-making tends to be more consistent across the *whole* early childhood age-group. Core understandings of young children, families and the purposes of ECEC (see Section 2.2), are elaborated in policy documents and framework curricula, from which flow agreed general goals to be elaborated in local services for children, aged birth to 6 or 7. Monitoring and evaluation of these goals take place regularly, although, as indicated below, in a rather different manner from the formal assessment or outcome measures used in other countries. The transition to school increasingly takes place as a two-way process developed in collaboration between ECEC and primary school settings. This collaboration leads frequently to mutual influence, *e.g.* to a better focus on goals and outcomes in ECEC settings, and to more appropriate pedagogical approaches in the early classes of the primary school.

In most countries, responsibility for the education and care of young children is split between ministries and among different administrative levels, and provision may include a large, loosely regulated private sector. In the past, policy was often formulated on the presumption of familial care, and early childhood services were organised along a social welfare or medical model for children whose families were unable to assume full care. As a result, wide divergences existed in the objectives set for services in different sectors, including with regard to the profiling, training and certification of staff.[29] Even today in most countries, services for the under-3s remain under-funded, and are not fully acknowledged as forming part of the educational and developmental services to which all young children have a right. Services may be seen primarily as a means of facilitating the growing participation of women in the labour market or as facilitating social integration of disadvantaged and immigrant children. In short, lack of policy co-ordination can make it difficult to maintain quality standards in a systematic way across the range of early childhood services. At the same time, several examples of cross-sector collaboration led by government departments are emerging, as outlined in Section 3.3.

What are the conditions of quality across a system?

Although definitions of quality are not agreed on internationally or even within a given country or community, there is general consensus among researchers that certain inputs contribute to positive short- and long-term outcomes for children. At the *systemic* level, these conditions include: adequate levels of investment; co-ordinated policy and regulatory frameworks; efficient and co-ordinated management structures in place; adequate levels of staff training and working conditions; pedagogical frameworks and other guidelines; and regular system monitoring based on reliable data collection (see Box 3.3). In addressing the issue of overall quality, many countries would also see features, such as equity and respect for diversity (expressed in eligibility and staffing policies), as conditions of a quality system.

There is general agreement that stable structural conditions are linked to quality ECEC...

At the *programme* level, other criteria of quality may be identified *e.g.*, sufficient duration and intensity of programmes, appropriate size and composition of children's groups, favourable adult-child ratios, and factors linked to the physical design of settings such as the quality of indoor and outdoor-environments.[30] Some of these variables are easily measured and form the basis of regulations, though countries accord different standards and priorities to the different variables. The interpretation of standards is influenced by national understandings about which pedagogical environments are suitable for young children, as well as financial and organisational constraints. For example, where child-staff ratios are concerned, there is a continuum going

---

29. This may not be a consequence of a divided system. Clear policy lines characterise infant-toddler services in Belgium and in many Italian municipalities.

30. A comprehensive listing and description of the major structural requirements of ECEC systems can be found in EC Childcare Network (1996a). The report sets out 40 targets across nine areas: policy; finance; levels and types of services; education targets; staff-child ratios; staff employment and training targets; environment and health targets; parents and community; performance targets.

Box 3.3 **The Early Childhood Observatory in the French Community of Belgium**
L'*Observatoire de l'enfance*

In 1991, as a result of the profound social and demographic changes that were taking place in Brussels, the French Community Commission (*Commission Communautaire Française*) for the Region took the initiative to create a permanent Early Childhood Observatory with two affiliated researchers from regional universities. The Observatory was given the task of generating indicators and collecting all necessary data about ECEC for young children in the capital. The Observatory researches and proposes solutions regarding four themes:

– The ECEC needs of parents with children from 0-3 years and proposals to improve access;

– The quality of ECEC received by infants and toddlers enrolled in services in the city;

– The ECEC needs of children aged 2.5-12 years in the school system, including out-of-school provision;

– The socio-demographic and intercultural dimensions of ECEC, with measures to improve equity.

The Observatory, in co-operation with several university researchers, publishes annually the basic quantitative data on ECEC in Brussels, matching a number of agreed analytic indicators. The health of children is reported; their social (including ethnic) and family backgrounds described; what types of early care and education services are available to them; and which children are using what services. Several action-research studies have been completed on the accessibility and quality of services, linked with socio-economic status and other indicators.

Persuaded of the key role of well-trained personnel in raising quality and the need to keep them in the sector, the Observatory collaborates with a training association for early childhood personnel in the Brussels region, called the FRAJE (*Centre de Formation Permanente et de Recherche dans les Milieux d'Accueil du Jeune Enfant*). The FRAJE, which began its training activities in 1970s, works to increase the access of ECEC personnel to high quality training. Seven psychologists lead regular evening discussions or on-site sessions for staff. The Observatory publishes a quarterly magazine – *Grandir à Bruxelles* – which provides up-to-date information about the current situation of young children in Brussels.

The contribution of the Observatory has been recognised by the French Community Government, through a formal agreement. The information gathered by the Observatory, in a rapidly changing urban environment, is considered a powerful means of monitoring early childhood services in the city, and as providing a well-informed basis for policy-making.

---

from the low child-staff ratios of centre-based provision in Denmark, Sweden, Finland, and Norway to ratios commonly found in school-based provision in Belgium (Flemish and French Communities), the Netherlands, Portugal, and the UK (see Table 3.3).[31] There are trade-offs, however, as in most countries, child-staff ratios are higher in schools than in centres, but participation in schools is usually free.

... but that quality needs also to be viewed as a dynamic and collaborative process.

In addition to structural *inputs*, quality may be defined in terms of *process* (what is occurring in programmes) and *outcomes* or *results* (what knowledge and learning children gain through programmes). Process quality variables are primarily related to health and safety features, interactions between children and adults, partnerships with parents, and the learning and social opportunities offered. Outcome variables measure children's progress in developmental and learning areas, and seek to evaluate the effectiveness of various ECEC approaches. Outcomes are defined and assessed at three levels: i) at programme level (*e.g.* the Dutch evaluations of Piramide and Kaleidoscoop

---

31. The EC Childcare Network recommended approximate staff-child ratios of 1:4 for children under 12 months; 1:6 for children aged 12-23 months; 1:8 for children aged 24-35 months and 1:15 for children aged 36-71 months.

Table 3.3. **Regulations for child-staff ratios in ECEC**

	0-3 years	3-6 years
Australia	5:1 (0-2 years) 8:1 (2-3 years)	10:1
Belgium (Flem. Com.)	7:1	18:1 (maximum)
Belgium (Fr. Com.)	7:1 (centre-based ECEC)	19:1 (maximum)
Czech Republic	m	12:1
Denmark	3:1	6:1
Finland	4:1	7:1
Italy	7:1	20:1-28:1
Netherlands	4:1-6:1	20:1 (*bassischool* only)
Norway	7:1-9:1	14:1-18:1
Portugal	10:1 (maximum)	15:1
Sweden	6:1	6:1
United Kingdom	4:1 (public) 8:1 (private)	8:1 (playgroup) 13:1 (nursery class) 30:1 (reception class)
United States	4:1-6:1 (varies by state)	10:1-20:1 (varies by state)

Note: Comparisons across countries are not always valid in terms of these ratios, as staff in some countries may be fully-trained professionals, whereas in other countries, contact staff may have little initial training (see Section 3.5).
m: missing data.
Source: Country reports (see Appendix 1 for more detailed information).

curriculum approaches); ii) at child level (*e.g.* the identification of special needs); and iii) at aggregate or national level [*e.g.* the British (except Scotland) national Baseline Assessment of children on entry into primary school]. There is growing agreement, in fact, that quality goals for children should be specified at multiple levels – local as well as national – and, with increasing customisation and specificity (Kagan and Cohen, 1997)· In addition, it is critical to investigate how quality objectives at whatever level are identified and prioritised, and how they evolve (Moss and Pence, 1994). Just as concepts of quality change, the process of defining quality also is expected to be dynamic and continuous, changing across programmes and time, and involving a wide range of groups with an interest in ECEC for young children (EC Childcare Network, 1996*a*; Woodhead, 1996).

From a structural perspective, with the exception of countries that have developed ECEC under unified administrative auspices, the situation of children under 3 years is generally less favourable both in terms of access and quality. Critical systemic elements that underpin quality are often lacking in programming for these children, *e.g.* coherent policy formulation, a unified regulatory framework, co-ordination across ministries or between central and local government, effective management structures, pedagogical frameworks, a solid professional corps. In many countries, for example, despite the presence of some excellent programmes and initiatives, the overall situation is characterised by weak public investment and high costs to parents, inade-

With some exceptions, these conditions tend to be less favourable in ECEC for children under 3.

quate regulatory frameworks, low training and status of staff, insufficient attention to pedagogical frameworks, wide variations in inspection and monitoring.

How is quality measured?

From a systemic perspective, the evaluation of quality is based, first of all, on the analysis of the structural conditions of quality. Questions such as the following are fundamental: what is the level of public investment in early childhood, including services and parental leave policies for infants and toddlers? What is the status and quality of the legislation that regulates and guides the sector? What is the volume and quality of the infrastructure? Are sufficient administrative and management resources being devoted to the sector at every level? What is the level of recruitment, training and status of staff? These, and other elements such as staff-child ratios, are crucial if the "trilemma" of adequate access, high quality and affordability for all parents is to be properly resolved. The different elements of quality as outlined above may be taken into account to measure the quality of particular programmes. Some countries use standardised observation scales and engage in external, research assessments of programmes. Other countries favour the co-construction of both objectives and evaluation processes at local level.

To assess programme quality, some countries use standardised observation scales in ECEC…

In Australia, Belgium (Flemish Community), Portugal, UK, US, the best known measures of process quality are the *Infant/Toddler Environment Rating Scale* – ITERS (Harms *et al.*, 1990) and *Early Care Environment Rating Scale* – ECERS (Harms *et al.*, 1998). Developed by researchers in the US, these scales are used to rate the quality of the physical, interactive and pedagogical environments of the early childhood setting. ECERS, for example, is a purpose-built, process observation scale. It evaluates seven aspects of centre-based provision for children ages 2.5 to 5 years: personal care routines, furnishings, language, reasoning experiences, motor activities, creative activities, social development and staff needs. Detailed descriptors are given for the 37 items within these seven categories, and each item is rated by the observer as minimal, good or excellent.

…which provide advantages as well as risks.

Some concerns are raised against the use of scales, pointing, for example, to the possibility that imported process scales may have little to do with the child-rearing patterns and educational ideals of a particular country or cultural group. Specialists fear too that scales may be used to assess and classify children or personnel in a normative and non-motivating manner that does not view child develop- ment as contextually-grounded in time and place. Yet, several positive aspects of these scales emerged from the review, in particular when scales have been carefully adapted to reflect national needs and contexts, and staff are trained sufficiently to understand not only the application but the theory behind the scales. Australia, for example, has elaborated a powerful instrument for accreditation and evaluation of centre-based ECEC called the QIAS (Quality Improvement and Accreditation System) (see Box 3.4) inspired by the NAEYC guidelines for Developmentally Appropriate Practice (Bredekamp and Copple, 1997) and the ECERS rating scale. The QIAS has been widely accepted as an instrument that assesses with some objectivity the care and education environments of young children. When trained permanent staff are engaged in this process, these scales also can provide a basis for discussion and self-evaluation.

Quality is measured increasingly in a few countries through child assessments…

Another approach – favoured particularly in the United States – is to measure quality by assessing children's performance in achieving specific outcomes. Data from such assessments are used increasingly for "high-stakes" decision making, for example, to judge programme effectiveness and to deter-

---

Box 3.4 The Quality Improvement and Accreditation System in Australia

Australia has put into place a national, government supported, accreditation system for its centre-based ECEC (long day care) that is directly tied to the provision of funding. The Quality Improvement and Accreditation System (QIAS) focuses primarily upon process components of quality. As centres are required to take part in the QIAS process in order for parents to be eligible for the Child Care Benefit (the main fee subsidy), over 98% of both private for-profit and non-profit centres participate. The QIAS system, developed in 1994, is based on the National Association for the Education of Young Children's (NAEYC) Developmentally Appropriate Practice, the NAEYC voluntary national accreditation system, and the Early Childhood Environmental Rating Scale (ECERS).

Centres undertake a self study against 52 principles related to staff-child, staff-parent, and staff-staff interactions; the programme; nutrition, health and safety practices; and centre management and staff development. The self study process is undertaken collaboratively between management, staff, and parents, and submitted to the National Childcare Accreditation Council. A peer reviewer then visits the centre and assesses the self study against his/her observations and discussions during a one or two day visit, depending on centre size. The reviewer's ratings are moderated by the Council. An independent Accreditation Decisions Review Committee is available to consider appeals against the Council's accreditation decision. All moderation, appeals and accreditation decisions are made on the basis of written documentation and without any knowledge of the centre's identity.

The QIAS process has been widely supported as having drawn attention to the quality of children's experiences in early childhood settings, and as a means of enabling centres to self-evaluate the quality of their service provision. The system focuses on both improvement and accreditation. Rather than being immediately censured, centres which at first do not achieve accreditation are encouraged to put in a plan of action to improve quality. Censure is based upon a centre's failure to participate in the system, or failing for a third time to become accredited after two previous unsuccessful attempts.

The QIAS has recently been reviewed by the Commonwealth Child Care Advisory Council. A revised system, aimed at streamlining and simplifying administrative requirements and ensuring greater validity and consistency in the accreditation process, will be implemented by 2002. The Commonwealth government is supporting the development of pilot quality assurance systems for family day care (start mid-2001) and out-of-school provision (start mid-2002). The New South Wales Office of Child Care is funding a pilot accreditation programme for pre-schools.

---

mine whether policies and programmes should receive continued funding (Bowman *et al.*, 2000). In the US, the method most generally used to evaluate the quality of major programmes, *e.g.*, Head Start and other programmes for poor children or children with disabilities, is to assess samples of children on the health, cognitive, socio-emotional and English language development that an "intervention" should help the children to achieve. Some researchers express ethical and professional reservations about child testing (Meisels, 1994; Schweinhart *et al.* 1993; Penn, 2000). They observe that young children have difficulty in understanding the demands of a test situation and may not be able to control their behaviour to meet those demands. Critics argue too that psychometric testing may be inappropriate to various cultures and day-to-day experiences of children (Schweinhart *et al.*, 1993). An obvious danger is to associate developmental status with the norms of the dominant middle-class culture (Bowman *et al.*, 2000). Child testing may be blind to other major aims of programmes, *e.g.* to increasing parental understanding of their child's potential and their own important role; to nurturing creativity and autonomy in children; to fostering educational relationships with parents and communities; to multi-cultural outreach, to catering for special needs and non-mainstream communication patterns. Moreover, there is little in this assessment method

...that can be used to inform pedagogical practice.

that directly supports educational practice or the professional development of staff, and there are dangers that some staff will leave aside broader aims to ensure that children meet primarily cognitive and school readiness outcomes.

These critiques are now being addressed by professional research teams who use assessment approaches which take into account more than just a cognitive functioning score on a standardised test.[32] The National Council on Measurement in Education (American Educational Research Association, 1999) in the US emphasises that important educational decisions should be grounded in *multiple* sources of information, including interviews, observations, work sampling and informal assessments over a period of time. Assessments are considered incomplete if they focus exclusively on intelligence testing and cognitive measures. Greenspan and Wieder (1998) have drawn up key areas for assessments that include the child's biology, interactive patterns and developmental environment, that is the patterns of family, culture and the larger environment.

According to Shepard *et al.* (1998) there are four main aims for assessing children: i) to support children's learning; ii) to identify special needs; iii) to evaluate and monitor programmes; iv) to make schools or programmes accountable. As noted earlier, assessment and evaluation measures have become an important criterion in many countries (the Netherlands, Portugal, UK, etc.) for comparing the effectiveness of different types of programmes and for justifying continued investment. Given the episodic course of development in any one child and the great variability to be found in any group of young children, it is important for staff to know what each child *brings* to the process. Assessment can provide an accurate idea of each child's prior knowledge, development of concepts and ways of interacting so that teachers can choose a pedagogical approach and curricular materials to support the child's further development and learning (Bowman *et al.*, 2000). Whether assessments are informal or carried out in a more formal way by external research teams or by staff, *e.g.* as in the British Baseline Assessment, they can help guide pedagogical practice in ECEC. The data provided can be used by staff and parents as part of an ongoing reflection and quality improvement process. This approach is evident in the documentation and self-evaluation processes increasingly adopted in OECD countries.

Other countries favour co-constructing aims and objectives at the local level...

Other countries have adopted a different approach, assuming that to achieve system goals requires co-construction of programme aims and objectives at local level, with children, parents, teachers and the social partners. In Denmark, Finland, Norway, and Sweden and certain regions of Italy, for example, well-educated teams of staff and parents, guided by municipal pedagogical advisors, will normally generate their own quality observation processes and evaluation mechanisms. Services aim to meet the broad goals established by the local authorities for the benefit of all children and parents. The quality of the setting is not measured according to the performance of individual children. The structural conditions of quality are already in place, and standardised process measures and assessments are deemed less neces-

---

32. Bowman *et al.* (2000) explain that though there is overlap in the use of the words "test" and "assessment", the former refers to a standardised instrument, formally administered and designed to minimize all differences in the conditions of testing. Assessments tend on the contrary to use multiple instruments (observations, performance measures, interviews, portfolios and examples of children's work, etc.) and take place over a longer period of time.

sary in a context where team planning, team evaluations, and goals monitoring are an ongoing feature of the work of the centre (see Section 3.6).

This participatory approach to evaluation is a means not only of finding out how children are developing but also of supporting the practice of educators, leading them to constructive self-assessment and change. With this intention in mind, the municipal pre-schools of Reggio Emilia – and institutions in other countries influenced by the Reggio approach – engage in intensive documentation of the individual child, the group class and the work of the centre (see Box 3.5). They aim both to understand each child's learning processes and to provide a platform for ongoing discussion within the pedagogical group. Staff, in fact, are seen as "reflecting practitioners", that is, professionals who are continually reviewing and reflecting on their own practice and learning theory. In Finland, too, child documentation and portfolios are viewed as important to improve quality and awareness. ECEC centres use these tools as a basis for developing individual "contracts" between parent, child and personnel. A profile of the child's work and interests is built up gradually and is made available to parents for comment and contributions. As in Reggio Emilia, the purpose of such documentation is not to evaluate children against external norms, but to lead to a common reflection by professional and parents on the practice of the centre and the well-being of the child.

...that support the actual practice of educators.

In sum, quality is understood as an adequate response to the needs of a particular group of children, and quality assessment is seen as primarily the responsibility of local administrations and staff. In this perspective, evaluation moves from conformity to external standards toward trust in local responsibility and the professional quality of staff, though guided by national frameworks. Such trust presupposes that government or local authorities have invested well in staff and in the pedagogical frameworks that can support their work. Staff are given the means to reflect on and assess their own practice, in the light of the guiding pedagogical frameworks, *e.g.* through thorough pre-service training, ongoing professional development courses and investment in self-evaluation instruments, such as the Effective Early Learning method discussed below. Quality assessment becomes an ongoing process of discussion and

---

Box 3.5 **Pedagogical documentation in Reggio Emilia, Italy**

Documentation, as developed in Reggio Emilia, is the recording the children's project experience in words, drawings, photos, videos, etc. The process as well as the final product of each group project is recorded, incorporating the ideas of the children, their memories and feelings, and the observations made by teachers on the dynamics of children's explorations and social engagements. Documentation serves three key functions:

1) It provides children with a concrete and visible memory of what they have said and done, using images and words to serve as a jumping off point to explore previous understandings and to co-construct revisited understandings of the topics investigated. Children become even more interested, curious, and confident as they contemplate the meaning of what they have achieved;

2) Documentation also gives the educators an insight into the children's understanding of everyday institutions, objects and events, and their own reactions to child learning and initiative. Documentation is thus a tool for research and a key to continuous improvement and renewal; and

3) Finally, documentation provides parents and the public with detailed information about what happens in the pre-schools as a means of eliciting their reactions and support. In turn, children learn that their parents feel at home in the pre-school, at ease with the teachers, and informed about what takes place.

71

evaluation involving different groups – children, parents, staff, the administrators and advisors attached to services. Checks and balances may also be present, *e.g.* monitoring by the relevant ministry through national research assessments, surveys, light inspections, etc. and/or client monitoring, in which training and information are provided to parents to assess early childhood institutions and their practice (see Section 3.7).

Who should ensure quality?

Governments ensure quality, but monitoring is increasingly devolved to local stakeholders.

In all countries, central governments have played and continue to play a crucial role in defining and ensuring quality. Governments and/or local authorities are expected to provide the broad goals, frameworks, and resources to foster quality. On the other hand, they are withdrawing increasingly from the day-to-day management of quality control, and engage only in "light" steering. Centralised enforcement instruments, such as detailed curricula, and external inspection are giving away to devolution of control and management to local authorities. Even in countries such as Belgium (Flemish and French Communities), the Czech Republic, Portugal and the UK, which have retained centralised pedagogical inspection, there is growing co-operation with staff and parents as to how inspections should take place. In Denmark, Norway, and Sweden, the traditional inspectors have been replaced for many years by municipal pedagogical advisors, who work alongside personnel, parents and authorities from the local institutions. In a growing number of municipalities in Italy, advisory services are organised to support teachers and centres to enhance their programmes and to document their progress. In sum, quality assurance and evaluation increasingly engages the participation and responsibility of a wider range of stakeholders in the early childhood field, including parents, staff, and (sometimes) children.

Staff are encouraged to evaluate their own work and practice...

Despite retaining a highly centralised inspection service (OFSTED), the UK has also developed instruments to encourage staff to reflect on and self-evaluate their work with children. The Effective Early Learning (EEL) project, for example, is a systematic process of self-evaluation undertaken by a whole centre, which is supported and validated externally. There are four key stages to the model as illustrated below (see Figure 3.3). The self-evaluation process is supported by an External Adviser, trained in EEL methodology, who acts as a change agent and source of expert knowledge. The self-evaluation model derived from the EEL project has formed a part of the national evaluation of the British government's Early Excellence Centre pilots. In addition, the EEL project has been introduced in the Netherlands, and along with other early childhood programmes (*e.g.*, Piramide and Kaleidoscoop) emphasise observation and self-evaluation processes. Under the super- vision of the Ministry of Education, an adaptation of EEL has been used in experimental kindergartens around Lisbon and Braga in Portugal. These examples illustrate a trend toward participatory quality improvement processes that involve staff, parents, and children.

...and parents contribute to maintaining quality standards.

National surveys and local consultation of parents ("clients" or "service users") are another way to ensure quality that is becoming more important in many countries (*e.g.*, Czech Republic, Denmark, Finland, Norway, the Netherlands, Sweden, US). In this approach, variables such as facility of access, convenient hours of opening, efficient administration and distribution of places, sensitivity to the family's cultural, religious, and linguistic background, parents' perception of the happiness and well-being of children, the provision

Figure 3.3. **Effective Early Learning (EEL) model of quality evaluation and development**

Following three days of intensive training in the EEL methodology, the evaluation and development cycle should take 12-18 months. There are four key stages to the model as illustrated below:

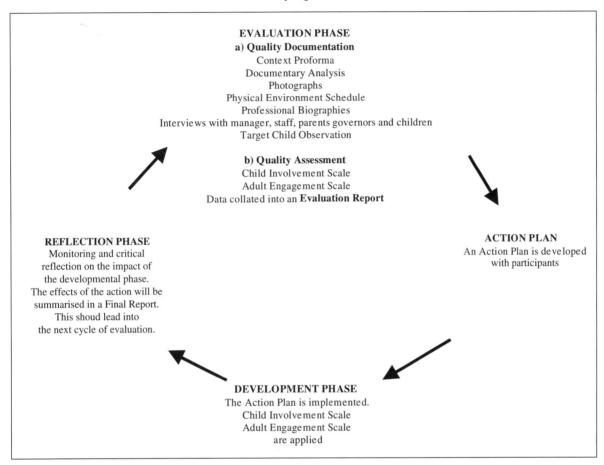

EVALUATION PHASE
a) **Quality Documentation**
Context Proforma
Documentary Analysis
Photographs
Physical Environment Schedule
Professional Biographies
Interviews with manager, staff, parents governors and children
Target Child Observation

b) **Quality Assessment**
Child Involvement Scale
Adult Engagement Scale
Data collated into an **Evaluation Report**

REFLECTION PHASE
Monitoring and critical
reflection on the impact of
the developmental phase.
The effects of the action will be
summarised in a Final Report.
This shoud lead into
the next cycle of evaluation.

ACTION PLAN
An Action Plan is developed
with participants

DEVELOPMENT PHASE
The Action Plan is implemented.
Child Involvement Scale
Adult Engagement Scale
are applied

Source: Pascal and Bertram (1997).

of meals and normal healthcare to children, amiable and informative relations with teachers are all important. The degree of parental involvement in the work of the early childhood institution is also key and can have a real impact on monitoring and raising quality (see Section 3.7).

What were the major quality issues that emerged during the review?

Fragmented policymaking raises quality concerns...

A major quality issue in many countries is the *lack of a coherent vision and national strategy for ECEC that embraces children from birth to 6*. This has wide repercussions throughout systems, leading to conflicting policies; fragmentation of services; poor pedagogical settings for the younger children or directive, didactic settings for very young pre-school children; wide disparities in the status and training of staff, making common in-service training and participatory evaluation extremely difficult; confusion, both in conception and practice, about out-of-school provision. The lack of coherence often means that very young children make numerous transitions in staff and setting in their early years. That these discontinuities are accepted in many societies relate not

...as does the limited monitoring of infant-toddler provision.

In countries with less universal systems, children from low-income families tend to receive lower-quality services.

only to longstanding divisions of administrative responsibilities, but also to the assumptions held about what is good for young children.

The *low status and training of staff* in the social welfare sector – not least in family day care – merit particular mention as the situation serves to undermine quality and negates the significant investments most governments are now making in the field. Another related issue that emerged in several countries relates to *quality of provision for children under* 3. The relative neglect of the sector is reflected in apparent *gaps in the statistical knowledge base*, most notably with respect to actual numbers of under-3s in services, their patterns of use of services, and the programme quality. There is often limited information too about the amount of government or municipal transfers and of public and private cash flows to institutions. Moreover, much of the quality monitoring that takes place is concerned with minimum standards of health and safety rather than the pedagogical quality of the settings. Given the low-levels of staff training and insufficient resources accorded to provision, it is not surprising that custodial care predominates and opportunities to foster children's early learning and development can be neglected.

Yet another quality concern is the tendency for *children from low-income families to receive inferior services* compared to their higher-income counterparts, particularly in countries with high levels of child poverty and with low public investment in ECEC. Evaluations in several countries (*e.g.*, Netherlands, Portugal, the UK and the US) have shown that even when disadvantaged children do participate in ECEC, they often do not receive the full range of child development, health, and parent services that are needed to optimise their learning (Kempson, 1996; US General Accounting Office, 1995). Children from lower socio-economic backgrounds are also more likely to experience lower-quality family day care and relative care (Galinsky *et al.*, 1994; NICHD, 1997). There is evidence that suggests that poor quality may be more detrimental for children from low-income families than for other children (Phillips, 1995). On the other hand, when access is close to universal, with strong public investment, quality tends to be more even across income boundaries. A related concern is the need for ECEC to support parents – particularly those from disadvantaged backgrounds – and their educational, social, and health needs. Increasingly, ECEC settings in many countries are developing a range of strategies to involve parents in their daily activities and in informal learning that takes place in the home, as well as links with supportive services. As noted earlier, however, the quality of out-of-school provision to support working parents needs to be addressed.

How are governments improving quality?

In addition to creating shared understandings about childhood, to formulating clear policies and goals, governments have at their disposal several indispensable instruments to improve the quality of early childhood services. They legislate and make regulations; they provide adequate funding and management; they fund selectively to reinforce particular elements of early childhood management or programming that need particular attention at a given moment; they train and set the working conditions for the early childhood profession; they ensure that adequate monitoring, research, data collection, and evaluation mechanisms are in place. In decentralised contexts also, the central government contribution is significant, even if perceived as steering monitoring. In co-operation with major stakeholders in the field – regional and local government, social partners, professional organisations, and parent groups – ministries may guide the system through:

- Framework documents and goals-led steering [*e.g.*, Belgium (Flemish and French Communities), Italy, Finland, Norway, Portugal, Sweden, UK];

- Supporting the creation of voluntary standards, codes of ethics, guidelines, recommendations, *e.g.* the support given to voluntary accreditation and quality improvement (*e.g.*, Australia, the Netherlands, UK, US);

- Dissemination of research and information to the public, parents and early childhood personnel [*e.g.*, Belgium (Flemish and French Communities), Finland, US];

- Judicious use of special funding, *e.g.* the major investments made in the Netherlands to provide improved ECEC for children "at risk";

- Providing support to building up technical competencies at local management levels (*e.g.*, the Netherlands, Sweden);

- Focusing on raising the education levels and status of early childhood personnel (*e.g.*, Italy, Sweden, Portugal, UK);

- Encouraging the move in early childhood services toward internal, centre-based, self-evaluation [*e.g.*, Belgium (Flemish Community), Denmark, the Netherlands, Portugal, UK];

- Building up a culture of quality in the system (*e.g.* Finland, UK) based on action research at local level, conducted jointly by universities and local early childhood centres; and

- Establishing a system of democratic checks and balances, in which genuine decision-making, access to information and some powers of supervision are given to parents *e.g.*, parent councils, representation on governing boards (*e.g.*, Denmark, Finland, the Netherlands, Norway, Sweden, US).

Many countries in the review give careful attention to the major structural requirements that contribute to strong early childhood systems, including adequate public investment and financing mechanisms; to clear policy and pedagogical frameworks that meet both child and family needs; and above all, to motivating and training professional staff. The approaches and issues concerning these structural elements of quality ECEC systems are discussed in later sections of the report.

3.3. Promoting coherence and co-ordination of policy and services

Key points

In most countries, policies for "care" and "education" have developed separately, with different systems of governance, funding streams, and training for staff, while in others, care and education have been integrated conceptually and in practice. Across countries, a more holistic approach is gaining ground as policy makers seek to improve the continuity of children's early childhood experiences and make the most efficient use of resources. OECD countries are recognising that coherent early childhood experiences are more likely to facilitate children's transitions from one sphere of life to another, and provide more continuity in their early learning and development. This section explores some of the trends and issues related to efforts to promote coherence and co-ordination of policy and services:[33]

- Unified administrative auspices can help promote coherence for children, as can co-ordination mechanisms across departments and sectors. In particular, there is increasing trend toward co-ordination with the educational sector to facilitate children's transition from ECEC to primary school.

- The trend toward decentralisation of responsibility for ECEC has brought diversification of services to meet local needs and preferences. The challenge is for central government to balance local decision-making with the need to limit variation in access and quality.

- At the local level, many countries have recognised the importance of integrating services to meet the needs of children and families in a holistic manner. Services integration has taken many forms, including teamwork among staff with different professional backgrounds.

The impact of administrative and policymaking responsibility on ECEC policy and provision

Countries may have divided or unified administrative auspices for ECEC policy and provision.

The degree of coherence of a country's ECEC system is linked, in part, to its organisation of administrative and policymaking responsibility. Countries follow broadly two models (see Figure 3.1. and Table 3.1): in the first, and dominant, model – found in Australia, Belgium (Flemish and French Communities), the Czech Republic, Italy, the Netherlands, Portugal, and the United States – ECEC policy and provision is *divided* into education and welfare systems. This division generally follows the age of the child, with "pre-school" arrangements for children from about the age of 3 based in education departments together with primary schooling. "Care" services for children under this age fall under the responsibility of social welfare or health departments. In Australia, Portugal[34], and the US, there is some overlap or *parallel* responsibility for the age groups served by the education, health and social affairs ministries, mostly in the two or three years prior to school entry. In the second

---

33. In this report, *policy coherence* refers to joint efforts across government departments and agencies to forge mutually reinforcing policy action towards achieving equitable access to quality ECEC. *Policy co-ordination* refers to the institutional and management mechanisms by which policy coherence is exerted among the various entities involved.

34. In Portugal, the Framework Law specifies that pedagogical supervision for 3- to 6-year-olds is the responsibility of the Ministry of Education.

model, policy and provision for children under compulsory school age are *unified* under one administrative auspice, either education, as in Sweden and the UK, social affairs, as in Denmark and Finland, or children and family affairs, as in Norway. In Denmark and Finland, there is some overlap in responsibility for the 6-year-olds between education and social affairs departments.

In the divided approach, the two systems of services may differ in terms of regulation, staffing, funding, and delivery, despite often overlapping goals and types of families served. These differences may create inequities and lack of coherence for children and families (EC Childcare Network, 1996*b*). For example, the welfare services tend to be far less developed in terms of coverage, and usually require a parental contribution, while education services are usually free and accessible to all, but are not available on a full-day, all-year basis. While levels of staffing (*e.g.*, staff-child ratios) in the welfare system are higher than in the education system, levels of training and working conditions are lower. If developments in different parts of the system are unconnected and isolated, as opposed to a seamless system, children may experience difficult transitions in their young lives. The division of policy and provision into education and social welfare systems is often based more on traditional divisions of competence among ministries than the practical needs of children and families. In the context of high maternal employment rates and concerns about quality outcomes for children, however, services in the welfare system are increasingly adopting a pedagogical, as well as a care role, while schools are pushed to respond to wider functions than education (including care for children of working parents).

A more unified approach facilitates policy coherence for young children in a number of ways. Placing the responsibility for ECEC under one department allows for common policies, social and pedagogical objectives, and budgets for early childhood to be organised. Regulatory, funding, and staffing regimes, costs to parents, and opening hours tend to be more consistent. Links at the services level – across age groups and settings – are more easily forged. In these systems, a common vision underlies education and care, in policy and practice, along with a real understanding of how together they contribute to children's development and learning. In Denmark, Finland, Norway, and Sweden, for example, age-integrated services have developed for children from 1 to 6, and sometimes older. This approach allows children to be part of the same group of several years before beginning school, giving children and parents opportunities to establish important relationships with professionals and other children over time. Care and education are implemented as integrated components of all programmes for young children across age groups. Services that have developed according to this model tend to support the holistic needs of children and their families.

Unified administrative auspices can promote coherence for children...

Administrative integration, however, is not the only way of creating coherence for children. At the national level, in recent years, countries have adopted a range of innovative mechanisms to increase co-ordination for children and youth across different departments and sectors. In the French Community of Belgium, for example, the Minister for Childhood is responsible for both education (*école maternelle* and *primaire*) and children's services (infant-toddler and out-of-school). Although "education" and "care" services are still administratively divided, the appointment of a political leader with policy responsibility for all children under 12 favours co-ordinated policy development in the French Community. In Denmark, an Inter-Ministerial Committee on Children was set up in 1987 as an interdisciplinary body of 15 Ministries

...as can other inter-departmental co-ordinating mechanisms.

with responsibility for matters relating to children and families. Chaired by the Ministry of Social Affairs, the main objective of the Committee is to create coherence in areas relating to children and families and to promote cross-sector initiatives to improve the living conditions for children and young persons. In 1996, Portugal set up an inter-ministerial bureau for the expansion and development of pre-school education. Guided by an advisory board (with representatives from municipalities, private profit/non-profit organisations, and researchers), the office produced joint legislation and set up communication strategies across the Ministry of Education and the Ministry of Labour and Solidarity. Several governments have established an Ombudsman or Council for Children as an autonomous institution that works across many different disciplines and areas of responsibility to promote children's rights and well-being, particularly through the implementation of the UN Convention on the Rights of the Child (Hodgkin and Newell, 1996). Despite these efforts, coherent policy may be difficult to implement in practice, especially if policy-makers, staff and parents do not share an integrated view of ECEC. In sum, the development of a coherent and integrated system of ECEC goes beyond issues of structure and organisation and deals centrally with how these services are understood by society.

Co-ordination between ECEC and the education sector to facilitate children's transitions

There is a trend toward closer co-operation between ECEC and compulsory schooling.

Even when services before compulsory school age are coherent, there is no guarantee that the relationship between these services and the compulsory school system will be coherent (EC Childcare Network, 1996*b*). Driven by efforts to facilitate children's transitions, there has been a trend toward more co-ordination of policy across ECEC and compulsory education, often following the lead at the local level. Every country, except Norway, has some form of non-compulsory school-based ECEC to provide a bridge to formal schooling (in the Netherlands this provision has been integrated into the *bassischool*). In Belgium (Flemish and French Communities), the Czech Republic, Italy, and Portugal, for example, the education system plays an important role in providing ECEC for children over 3, and consistent regulations, funding, and curricula have been developed across the education system. However, since policy and provision for younger children under 3 and out-of-school activities fall under different administrative auspices, there is still the risk of fragmentation.

Sweden is the only country participating in the review that has fully integrated all early childhood services *and* the compulsory schools into the education system under the Ministry of Education, but there are signs that other countries may follow this model.[35] England, for example, has taken the step of transferring child care services from the Department of Health to the Department for Education and Employment. The recently created "Early Years and Childcare Unit" now has responsibility for the development and implementation of ECEC policy. Within the Scottish Executive Education Department, the "Early Education and Childcare Division" administers government policy for all ECEC, and a Children and Young People's Group seeks to co-ordinate and integrate policies and resources affecting children and young people. Most recently, in Italy, there are political proposals to shift

---

35. Two other OECD countries have fully integrated all responsibility for ECEC under education auspices: New Zealand in the late 1980s and Spain in 1990.

national responsibility of services for children under 3 to the Ministry of Education in order to provide more coherence in policy and practices for young children and to improve the emphasis on education within the *asilo nido*. In federal systems, administrative integration may be more feasible at the state level. In Australia, three states and territories – South Australia, Australian Capital Territory, and Tasmania – have integrated children's services and education portfolios to facilitate coherence and co-ordination for young children.

Consolidating administration under education auspices provides an opportunity to strengthen the articulation between ECEC and school and to develop a coherent policy framework for regulation, funding, training, and service delivery across the different phases of the education system. This strategy can facilitate co-operation between ECEC and primary school staff and promote pedagogical continuity for children as they transition from one level of education to another. In Sweden, integrating responsibility for pre-schools, family day care, open pre-schools, and leisure-time activities has led to an increasing public understanding that early childhood services combine care and learning – and represent a first and important phase of lifelong learning. However, there are risks to this approach. There are concerns in some countries that as ECEC becomes more integrated with compulsory schooling, early childhood services will become more isolated from child welfare, health, and other policy areas for children, which underlines the importance of creating cross-departmental links. In addition, specialists in some countries (*e.g.*, Belgium, Denmark, and the UK) fear that the dominant culture of the school system has eroded some of the specific pedagogical methods and traditions of early years provision – particularly the emphasis on children's creativity and self-initiative – in favour of more formal teaching approaches. However, this has not been the experience in Sweden where ECEC has been recognised as a distinct stage of education, with its separate curriculum framework and staff with specialised training to work with children under 6. The new Foundation Stage in England also seeks to create a strong framework for early years provision as a unique educational phase (see Section 3.6). Finally, making early childhood an important part of the educational system suggests that these services should be accessible to all children, like public schooling, which raises important cost issues.

Consolidation under the aegis of education provides opportunities as well as risks.

There is a trend toward collaboration across the range of ECEC provision – centre-based, family day care, out-of-school – in order to create a network of services that work together. It is quite common, also, for ECEC and primary schools to be co-located, but increasingly, staff from the two institutions are also working more closely together. In Portugal, E*scolas Básicas Integradas* (Integrated Basic Schools) have been created to enable all children to stay in the same school environment from pre-school to the completion of compulsory education, facilitating coherent learning conditions for children and improved management of educational resources. Pre-school classes are staffed by *educadores de infância*, who are considered as equal members of the school staff and often participate in in-service training with their colleagues from other levels of the school system. Whenever possible, children are followed by the same group of teachers within the compulsory school system in order to promote a strong interaction between the staff, families, and the community.

Working in multi-disciplinary teams across age groups and settings...

In some countries, attention to children's transitions has led to the integration of pre-school, school, and out-of-school programmes into a seamless full-day service (see Box 3.6). Multi-disciplinary teams of staff have developed new ways of working together to overcome professional boundaries and

... is a way to bridge children's experiences from ECEC to primary school.

Box 3.6 Integrated ECEC services in Maria Gamla-Stan, Sweden

Administrative integration: Maria Gamla-Stan is one of the largest districts in Stockholm (60 000 inhabitants), located in one of the oldest parts of the city. The district has one of the highest densities of children in all of Europe. In order to better serve this young population, Maria Gamla-Stan has formed a Department of Children and Youth, with responsibility for ECEC, education, as well as youth and preventive services. In the Department, a multi-disciplinary team of staff work together to serve the multiple needs of children and youth. As one municipal official noted, "We now look at children and youth together as our collective responsibility." By combining funds into one stream, forming 51% of the total budget, the district can more efficiently allocate resources for children than if the money was distributed across various agencies. Three out of 18 districts in Stockholm operate following this model.

Services integration: a holistic approach has also been adopted in the many programmes that the district offers, *e.g.* Lilla Maria, a municipal school in Maria Gamla-Stan, has integrated pre-school classes, compulsory school, and leisure-time activities for 200 children between the ages of 6 and 9 years old. Initiated by the teachers, Lilla Maria has aimed to take the best features of the three sectors and bring them together into one seamless programme. The school is open from 7h30 to 18h00 each day, and children easily transition from one hour of leisure-time in the morning, to five hours of school, to leisure-time activities at the end of the day. Parents pay only for the leisure-time hours.

Age- and staff-integration: the 6-year-olds have the opportunity to interact with older children, while following their own developmentally-appropriate activities. Children are organised into age-mixed groups of 36, with one school teacher, one pre-school teacher, and two leisure-time pedagogues. These groups are broken down into smaller "family groups" of 10 children with one responsible adult. In this way, Lilla Maria encourages staff with different disciplinary backgrounds and training to work together and to establish close relationships with children of different ages. Since all staff work some mornings and some afternoons, they have the opportunity to meet informally with most parents. In addition, they formally monitor children's development, using checklists and work sampling, and organise regular meetings with parents to discuss their documentation of each child's progress.

promote coherence in children's lives. In some schools in Denmark, teams of pedagogues and primary teachers plan and organise activities for mixed-aged children from 6 to 9, bringing together the traditions of both ECEC and school to ease children's transition from one institution to the other. Often the same *pedagogues* work with children during the school day and in leisure-time activities. This collaborative strategy promotes continuity in children's relationships with adults on a given day and over time, and gives parents more opportunities to communicate with staff. Working in multi-disciplinary teams has led staff to rethink respective pedagogical methods in ECEC and schools (*e.g.*, more emphasis on learning through play, age-mixed activities, and organisation around themes). Children have the opportunity to become more accustomed to the routines and styles of working in the primary years, while retaining some of the familiar aspects and traditions of the ECEC settings. However, it is important that different workers are respected as equal members of the team, bringing different, but equally valuable, skills, knowledge and experiences to work with young children. In this way teamwork can provide opportunities for staff from different fields to exchange information and reflect on their own practices.

Trends toward decentralisation and diversification of provision

In several countries, there has been a trend across the social and educational services toward decentralisation and devolution from the central government to the municipalities. This shift has been motivated by efforts to bring decision-making and delivery closer to the people being served and to adapt services to meet local needs and circumstances. It is hoped that decentralisation will facilitate the development of services that are more "client-oriented", address individual needs, and reinforce diversity of choice. Decentralisation and devolution have facilitated the diversification of the types of provision, and in some cases the privatisation of services. Countries with more decentralised systems now face the difficult task of balancing power and responsibilities between the national and local (and in some cases regional) authorities, which is particularly challenging when it comes to issues of funding, access, and quality monitoring. The impact of decentralisation on the coherence of local service delivery often depends on the current political climate and the historical context of specific ECEC systems (Oberhuemer and Ulich, 1997).

In some of the Nordic countries, for example, there is a strong tradition of self-government, based on the principles that citizen needs are best determined and met locally. Decentralisation has built on a well-developed existing infrastructure for ECEC with clear targets for access. Whereas in the past, ECEC services had to meet rather detailed and strict national guidelines and standards, responsibility has been increasingly devolved to the municipalities. While general regulatory frameworks exist, municipalities now decide the appropriate balance of services (*e.g.*, between family day care homes and centres). They also are free to contract with private services as they see fit, though in general, these providers must meet the same quality standards as those run by the municipality. Local authorities have considerable discretion in fixing staffing ratios, and are responsible for supervision and inspection of services, which has led to some concerns about variation in quality across municipalities and regions.

Decentralisation can promote local decision-making and diversification of provision.

Decentralisation often goes beyond the local authority, giving considerable discretion and autonomy to institutions, and to staff and parents. In Denmark, the Netherlands, and Norway, parents have a clearly-defined role in planning and running centre activities, including financial and staffing decisions. In Italy, the Netherlands, and Portugal, new legislation giving schools autonomy and control over staffing and budgets is likely to have implications for the delivery of services for children under educational auspices. In the Czech Republic, trends toward decentralised decision-making, increased parental influence, and the development of privately- or church-operated alternatives have contributed to greater diversity in the pre-school sector than was the case before 1989. The success of these reforms depends to a large extent on the degree to which a wide range of stakeholders are involved in negotiating local standards and patterns of provision, as well as the availability of technical expertise within the local or regional authority to support the transfer of power to the institutional level.

In some countries, decentralisation, sometimes accompanied by deregulation, has been used as a mechanism to introduce market-driven policies to expand provision for young children. In the Netherlands, decentralisation and private provision have been supported in the interests of democracy, empowerment, and local responsiveness. The Dutch government and municipalities contract with the non-profit and for-profit sectors to provide many early childhood services, including work-site childcare and services targeting groups that are difficult to reach through mainstream provision. In England, local Early Years and Child Care Development Partnerships have been given the respon-

Decentralisation may lead to a greater role for market provision.

sibility to expand ECEC provision in partnership with state, private, and voluntary providers (see Box 3.7). Although the funding is decentralised to the local and services level, national standards and regulations remain. The US has traditionally relied on market approaches with little government regulation. Responsibility for ECEC is devolved almost completely to the individual states, giving authorities considerable flexibility toward meeting the needs and preferences of children and families. Few regulations or guidelines exist at the central level, leading to widespread variation in staff training, staff-child ratios, and even health and safety requirements across and within states. There is concern that the limited role of government, at both federal and state levels, has led to variation in quality and access to services. Australia – another federal system – has sought to address this issue by linking federal funding for child care to an accreditation scheme with nationally-recognised standards (described earlier).

Decentralisation may foster more coherent and efficient policy development and implementation.

In spite of the risks, decentralisation can also lead to more coherence in local policy and provision. With loosening central control, some local authorities have combined funding streams and experimented with integrating administration and policy development across age groups and sectors. In Denmark, Italy, Norway, Sweden, and the UK, for example, an increasing number of local authorities have reorganised local administrations and political committees to bring together ECEC and schools (and sometimes other services for children), often under education departments. Municipalities in parts of Norway have integrated *barnehager* for children under 6, leisure-time activities, schools and child welfare services into a Department for Growing Up, with responsibility for a child's total environment; a few have brought together a range of other services such as health, social security and eldercare under one department. Despite the inherent challenges of bringing together various services and professionals, administrative integration has helped to promote co-ordinated and inter-disciplinary ways of working, as well as a more coherent, and possibly more efficient, allocation of resources to young children in their communities.

The challenge for government is to maintain equitable access and even levels of quality.

Across countries, decentralisation and devolution have allowed for freedom, adaptation and variation at the local level. In particular, decentralisation has led to the development of a variety of ECEC provision rather than one standardised type, giving more choice for parents. In addition, since municipalities are now charged with making important funding decisions regarding

---

Box 3.7 **Early Years Development and Childcare Partnerships in England**

In England, the Early Years Development and Childcare Partnerships (EYDCP) function in local authorities as the primary mechanism by which the provision of universal early education for 3- and 4-year-olds, and childcare targets will be realised. The Partnerships consist of representatives from the maintained, private, and voluntary sectors, local education, health, and social services, employers, trainers, advisors, and parents. Members of the partnership serve on a volunteer basis. Their role is to assess the current provision of care in local areas and to develop plans for future expansion. Working in co-operation with its partner Local Education Authority, each local Partnership draws up an annual local Early Years Development and Childcare Plan. The EYDCP plans are linked to national targets for the provision of early education places for 3- and 4-year olds and are required to address the need for expansion of child care provision in their area. The Plans need to address issues of quality, affordability, and accessibility across the range of services in their area and to consider how to provide parents with access to information they need by developing Childcare Information Services (CIS) for their area.

early childhood services, ECEC policies have become an integral part of local politics. Decentralisation may promote more co-ordinated ways of working, and more efficient use of resources. On the other hand, local decision-making may lead to disparities in quality and access from one municipality to the next, depending on local political priorities, especially if these are driven more by economic considerations than by quality concerns. In Sweden, for example, decentralisation occurred during a period of recession, and was accompanied by funding cuts and the lowering of local standards (though quality remains high by international standards). This suggests that there is a role for the national (and state) government in ensuring that local and regional authorities secure adequate resources to implement their policies. In sum, while in some cases decentralisation and devolution have been associated with increased local involvement, democratic structures and matching provision to local needs, in others it has led to regionally diverse levels and standards of provision. These differences are found within and across countries. The challenge is for central government to foster decentralisation and promote local discussion and negotiation, while retaining the authority and capacity to monitor fair access to ECEC and maintain quality across regions and forms of provision.

Links between ECEC and other services at the local level

Many countries have recognised the importance of integrating services in order to meet the wide-ranging needs of children and families, particularly those at-risk, in a holistic manner. By working together, social welfare, health, and education sectors can provide more effective and appropriate services for young children, often at a reduced cost to government. In addition, services integration is particularly valuable in communities with large numbers of disadvantaged children and families. Close co-operation among ECEC, school, and allied services, can help promote continuity in children's development and learning during important transitions, such as the critical passage from home to ECEC or from ECEC to school. The Netherlands has developed the *brede school* (broad-based school) which, in addition to its regular educational tasks, offers a range of services to the community outside school hours in co-operation with volunteers and professionals (see Box 3.8).

Several countries have developed approaches to encourage links across ECEC, schools, and other community services to promote coherence for children and their families. These multi-agency initiatives sometimes target individual children and families, but more often they serve an entire community identified in need of special support. Perhaps the most well-known comprehensive early intervention programme is *Head Start*, a federally-funded, community-based initiative in the US, which provides comprehensive education, developmental, mental health, nutrition, and social services to poor families with young children, and includes an intensive parent and community involvement component. While Head Start has traditionally co-ordinated with the health, social, and mental health fields, increasingly, programmes are establishing links with child care services to provide full-day, year-round coverage for children of working parents. The UK recently introduced the interdepartmental anti-poverty initiative *Sure Start*, which draws on the Head Start model, but is area-based, and includes all children under four regardless of family income. Sure Start uses a partnership approach to local service delivery which includes public, private, and voluntary sectors, community organisations and parents. In Belgium (Flemish and French Commu-

Comprehensive early intervention strategies target areas in need of special support.

83

Box 3.8 **Developing the broad-based school in the Netherlands**

In the Netherlands, there is a trend toward integrating educational and welfare services as broad-based schools. There are many different types of broad-based schools, but all are based on the idea of service integration. Educational facilities, recreational facilities, childcare services, child health services, etc., are integrated in an area-based network or even in one multifunctional building. The development of broad-based schools can be seen as a consequence of decentralisation policy. As a bottom-up initiative which adapts to meet neighbourhood and user needs, there is wide variety in arrangements and goals of broad-based schools in different municipalities. Yet the underlying rationale is similar. Schools are viewed as places where other services and organisations can find and reach all children and youth. They are confronted with a wide variety of social and health problems among their students, which often need to be addressed before the child can fully participate in education. Schools can co-operate with other services to meet children's holistic needs, and also are increasingly seen as and functioning as supports to enable parental employment. This relatively new demand on schools does not coincide with the way schools are organised, *e.g.* school opening hours and lunch arrangements. Schools have developed links with other professional services, such as out-of-school care and educational and recreational services, to provide for children during the full workday of their parents. Broad schools often stay open late at night and function as a centre for cultural, sporting, and educational activities for parents and youth in a neighbourhood. One of the main aims is to strengthen community ties and trust between parents and the local school.

---

nities), the Netherlands, Portugal, and the UK (also France), *educational priority policies* allocate extra resources to pre-schools and schools located in designated socially, culturally, and economically disadvantaged zones in order to improve the quality of children's educational experiences through a collaborative and multi-service approach. By targeting geographical areas, these programmes promote equal educational opportunities without stigmatising individual children.

Flexible forms of family support complement mainstream ECEC provision.

Complementing mainstream ECEC provision, there is also a movement toward the development of more flexible services that respond to a broad set of cognitive, social, physical, and psychological needs of young children and families. Many countries recognise that very young children and their mothers or caregivers can benefit from an informal group experience that enhances child development and supports parents. These programmes tend to include part-time early childhood services, combined with parent outreach and language training, as well as other forms of family support (*e.g.*, health, mental health) (Kamerman and Kahn, 1994). Like the educational priority zones, these projects link and network with other services, and often employ staff from the community in which they work. These programmes may take many forms. In England, *Early Excellence Centres*, government-supported models of exemplary practice, offer a range of integrated services, including early years education for 3- and 4-year olds, full-day care for children birth to 3 years, drop-in facilities, outreach, family support, health care, adult education, and practitioner training. In Italy, *nuove tipologie* (new typology) services have developed to provide flexible learning and socialisation opportunities for children and families who do not need full-time ECEC (see Section 3.7). In many countries, open pre-schools or playgroups offer part-time activities for children who are accompanied by a parent or another caregiver *e.g.*, a family child care provider. These services may be particularly valuable for immigrant families to become familiar with the rhythm of more formal ECEC and develop their social networks and language skills. The trend is for these flexible services to be open to all families, though they may give priority to those with special needs.

Finally, in most countries, groups of family day care providers have been organised into networks, which effectively reduce isolation among providers and link them to family support, schools, and other community institutions, and services. Such linkages across services can help to address unmet needs, expedite service delivery, minimise duplication of services, facilitate children's transitions, and assist parents in navigating available services. Not surprisingly, integrating services for young children has been found to be a cost-effective strategy, particularly for those in need of special support (OECD, 1998a). However, there are challenges to adopting a more holistic approach. Service providers may hold different visions, come from different professional backgrounds, and work in isolation from counterparts in other fields. In addition, fragmented funding and delivery systems may present a barrier to integrating services. Thus, while in some countries efforts to co-ordinate services for young children are common, in others they are only emerging.

3.4. Exploring strategies to ensure adequate investment in the system

Key points

Adequate funding is essential to ensuring that all children have equitable access to quality ECEC and that their parents have choice in selecting services. The economic arguments for public investment in quality ECEC are strong (EC Childcare Network, 1996a; Vandell and Wolfe, 2000; Verry, 2000). As many countries have recognised, public intervention also can be justified by the goal of equal opportunity so that children in low-income families may have the same chances to benefit from quality ECEC as children in high-income families. The costs to education systems and economies become incalculable if children at-risk of educational failure are not detected and supported from the earliest age. The benefits of public investment in quality ECEC are more widespread and include social, economic and educational gains to children, parents, and families, and economic benefits to society in general through the increased labour force participation of women. Much of these costs will be offset by more efficient education systems, increased tax revenue, and reduced welfare payments. While most countries have recognised the important role of public investment, the levels of expenditures, financing mechanisms adopted, and the reliance on private funding sources vary across countries:

- In almost all countries in the review, governments pay the largest share of costs, with parents covering about 25%-30%. The two or three years of ECEC prior to compulsory schooling are often free.
- Direct provision through services and schools makes up the bulk of government assistance in most countries. Even when the mix of public and private providers is great, a high percentage of services receive direct or indirect public funding.
- Countries have adopted a range of financing mechanisms to improve affordability including: direct funding, fee subsidies, tax relief, and employer contributions. Affordability remains a barrier to equitable access, particularly in systems where the cost burden falls on parents.
- While most countries seek to expand supply and raise quality through direct subsidies to providers, a few countries favour indirect demand-driven subsidies – fee subsidies and tax relief to parents. In both cases, there are equity concerns about access to and quality of provision.
- Regardless of the financing strategy adopted, it is clear that substantial *public* investment is necessary for the development of an equitable and well-resourced *system* of quality ECEC.

Public investment in ECEC

Government have recognised the importance of public investment in ECEC.

In most OECD countries, there is substantial public investment in ECEC systems, at least for pre-schools and kindergartens for children from the age of 3. It is difficult to aggregate expenditure for all forms of ECEC given the variation in institutional and funding arrangements, as well as in parental contributions. While there are few comparable, reliable figures on total expenditure, available data suggests that public spending on ECEC (covering the age group birth to 6), in terms of percentage of GDP, tends to be the highest in the Nordic countries, in middle range in the continental European countries, and the lowest in Australia, UK, and the US (Rostgaard and Fridberg, 1998; Meyers and Gornick, 2000). In terms of trends, countries with comparatively low public expenditure (*e.g.*, Portugal, the Netherlands, the UK, US) have increased spending significantly over the past five years. In Portugal, for example, the budget for pre-school education has more than doubled since 1996, and in the UK, it is estimated that the investment over the period 1998-2002 will amount to almost £8 billion.

Most countries spend more per child on primary education than on the early years.

Given the gaps in comparative ECEC data and indicators, this section relies primarily on ISCED data.[36] As Figure 3.4 shows, the highest public expenditure for pre-primary education as a percentage of GDP is about 0.9% in Denmark. Most countries participating in the review spend between 0.4% and 0.6% of GDP. As these data refer only to educationally-oriented provision for children over 3, total expenditure on ECEC is underestimated. As an example, when all ECEC for children under 6 is included, the total expenditure in Sweden rises from 0.6% to 2.3% GDP. In most countries, total expenditure would increase significantly if public funding for maternity and parental leave, child allowances, and other transfers to families with children were included along with educational investment data. Another way to look at levels of investment within countries – and the priority accorded to young children – is to compare per child expenditure for pre-primary and primary education (again limited to the narrow definition used by ISCED). With the exception of the Czech Republic, Norway, the UK, and the US, countries in the review spend more per student on primary education than on pre-primary education (see Figure 3.5), even though the recommended child-staff ratios and group sizes are much smaller for young children than for compulsory school students. According to these data, Norway spends by far the most per child in the pre-primary years (almost $8 000 per child).

There is a need for co-ordinated financial data collection and planning.

Effective resource allocation requires careful financial planning, yet divisions in responsibility between ministries and levels of government make it difficult to aggregate expenditure for ECEC. While in some countries, it is possible to obtain accurate financial data on expenditure for young children, in others data are unreliable or inexistent. Without a coherent and co-ordinated system of funding, in which all aspects of expenditure on ECEC are considered as a whole, policies are less likely to be fully implemented, and inefficiencies and duplication in the system will be more widespread (EC Childcare Network, 1996b). There are some promising strategies, in line with recommendations made by the UN Committee on the Rights of the Child. In Norway, for example, the Ministry of Children and Family Affairs compiles the annual expenditures on children across all Ministries into one document to

---

36. See explanation in Chapter 1. The review has used a broader definition for ECEC than used by ISCED.

Figure 3.4. **Public expenditure for pre-primary[1] education as a percentage of GDP, 1998**

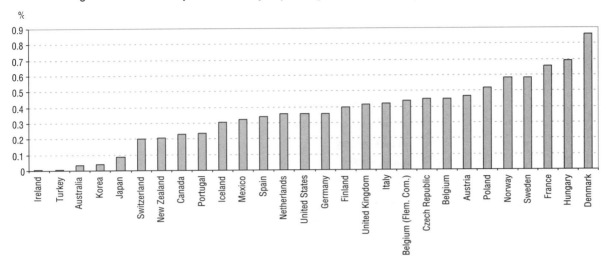

1. The data refer to pre-primary education, which is limited to organised centre-based programmes designed to foster learning and emotional and social development in children for 3 to compulsory school age. Day care, play groups and home-based structured and developmental activities may not be included in these data.

Source: OECD Education Database (2001).

demonstrate what share of the budget is spent on children, as well as to formulate government objectives and policy for children across sectors. In Australia, the Productivity Commission produces an annual report which details expenditure by Commonwealth and state and territory governments on children's services. In general, there is a need for consistent and comprehensive data collection on expenditure at both national and international levels. There is also a longer-term need for regular research and monitoring of the impact of levels of resource allocation and different financing mechanisms for children and families across countries.

Cost sharing by government, parents, and business

In order to maximise constrained resources, the main cost of providing ECEC is usually shared among different levels of government (national, regional, and local), parents, and sometimes business. However, this distribution varies greatly across countries, as well as within countries, and usually by sector (education, social welfare). In terms of *government* funding, federal and state governments share financial responsibility for ECEC in the US, while local authorities bear most of costs in the UK. In Australia, national, state/territory, and local governments finance non-school based ECEC, and states/territories mostly finance pre-school education. Financing arrangements vary among other countries, as well. For *non-school* provision, financing is shared by national, regional and local authorities in Belgium (Flemish and French Communities), national and local authorities in the Netherlands, and regional and local authorities in the Czech Republic, Italy, and Portugal. National governments play a substantial role in financing *pre-school* education in Belgium (Flemish and French Communities), the Czech Republic, Italy, the Netherlands, and Portugal; Italy relies also on regional and local funding. In Denmark, Finland, Norway, and Sweden, there is a uniform system for all ser-

Governments at different levels bear most of the costs for ECEC.

87

Figure 3.5. **Expenditure per child (US dollars converted using PPPs) on public and private institutions by level of education (based on full-time equivalents), 1998**

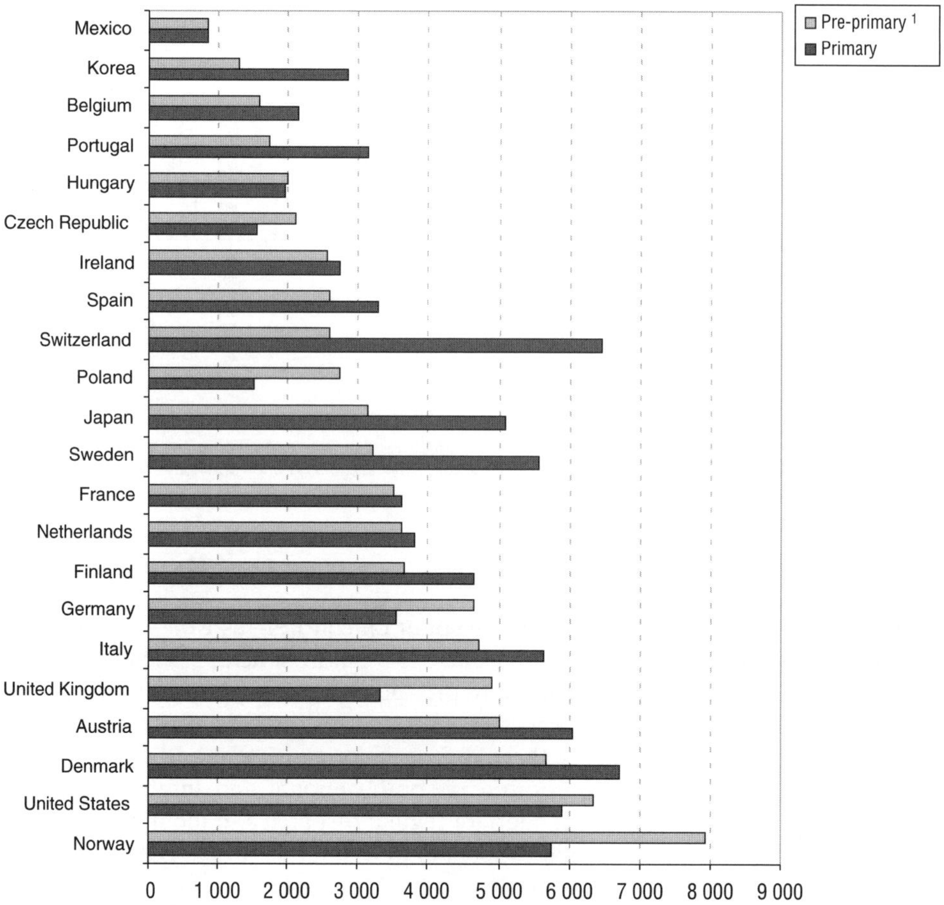

1. The data refer to pre-primary education, which is limited to organised centre-based programmes designed to foster learning and emotional and social development in children for 3 to compulsory school age. Day care, play groups and home-based structured and developmental activities may not be included in these data.

Source : OECD Education Database (2001).

vices below compulsory school age, with shared financing by national and local authorities. In Norway, the state has assumed a larger share of the costs in the 1990s, while in Finland and Sweden, decentralisation has increased the financial responsibility of the municipalities (Meyers and Gornick, 2000).

Parents contribute between 25-30 % of the costs in most countries.

In most European countries, *parents* generally cover one-quarter to one-third of operating service costs, but only 15% in Finland (see Table 3.4). Only in Australia, the UK, and the US do parent fees make up most of the costs. However, these fees are heavily subsidised by government in Australia and the UK.[37] In the US, where ECEC is underfunded relative to other publicly-funded

---

37. Depending on family income, subsidies cover up to 70% of costs in the UK and 100% of costs in Australia.

Table 3.4. **Parental contributions to the costs of ECEC settings**

	Aged 0-3	Aged 3-6 years*
AUS	Varies according to income via Child Care Benefit (Average 9% of disposable income)	Free for 4-year olds in State-funded reception classes
BEL(FL)	Varies according to income Parents pay maximum 28% of costs	Free from 2.5 years
BEL(FR)	Varies according to income Ranges from 17-25% of costs	Free from 2.5 years
CZE	Not applicable, as few services exist	Varies according to income Parents pay maximum 30% of costs
DNK	Varies according to income and municipality Parents pay maximum 33% of costs	Varies according to income and municipality Max 33% of costs
FIN	Varies according to income, usually 10-15% Maximum fee for parents is 1 100 FIM per month	Varies according to income, usually 10-15% Max 1 100 FIM per month
ITA	On average, parents pay 36% of costs (12% of disposable income)	Free in public (except meals) Fees vary in private
NLD	Varies according to income Overall, parents pay 44% of costs (6-21% of net family income)	Free from 4 years
NOR	Varies according to income Parents pay from 28% to 45% of costs in public centres	Varies according to income Parents pay from 28% to 45% of costs in public centres
PRT	Costs to parents average 11% of family income	Free in public Jardims
SWE	Varies according to income and municipality, from 2% to 20% of costs.	Free pre-school class from 5 years.
UKM	Varies according to income via tax credit schemes Parents normally pay from 30% to 60% of costs	Free nursery education for all 4 years olds, and increasingly for 3 year olds.
USA	Varies according to income Unless exempt, parents pay on average 60% of childcare costs (18-25% of income)	Parents pay on average 60% of childcare costs Free access for some 4 year olds in State-funded Pre-K and for most 5s in Kindergarten classes

Source: OECD background reports.

* Free services in this column are generally part-day. Parents generally have to pay for supplementary care.

education programmes and social services (Casper, 1995), parents pay an average of 60% of the costs (rising to 70-80% of costs of ECEC outside the school system), at a time in their life when their earnings are likely to be the lowest (Barnett and Masse, 2000; CQCO Study Team, 1995).[38] This imbalance between public and private funding reflects deeply ingrained attitudes concerning individual and collective responsibility for ECEC. The education and care of young children are predominantly seen as private tasks to be managed by individual families, not as issues which demand strong public commitment.

The role of *employers* in financing services outside the education system varies across countries, depending, in part, on the extent to which these services are viewed as a labour market support. In Belgium (Flemish and French

Employers have played a minor role, except in the Netherlands.

38. In the US, families pay higher fees for child care (an average of $4 000 a year) than they pay for higher education tuition and also a larger share of the total cost (Barnett and Masse, 2000).

Communities), employers contribute 0.05% of the wage bill for services for children under 3, and in Italy, they pay 0.1% of the wage bill for social services (including child care), which represents only a small contribution to the costs (Meyers and Gornick, 2000). In Australia, the Netherlands, and the US, the tax system stimulates employer contributions by allowing employers to deduct the cost of child care for employees from their taxable earnings (or through a tax exemption in Australia). The Netherlands has taken a unique approach by aiming for a tripartite arrangement in which government, employers, and parents share the major costs of child care provision. In 1990, the government initiated a *Stimulative Measure on Child Care* which has succeeded in attaining cost sharing as follows: employers 21%, government 35%, and parents 44%. In moving toward greater reliance on employer-sponsored ECEC, the Netherlands is acknowledging that employers are a major stakeholder in ECEC and that providing supports for working parents can reap benefits for both employers and employees. In the Nordic countries, it is not common for employers to contribute directly financing ECEC. Services are viewed as a public responsibility, and admission is a social right, rather than a benefit for employees.

Financing mechanisms and delivery systems

The most common mechanism is direct funding to public services.

The choice of funding and financing mechanisms varies across countries and reflects different political traditions toward the role of government and public services. Most OECD countries favour public delivery of services, but costs are often shared with parents, as noted earlier. The direct provision of ECEC through services and schools constitutes the bulk of government assistance. Providers in Belgium (Flemish and French Communities), Czech Republic, Denmark, Finland, Italy, Norway, Portugal, and Sweden are either public authorities (*i.e.*, state or municipalities) or a mixture of public and private (primarily non-profit) organisations that are funded and regulated by public authorities. In Sweden, most private providers are parent co-operatives. There is a slight trend toward greater reliance on privately-delivered but publicly-financed providers in order to reduce costs for the municipalities and provide parents with more diverse options.[39] In the Czech Republic, changes in the political and economic system have opened up the opportunity for privately and church-organised ECEC settings for 3- to 6-year olds, although to date on a small scale (covering less than 2% of children). In general, private providers must meet the same quality standards as public providers in order to receive direct subsidies.

Private providers tend to receive public funding and are expected to meet quality standards.

In Australia, the UK, and the US, the public-private mix is greater, and for-profit providers for children under 5 are more common. For example, 90% of provision is private in the US (60% of which is not-for-profit and 30% for-profit) and in Australia 73% of long day care centres are private, for-profit, while other forms of ECEC are predominately community-based, not-for-profit. The involvement of the private for-profit sector has increased in Australia in the past decade and has been concurrent with a shift from funding direct provision

---

39. Publicly-funded, privately-operated provision currently covers 7% of children in Finland, 13% in Sweden, 30% in Denmark, and 42% in Norway. In Belgium, which has a strong tradition of private, non-profit (often confessional) schools, the figures are higher (64% in Flanders and 40% in the French Community).

and funding of services to subsidising the consumers. Recently, the Commonwealth removed the operational subsidies to community ECEC centres in order to "level the playing field" for for-profit providers.[40] For-profit provision also exists in Belgium (Flemish and French Communities), Italy, the Netherlands, and Portugal, primarily for children under 3, and to a much more limited extent in Finland and Norway. Profit-making is almost inexistent in Denmark and Sweden. Again, most countries require quality standards for private and public provision if they are to receive direct or indirect public resources, and in many instances, if they are to operate at all [*e.g.*, Belgium (Flemish and French Communities), Denmark, the Netherlands].

In some countries, parents receive subsidies to purchase care. *Fee subsidies* – vouchers or cash grants – enable access to a wide range of services for many parents who could not otherwise afford the full cost. In Australia, for example, parents receive fee subsidies through the new Child Care Benefit (CCB) for private and community-based centres, family day care and out-of-school provision. All families who use formal approved child care are eligible for a minimum amount, and assistance increases as family income decreases. Families must send their children to an approved Quality Improvement and Accreditation System (QIAS) centre to be eligible for the CCB. A minimum level of CCB is also available to working families using informal (registered) care. In Finland, parents with children under school age are entitled to a fee subsidy (Private Care Allowance) to purchase private centre-based or home-based provision. Local authorities pay the allowance – which consists of a basic allowance and supplement related to income and family-size – directly to the provider. In the US, there have been substantial increases in federal and state funding for subsidies for low-income parents.

Other financing mechanisms include *tax relief* to enable parents to purchase private care, and incentives for *employer contributions* (discussed earlier). In most countries, tax relief allows families to deduct ECEC expenses from their tax liability. This strategy may not help very low-income families if they do not earn enough to pay taxes. In contrast, the new Childcare Tax Credit in the UK (part of the Working Families Tax Credit) is targeted to make childcare services more affordable for low- and middle-income families. The Childcare Tax Credit is worth up to 70% of eligible childcare costs up to a maximum cost of £100 per week for families who pay for one child, and £150 a week for families who pay for two or more children. Eligible childcare must be registered with the local authority (*e.g.*, family day-care, play schemes, day nurseries or out-of-school clubs) or accredited. While fee subsidies, tax relief, and employer contributions are mechanisms to supplement publicly-subsidised provision in most countries, they form the majority of government assistance in Australia, the UK, and the US – especially for the non-school sector. In contrast to direct funding and provision, these mechanisms represent a greater reliance on family or the private sector to provide services, and in some cases, to absorb the costs (Myers and Gornick, 2000). If such is the case, relationships between supply, demand, quality, and affordability may become problematic.

Other financing mechanisms include fee subsidies, tax relief, and employer contributions.

---

40. New South Wales and Northern Territory continue to provide ongoing funding in the form of operational subsidies to community-based long day care.

Affordability and access

A shift in policy toward a more universal education approach.

One way to determine affordability is by the percentage of disposable income that families accord to ECEC services. Reflecting the growing consensus that participation in ECEC is desirable for 3- to 6-year-olds, countries have sought financial incentives for children to attend services. In order to promote equal educational opportunities, Portugal now provides a free daily five-hour session for 5-year-olds in *jardins de infância*, and in the next two years, Sweden will subsidise a free half-day session for 4- and 5-year olds in the *förskole* (most of whom are already attending centres on a fee-paying basis). These recent changes suggest a shift in policy toward a more universal educational approach that has long been adopted in the education sector in Belgium (Flemish and French Communities) from 30 months, in Italy from age 3 (in state-run and municipal schools), and in the Netherlands from age 4.

Due to the high costs for infant-toddler provision and the different delivery systems, parents tend to pay much more for services for children under 3 than for older children. In most countries, publicly-funded services charge parents on a sliding scale according to income, and in many cases the fee is waived completely for low-income families or children with special needs. Fees are often reduced for additional siblings (*e.g.*, by 50% in Denmark and Finland). As a result of such subsidies, parent fees for publicly-funded ECEC take up less than 10% of the average family income in most European countries and Australia.

Yet, affordability is still a barrier to access for low-income families in many countries.

Affordability is a major criterion of access, especially in systems where most of the costs are expected to be covered through parental fees. In the US, parent payments are generally very low for means-tested public provision (*e.g.*, Head Start), but access to these services and other subsidies is limited.[41] Moreover, due to the limited supply of licensed ECEC and scarce knowledge of subsidies, many eligible poor families do not use subsidies for which they are eligible and rely instead on unlicensed provision (Fuller *et al.*, 2000). Lower-income families who do pay for services often end up paying a higher proportion of their income for services than higher income families. Research found that families earning less than $1 200 per month paid 25% of their incomes for child care, while families earning over $4 500 per month paid only 6% of their incomes (Casper, 1995). Despite availability of fee subsidies, affordability is cited as a major barrier to access to non-school ECEC services in countries including the UK, the Netherlands and the US, leading to a lower percentage of low-income families enrolled in ECEC than higher-income families. In the US, for example, only 45% of 3- to 5-year-olds from low-income families were enrolled in pre-school programmes, compared with almost 75% from high-income families (National Education Goals Panel, 1997). Even in heavily subsidised systems, country reports document that some children are excluded due to their families' economic situation or their parents choose to rely on private, informal arrangements. As children with limited access to services are often those who would benefit the most from quality ECEC, for equity reasons, there is a need for better monitoring of the consequences of public expenditure and mechanisms for distributing resources.

---

41. In the US, only about 10% of income-eligible children under federal guidelines received the main federal subsidy, the Child Care and Development Fund (U.S. Department of Health and Human Services, 1999).

With trends toward increased decentralisation and deregulation, both fee increases and greater variation in fees across regions have become prevalent in many countries (*e.g.*, Australia, the Czech Republic, Denmark, Finland, Sweden, Norway, the Netherlands, US). There is some concern that these substantial fee increases have led to decrease in utilisation, particularly among middle- and low-income families. In Australia, for example, fees, which are not regulated by government, have increased by 7% each year between 1991-1999, representing a total increase of 58%. Well-targeted public investment may help address these concerns. Since its introduction in July 2000, the new Child Care Benefit in Australia has improved the affordability of child care for most families (for many very low-income families, services are now free or require a nominal payment). According to official reports, there has been an increase in demand among families not previously using provision and existing families have increased their hours of usage. Another mechanism to limit fee increases and variation, is to introduce a maximum fee set at a low level, as in Finland and Sweden, to ensure that no parent pays more than a set amount on ECEC. In the Czech Republic and Denmark, fees may vary, but parental contributions must not exceed 30% of costs.

Concerns about increases and variation in fees.

Financing strategies to expand supply and raise quality

Government subsidies can help promote the development and enhancement of ECEC provision. Although it is difficult to gauge the impact of public subsidies on accessibility to ECEC (EC Childcare Network, 1996*b*), waiting lists for places in publicly-funded programmes suggest that funding is inadequate to ensure equitable access – even in some nations with entitlement policies. One of the major financing issues centres on the following question: what is the desirable mix between *demand-side* subsidies (allocating government resources directly to families) and *supply-side* subsidies (allocating resources to create and support a stable infrastructure of services)? As noted earlier, most countries seek to expand supply through subsidies to providers, generally via municipal block grants for non-school services and via earmarked per capita grants for educational services. The exceptions are Australia, the UK, and the US, which have adopted a mixed-system of demand-side subsidies to parents who need "child care" and supply-side funding to providers to expand "early education," usually for 3- and 4-year-olds. In the former approach, it is anticipated that the demand for services will both stimulate the expansion of supply and increase affordability. The use of subsidies to parents rather than direct support to providers also reflects a preference for supporting individual choice at family level.

However, it is argued that a completely demand-driven system only works in a more or less perfect market. Markets for ECEC are far from perfect: buyers lack both financial resources and full information on quality and accessibility (Vandell and Wolfe, 2000; Verry, 2000). There is also evidence that demand-driven systems can lead to inequitable development of services. In Australia, in the early 1990s, fee subsidies were extended to parents using private, for-profit provision. This led to uneven and unforeseen growth, with some areas experiencing an oversupply, while gaps in supply, such as places for infants and toddlers, still existed in some regions. To address these long-standing problems, a national planning system has been devised to support the viability and sustainability of existing services and to encourage providers to offer services in disadvantaged communities. The Disadvantaged Area Sub-

Equitable access calls for a balance between supply-side and demand-side funding.

93

sidy provides direct funding to community-based services in rural areas. The UK and the US, as well, have allocated additional subsidies to help attract private providers to low-income and rural areas (see Section 3.1). This suggests a need for a combined approach: supply-side investment to the full range of providers in exchange for guarantees of improved access and quality can be strengthened by demand-side subsidies to make programmes more affordable for middle- and low-income families. There is also a need for better consumer information on quality, affordability, and accessibility of ECEC (see Section 3.7 for examples).

In funding systems relying mostly on supply-side funding, there also may be a need for more parity in funding across regions and sectors to achieve more equitable access. In countries with wide differences in regional wealth (e.g., Italy, Portugal), there is a need for *differential funding* to even out geographic disparities in provision. Finland and Sweden address this problem through a special levelling mechanism that takes into account differences in local tax bases and redistributes tax revenue more evenly among municipalities. In addition, some countries (e.g., Norway, Portugal), rely on non-profit and for-profit providers to expand provision toward universal access, but these services receive lower levels of public funding than public providers. Without more equitable resource allocation, private services may be forced to cut costs and have difficulty in meeting quality standards. The Netherlands has addressed this issue by providing, under certain conditions, public funding to private providers, both non-profit and for-profit, as long as the latter meet the defined quality standards. In Australia, all families using private for-profit and non-profit provision are all eligible for the same level of Child Care Benefit.

Financing mechanisms can be used to raise quality.

Financing strategies are not limited to enhancing supply. Indeed, there are several financing strategies used to enhance quality. As mentioned earlier, most countries require ECEC (including family day care) to meet *quality standards in order to receive public funding*, and in some cases in order to operate at all. Funding for Head Start is now linked to national performance standards. Some countries provide financial incentives for programmes to achieve national *accreditation*, as in Australia or the US.[42] In addition, governments can *earmark decentralised funds* so that a proportion of resources will go to quality improvement efforts, including workforce training and the reduction of child-staff ratios and class sizes. In the US, the federal Child Care and Development Fund block grant, includes a 4% set-aside for quality improvement, which states can spend in various ways (e.g., staff training, improved ratios; parent information; facility improvement, etc.). The UK gives grants to local partnerships to develop the infrastructure and services which support quality assurance. Another approach is to *target scarce resources* to children who are more at risk of receiving inferior quality services. In the Netherlands and the Flemish Community of Belgium, for example, a "pupil weighting system" allocates additional funding to finance additional staff, teaching hours, or special programmes based on the number of children from ethnic minority backgrounds or families with low educational attainment in a given school.

---

42. In the US, 16 states pay a higher per child reimbursement rate to programmes achieving NAEYC voluntary accreditation.

Cost and quality

When services rely primarily on revenue from families with limited budgets, they must keep the costs down. There is a tension between the financial viability of services, affordability for parents, and high quality for children (Press and Hayes, 2000). Services may cost too little to achieve high quality, but too much to be affordable for many parents. In systems with limited public support, services compete to keep fees low and earn a profitable return on capital. The need to contain costs may result in programmes that do not invest sufficiently in personnel or facilities (Cochran, 1993). Without adequate resources, staff often subsidise underfunded systems with foregone wages and benefits, leading to difficulties in recruiting and retaining a well-qualified workforce (CQCO Study Team, 1995). These hidden costs are rarely made visible in cost-effectiveness analyses. Low public investment in ECEC jeopardises children by forcing services (both for-profit and non-profit) to operate with inadequate funds to provide quality. It also constrains the choices of lower-income parents who cannot afford the full cost of ECEC and may force them to settle for lower quality care for their children (CQCO Study Team, 1995).

There is a need for public investment in services and the infrastructure.

As the previous sections have argued, ECEC provision needs to be supported by a quality *infrastructure* for planning, monitoring, support, training, research and development. Without secure and adequate resources, in both services and the infrastructure, it will be difficult to ensure ongoing quality improvement efforts. In particular, raising the qualifications of staff (see Section 3.5) carries cost implications, since it would involve a major revaluing of early childhood work in many countries. Similarly, there is a need to invest in higher wages and benefits for staff in order to recruit and retain a qualified workforce which carries significant financial implications, as staff costs make up the bulk of programme costs (roughly 80% in most countries). Investment in other structural characteristics of quality (child-staff ratios, group size, facilities) also requires ongoing investment in the infrastructure. Regardless of the financing strategy adopted, it is clear that substantial public investment in ECEC is necessary for the development of a coherent and well-resourced *system* of quality services for all young children (Gallagher and Clifford, 2000; Kagan and Cohen, 1997).

3.5. Improving staff training and work conditions

Key points

It is widely recognised that staff working with children in ECEC programmes have a major impact on children's early development and learning. Research shows the links between strong training and support of staff – including appropriate pay and conditions – and the quality of ECEC services (Bowman *et al.*, 2000; CQCO Study Team, 1995; EC Childcare Network, 1996a; Whitebook *et al.*, 1998). In particular, staff who have more formal education and more specialised early childhood training provide more stimulating, warm, and supportive interactions with children (CQCO Study Team, 1995; NICHD, 1997; Phillipsen *et al.*, 1997). This section discusses the links between the structure of a county's early childhood system and the structure of staffing, and in turn, the implications for training, pay, status of professionals.[43] This section will focus first on centre- and school-based provision and then on family day care:

- Countries have adopted two main approaches to staffing: a split regime with a group of teachers working with children over 3 and lower-trained workers in other services; or a pedagogue working with children from birth to 6, and sometimes older in a range of settings. There is a cross-national trend toward at least a three-year tertiary degree for ECEC staff with the main responsibility for pre-school children.

- While the degree of early childhood specialisation and the balance between theory and practice vary across countries, there appear to be common training gaps in the following areas: work with parents, work with infants and toddlers, bilingual/multi-cultural and special education, and research and evaluation.

- Opportunities to participate in in-service training and professional development are uneven. Staff with the lowest levels of initial training tend to have the least access;

- Low pay, status, poor working conditions, limited access to in-service training and limited career mobility are a concern, particularly for staff working with young children in infant-toddler, out-of-school, and family day care settings.

- As ECEC provision expands, recruitment and retention are major challenges for the field. Many countries are seeking to attract a diverse workforce to reflect the diversity of children in ECEC. Another major issue is whether a more gender-mixed workforce is desirable, and if so how it can be achieved.

The structure of staffing and its implications

Most countries have developed a split staffing regime…

Different approaches to staffing relate to diverse views of the role of early childhood workers, the nature of their work with children, as well as how that work is valued by society (Moss, 2000). Earlier sections have discussed the divided systems of "care" and "education" provision between social welfare and education authorities in most countries [*e.g.*, Belgium (Flemish and French Communities), the Czech Republic, Italy, the Netherlands, and Portugal]. The length, level, and orientation of training, as well as pay and work conditions,

---

43. In this report, the term *training* refers to instruction and education courses offered to ECEC staff by public authorities, community organisations, and/or professional associations/unions. Included in the definition are more formal academic courses offered by secondary, post-secondary, and tertiary institutions. The term *initial (pre-service) training* refers to education to prepare staff for work in the ECEC field. *In-service training* refers to education intended to improve the knowledge and skills of staff currently employed in the sector.

considered appropriate for staff who work within the welfare and education systems tend to follow this dividing line. In these countries, one finds a mixture of highly-trained staff working as teachers in pre-schools in the education sector and various types of child care workers employed in the welfare sector, usually in infant-toddler and out-of-school provision (see Table 3.5 for an overview of staffing). The latter group tend to have lower levels of training, less specialisation in early childhood, lower compensation, and poorer working conditions than their early childhood counterparts in the education system.

When all early childhood services are under the responsibility of one Ministry, there is usually a unified training system with a high level of qualification for staff working with all children from birth to 6. In the UK, where administrative integration is fairly recent, it is not clear whether or not a new staffing structure will emerge, and if so, whether or not it will include a more integrated approach to staff working with children under 6. In early childhood systems with a longer history of integration (*e.g.*, Denmark, Finland, Norway, and Sweden), staff are trained to work with children across the early childhood period, birth to 6 (and sometimes older children), in non-school settings. These countries have adopted a simple staffing structure – a highly-trained pedagogue as the main worker, supported by less-trained assistants – with reasonable working conditions across the ECEC field. Pedagogues are considered to have a different, but equally important, role to school-teachers, and often enjoy equivalent status, pay, and working conditions.

...while other countries have developed a more unified staffing approach.

Countries also vary with regard to the emphasis on specific age groups within their initial training programmes. In Australia, the Netherlands, the UK[44], and the US, early years teachers and primary teachers are often trained together. While this ensures that professionals working with children from age 4 and older in schools share basic knowledge and professional identity, there is some evidence that time spent on learning about the early years tends to lose out to the weightier status of compulsory schooling. Other countries such as Belgium (Flemish and French Communities), Czech Republic, Italy, and Portugal consider that a high degree of specialisation is necessary for quality work with young children from 3 to 6. Early childhood educators are trained separately from primary teachers, at the same level and institutions. They are not qualified to work in primary schools, except in Belgium (Flemish and French Communities).

The degree of early childhood specialisation varies.

Given the range of educational, social, and community contexts in which they work, pedagogues in the Nordic countries view their multi-purpose roles as fulfilling social, cultural, and educational objectives. In Norway, pre-school teachers may work with children from birth to 6 years in ECEC, with 6-year-olds in grade I of primary school, with children from birth to 8 years in out-of-school provision, and with children with special needs.[45] Denmark trains its *paedagoger* to work with people from *birth to* 100 in all early childhood services, out-of-school provision, *and* in range of services for children and adults with special

---

44. It should be noted, however, that in the UK, half of early education settings are in the non-maintained sector and largely staffed by practitioners who are not trained as teachers.

45. After completing one more year of higher education, pedagogues may teach children up to the age of 10 in schools.

Table 3.5. **Overview of trained staff in centre- and school-based ECEC**

	Main type of staff	Initial training	Age range covered	Main field of work	Work in primary?	Men in ECEC (% of all staff)	In-service opportunities	% of primary teacher salary earned by staff with highest level of training
AUS#	Teacher	3-4 years university	0-5	Preschools	No	3.3% childcare 2.3% pre-schools	Commonwealth and state funding to centres	
	Child care worker	2 year post-18 to 4 year university	0-5	Long day care	No			
BEL (FR)	Institutrice de maternelle	3 years pedagogical higher education	2.5-6	École maternelle	Yes	Less than 1%	Funding decentralised to schools	100%
	Puéricultrice	3 years post-16 vocational secondary	0-3	Crèches (or assistant in école maternelle)	No			
BEL (FL)	Kleuteronderwijzer(es)	3 years pedagogical higher education	2.5-6	Kleuterschool	Yes	Less than 1%	Funding decentralised to schools	100%
	Kinderverzorgster	3 years post-16 voc secondary	0-3	Kinderdagverblijf	No			
CZE	Učitel mateřské školy	4 years secondary pedagogical schools or 3 years higher vocational schools or university education	3-6	Mateřská škola	No	Less than 1%	Voluntary Offered by regional centres	75%
	Detská sestra	4 years secondary nursing school	0-3	Creche	No			
DNK	Paedagog*	3.5 years vocational higher education (depending on prior experience)	0-100	Educational, Social care, special needs institutions (including day care)	No	14% 3% in pre-school class	Funding decentralised to centres	88-96%
FIN	Lastentarhanopettaja* (Sosiaalikasvattaja) Lähihoitaja	3-4.5 years university or 3.5 years polytechnic 3 years secondary vocational	0-7	6-vuotiaiden esiopetus Päiväkoti Avoin päiväkoti	Yes - with 6-year-olds	4%	Funding decentralised to municipalities	81%
ITA	Insegnante di scuola materna	4 years university	3-6	Scuola materna	No	Less than 1%	Municipality or director/ inspector decides	100%
	Educatrice	Secondary vocational diploma	0-3	Asilo nido	No			
NLD	Leraar basisonderwij	4 years voc. higher ed (PABO)	4-12	Basisschool	Yes	25% in primary - few with 4-6 year olds	Funding decentralised to municipalities	100%
	Leidster kinder centra	MBO (3 years) or HBO (4 years)	0-12+	Kinderopvang Buitenschoolse opvang Peuterspeelzaal	No	Less than 1%		
NOR	Pedagogiske ledere*	3 years higher education at state colleges	0-7	Barnehager SFO Grade 1 primary	Yes - in Grade 1 (and Grade 2-4 with one extra year of higher education)	7%	A plan for access is part of an agreement in the public sector	88-96%
	Assistents	2 year post-16 apprenticeship	0-7					
PRT	Educadora de infância	4 years university or polytechnic	0-6	Jardim de infância Crèches ATL	No	Less than 1%	Offered by regional teacher centres and universities to teachers in public/private sectors	
SWE	Förskollärare* Fritidspedagog*	3 years university 3 years university	0-7	Förskoleclass Förskola Öppen Förskola Fritidshem	Yes - with 6-year-olds and in teams with 6-9 year olds	5%	Funding decentralised to municipality	84%
	Barnskötare	2 years post-16 secondary	0-7		No			
UKM	Qualified teacher Trained nursery teacher	4 years university	3-11	Reception class Nursery school/class Day nursery Playgroup	Yes	1% in non-school ECEC	Regular access for teachers Limited in child care	
	Nursery nurse	2 years post-16 secondary	0-5	Nurseries (or as assistant in above)				
USA+	Public school teacher	4 years university	4-8 (0-8)	Public schools	Yes	3%	Most states require a certain number of hours per year	100% school
	Head Start teacher	CDA = 1 year higher education	0-5	Head Start	No			42% in childcare
	Child care teacher	1 course to 4 year university	0-5	Child care centre	No			

Staffing varies according to the regulations of each state and territory.
* These are "core workers" with group responsibility. They may be assisted by other workers (trained and untrained) which form the minority of the workforce in integrated ECEC systems.
+ There are wide variations in how these credentials are valued from state to state.
Source: OECD Country Reports; Oberhuemer and Ulich (1997).

needs. A more general, broad-based training in social care, though at a lower level, is available in Australia, Finland, and the Netherlands, as well.

Increasingly, pedagogues and other early childhood staff are working in teams with primary school teachers in the early years of schooling (see Section 3.3). To support such collaboration, in Sweden, there is a proposed reform to partially integrate the training of different teachers who work with children, while encouraging them to develop a variety of knowledge profiles. The proposal would extend the education for pre-school teachers and leisure-time pedagogues another six months to three-and-a-half years. The new study programme would consist of joint training so that students who will work in pre-school, compulsory school, and upper secondary school obtain a common core of knowledge in areas such as, teaching, special needs education, child and youth development, and interdisciplinary subjects. The remaining training would include specialised studies and *practica*. Teachers in pre-school, the first years of compulsory school, and out-of-school provision would have the same qualification, strengthening teamwork among the professionals, and building closer links across different phases of lifelong learning.

A trend toward multi-disciplinary staffing approaches?

Trend toward longer and higher levels of initial training

Whatever the organisation and emphasis, there is widespread movement toward longer and higher levels of basic training for the professional staff working with children *from the age of* 3, and sometimes younger. In the Western European countries, centre-based and school-based staff with primary responsibility for young children are required to complete at least three years of training at the tertiary level – either in universities as in Italy, Finland, Portugal, and Sweden or in higher education institutions, as in Denmark, Belgium (Flemish and French Communities), Norway, the Netherlands and the UK. In the Czech Republic, almost all staff working in pre-schools have completed four-year secondary level programmes with a pedagogical orientation, and discussions are underway to move the training for pre-school teachers to the tertiary level. In part due to the federal systems in Australia and the US, there is currently no agreed national framework for staff qualifications, and regulations vary across states and territories. A very complex system of staffing has evolved with multiple roles, training, and qualifications to reflect the diverse set of services found in these two countries, though staffing regulations tend to follow the "care" and "education" division.

At least three years of tertiary education is the norm for pre-school staff in Western Europe.

The training situation is more varied for staff working with infants and toddlers. As noted earlier, in more integrated systems with unified staffing regimes, staff with group responsibility working with all children under compulsory school age tend to have the same (high) level of training. In Belgium (Flemish and French Communities), Italy, and the UK, staff with group responsibility for infants and toddlers tend to have completed about two to three years of post-16 vocational training (comparable to the level of staff training among auxiliary staff in Finland and Sweden), which is a lower qualification than their counterparts working in the educational system. A matter of concern is that countries with large private and voluntary sectors still have a considerable group of low-trained and untrained staff working in ECEC, particularly with infants and toddlers (*e.g.*, Australia, the UK, and the US). In contrast, 98% of staff in Sweden are trained to work with young children.

Staff working with infants and toddlers tend to have less training.

Until recently, *out-of-school provision* has not been a high priority in most countries, and this neglect is reflected in the lack of attention to the workers who staff such services. In most countries, work with children is divided

Training for staff in out-of-school provision also has been neglected.

between school time and "wrap around provision" staffed by a different set of workers. With few exceptions, there is no framework for qualifying or regulating personnel working in out-of-school provision. Sweden is the only country to have a specific qualification for work in leisure-time centres. Training for *fritid-spedagoger* takes place at university level alongside pre-school and primary school teachers, but (currently) in a separate track. Denmark follows a more general approach. Qualified pedagogues in Denmark who wish to work in out-of-school provision may specialise in school-age recreation work within their broad training. In the Netherlands, qualification requirements for staff in out-of-school provision are identical to those working in settings with children under 4. With the expansion of out-of-school provision in many countries, there is recognition that there will be a need to clarify the nature of the work, qualifications, and training necessary to work in such services in the near future.

Initial training: what it covers and what it does not

The balance between theory and practice is under discussion in many countries.

In many countries, responsibility for developing training curricula has been decentralised. General study plans, focusing broadly on the purpose, content, and structure of training are articulated at the national level, and the details are developed by individual training institutions. This can lead to some variation, but also allows for tailoring courses to local needs and increasing the involvement of local institutions and community members (Pritchard, 1996). In general, training for staff to work with children under 3 often emphasises a paramedical, health, or care orientation. Training for staff working with 3- to 6-year-olds tends to focus on broad education-related courses, such as psychology, sociology, history, philosophy, along with subject-based courses including music, art, and movement. Supervised work placements are usually part of the training course, with the longest period in the final year. These *practica* may include placements in remedial, sociocultural, and special needs settings, along with more mainstream forms of ECEC.

The balance between theory and practice is an issue under discussion in many countries, particularly in countries where training has recently shifted to the university sector (*e.g.*, Finland, Italy, Portugal), as well as in the Czech Republic where there are proposals to upgrade training to the tertiary level. In sum, across Europe, a good general level of education and field-relevant knowledge-base, complemented by practical work experience, are considered essential ingredients for preparing staff to work in posts of responsibility with young children. In contrast, in Australia and the US there is less professional and public consensus regarding the level of education and knowledge necessary to work in the field, and this ambiguity is reflected in pre-service qualifications, which can be quite low by comparative and professional standards.

There are common training gaps across countries.

Looking ahead, there is a need for initial training to address some of the challenging issues facing early childhood practitioners. Across countries, there seems to be little emphasis on adult-related issues. Few staff training courses focus on professional issues in the field and strategies to *work with parents and family members*, even though these are an important part of programme goals in most countries. There is a lack of specialised training for those who *work with infants and toddlers*, even though provision for this age group is expanding in many countries. With changing patterns of migration, there is a need for more focus on bilingual/multicultural education and *work with diverse communities of children and families*. Similarly, trends toward inclusion mean that many mainstream staff need specialised training to *work with children with disabilities and other special educational needs*. In countries with complex funding streams, staff are expected to be *social entrepreneurs* to juggle various funding sources (public and private), compete for scarce resources and grants, etc. Finally, some countries encourage staff to develop their own theories based on their observations, research, and exploration of values and assumptions. In other countries, there is a need for more training for staff as researchers, including approaches to *observing and assessing children*, using assessments for purposes that advance early childhood pedagogy, as well as *self-evaluation strategies* that promote reflective practice.

Ongoing training and professional development: opportunities are uneven

Access to in-service training is important to improving early childhood practice (see Box 3.9). It is difficult to obtain information on access to or participation in in-service training, because in many cases, budgets from the central government are decentralised to municipalities or institutions to be used at the discretion of the municipality or programme director. In a few cases, the right to in-service training is determined by collective agreements, but in general, provision of and participation in continuous training is voluntary. Workers face many practical challenges to accessing in-service training, especially the difficulty of obtaining release time with pay to attend courses. This problem is aggravated for small centres in rural areas, where there may be only one staff

Practical challenges limit access to co-ordinated in-service training.

Box 3.9. **BUPL: a strong partner in raising quality in Denmark**

BUPL is the Danish National Federation of Early Childhood Teachers and Youth Educators, with more than 50 000 trained staff members in infant-toddler centres, kindergartens, leisure-time centres and youth clubs across Denmark. BUPL is at once a traditional trade union, protecting its members working conditions and salary levels, and a professional association committed to raising quality in Danish ECEC. BUPL positions itself in relation to the competent ministries (the Ministry of Social Affairs and the Ministry of Education), as an independent consultative partner, and supports them in implementing national policy. It attempts to maintain a presence in all the arenas important for ECEC, ranging from informal meetings with local authorities, civil servants, parents and parliamentarians to membership of councils and committees at central and local levels. BUPL starts from the premise that the quality of personnel is fundamental to the well-being of children in ECEC settings.

In the last two years, BUPL has actively taken part in the programme *Folkeskole* 2000, in particular to strengthen co-operation between the kindergarten and the primary school, and between schools and the educators in out-of-school provision. The municipalities – which, in Denmark, have full responsibility for the organisation, management and funding of ECEC at local level – have nominated its members as pedagogical advisors with the task of raising education standards and improving pedagogical methods. BUPL's Education Division is researching at the moment the issue of children's development of competencies – personal, developmental, cognitive and social – in wide consultation with ECEC settings, parents, experts and local employers. With pedagogues in the field of special education and residential care for children and adults with disabilities, BUPL has created a Foundation for Development and Research, which finances, from its own funds, projects on ECEC and special education.

BUPL publishes reports and guidelines on the rights and duties of the education partners (including children), and initiates discussions on pedagogical issues with parent and professional groups. It provides extensive in-service and continuous training, not only of its own members, but also at community level for all those involved with early education and care matters. BUPL has been closely involved also in the discussions setting up a common Educational University for teachers and pedagogues.

member for each group of children, and for family day care providers. If training is not subsidised, low wages prevent many workers, especially in the welfare sector, from taking advantage of in-service training. Consistent with trends in other sectors of employment, workers with the lowest levels of basic training are the most likely to have the least access to in-service training (OECD, 1999c). There is wide variation in the quality of in-service training offerings and in the transferability of training credits toward degree programmes, which is essential for enhancing career mobility in the field. In terms of content, trends toward devolution of responsibility to the institutional level mean that staff in management positions will need to develop budgeting, organisational, and human resource skills. There currently is little professional development opportunities for such management and leadership roles.

In addition to providing access to co-ordinated in-service training courses, well-run workplaces include regular opportunities for staff discussion and planning. In most countries, developing good working relationships amongst staff – their mutual support and collaboration – is viewed as essential to fostering good relationships with children and promoting co-operative relationships amongst children. In Belgium (Flemish and French Communities), Italy, Norway, and Portugal, non-contact time is set aside for staff development as an essential part of forging staff relationships and of undertaking an ongoing critical evaluation of the curriculum being offered to children (EC Childcare Network, 1996a). In Italy, six hours a week are set aside as non-contact time to allow staff to undertake, for example, the process of pedagogical documentation (discussed earlier), which is a very useful tool to deepen understanding among staff and children, and to encourage reflective practice.

Concerns about working conditions, status and pay

Low wages and high turnover are major challenges in the field.

The need to improve the work conditions of ECEC staff – organisational climate of the ECEC setting, remuneration, and benefits – is an issue in most countries. In many countries, staff receive poor pay and benefits, relative to workers in similar occupations, including those working in other levels of education. The growing diversification of providers, including higher proportion of private for-profit and not-for-profit providers and family day care settings has introduced greater variations in employment, working conditions, and career prospects within the sector (Christopherson, 1997). In particular, staff working with the youngest children in the welfare system have difficulties getting public recognition for the educational role of their work and have the lowest levels of training, least access to in-service training, lowest pay, poorest work conditions, and highest turnover rates of the ECEC workforce. It is not surprising that staff dissatisfaction and turnover are huge challenges for the field. In Australia, the UK and the US, where pay can be close to the minimum wage and many ECEC workers do not receive paid sick leave and holidays, annual staff turnover may reach over 30% in centre-based ECEC. High turnover rates interfere with the continuity and consistent relationships that are so important to young children's development and learning. Research shows that wages are the most important determinant of staff turnover and a strong predictor of programme quality, yet child care workers in the US earn less than bus drivers and garbage collectors (US Department of Labor, 1999).

There is a tension between keeping costs low and paying staff a fair wage.

Policy to improve staff qualifications and reduce turnover must also address the low wages in the field, as higher trained staff will expect improved compensation. The cost implications are even greater if a high level of basic training is linked to a system of professional development which gives regular non-contact time to staff. Yet, there is a conflict in many countries between policies which attempt to reduce the cost of services by employing workers at very low wages and those which recognise that quality ECEC requires highly-trained workers. Increasingly, there is a bifurcated workforce with a small number of well-trained staff, and a larger and faster growing sector of low-trained, low-paid workers. In largely market-driven systems, this less-skilled workforce provides labour flexibility and cost competitiveness (Christopherson, 1997). Without adequate public funding, either the early childhood workforce subsidises the costs of provision with their low wages or costs are passed on to parents through higher fees. In light of budget constraints, some countries perceive a trade-off between cost and access, fearing that employing highly-trained workers at reasonable wages will lead to fewer places and/or limited access to lower-income families. While most countries invest heavily in staff working with children over 3, Denmark, Finland, and Sweden are unique in their commitment to high levels of public funding across the early childhood workforce covering all centres for children under 6 or 7. Pay and conditions for staff are similar to, if not the same as, those of school teachers *and* services are affordable to families (see Section 3.4). This suggests a need to address the underlying issue leading to the low status and pay of workers in some countries: how the profession is valued by society.

Staff recruitment and retention: who in the future will do early childhood work?

As early childhood provision expands, it has been challenging to meet the increase in demand for trained staff. In the Netherlands, for example, with the rapid growth of welfare services on the one hand, and efforts to reduce class size and the greying of the teaching population in schools on the other, there has been an increasing demand for, and shortage of, qualified staff in both education and welfare sectors. Thousands of former teachers have been offered refresher courses to meet this demand. In Norway, there has been a drop in applicants and a decline in the grades of students admitted to training colleges for ECEC. Just over a third of the workforce are trained pedagogues. In 1999, about 15% of pre-school staff who did not hold the necessary qualifications received dispensations to address this staffing shortage. Within countries, these recruitment problems are more acute in remote and rural areas of countries including Australia and Portugal, and in areas with higher levels of economic and social deprivation in countries such as the Netherlands, UK, and the US. This suggests that there is a need for providing incentives for qualified personnel who accept such placements. As the demand for staff increases, employers have turned to entry level, less skilled and credentialed workers to make up the gap, which may compromise the quality of provision. Attracting workers who have not previously been employed in significant numbers – ethnic minority groups, staff with disabilities, and men – may help solve the staffing crises faced by several countries in the short-term (see discussion below). As a long-term solution, however, it would seem that the status, pay and working conditions of the workforce will need to be addressed.

It is unclear whether recruitment and retention problems are a temporary problem or a long-term difficulty for the sector. It may be part of wider issue in the care, educational, and social services, in economies in which women are better educated and have a wider range of employment opportunities with better pay and stronger career possibilities. In many countries, the ECEC sec-

Shortages of well-trained staff are a growing concern.

103

tor is competing with other employment areas, particularly the rapidly expanding field of elderly care. One concern in the Czech Republic, for example, is the low number of students who graduate from the training programmes and then actually start to work as kindergarten teachers. In addition, recruitment and retention difficulties may be linked to strenuous working conditions, particularly high child-staff ratios, long hours, and increasing demands on early childhood professionals. In several countries, particularly those where major policy changes are impacting the profession, practitioners speak of "change fatigue" as they try to cope with a large number of reforms in a short period of time – in addition to their regular roles and responsibilities with children. Many countries also document that practitioners currently take on a significant amount of unpaid overtime to prepare activities, complete forms and other administrative responsibilities, attend meetings, work with parents, and participate in professional development.

There are several strategies to address recruitment and retention concerns.

What are some strategies to address recruitment and retention issues and create training incentives for employers and employees?

– Where *joint training requirements* and systems exist for pre-school and primary school teachers – as in Belgium (Flemish and French Communities), the Netherlands, Portugal and the UK – teachers of young children receive the same compensation as counterparts working with older children in the school system and enjoy similar status. Early childhood professionals may also have more chances for career mobility within the school system, which may contribute to attracting and retaining a motivated workforce.

– In Denmark, where demand for training far exceeds available places, students may start training after working in the field, so they have the opportunity to get to know the nature of the profession *before* they are fully-qualified. Since 1997, students can be employed as paid trainees by local or regional authorities during an 18-month period in which they alternate courses with field practice.

– *Unions and professional associations* in many countries have been successful in drawing public attention to industrial issues, though membership and power vary from country to country (see Box 3.9). In the Netherlands, for example, collective labour agreements apply to private settings, regardless of how they are funded, ensuring the same minimum level of salaries and working conditions for staff working throughout the sector.

– *Mentoring programmes* have been developed in the US to offer experienced staff an opportunity to share their skills with others, grow in the profession, and receive improved compensation. Mentoring also offers novice staff a practical and supportive way to learn and to overcome the many hurdles of the critical first years on the job (Whitebook and Sakai, 1995).

– In the US, the TEACH Early Childhood Project provides scholarships to individuals already working in the field so that they can attend courses (see Box 3.10). They must commit to continue working in the setting that releases them for an agreed length of time, thereby increasing staff training and retention.

– In the UK, a new *recruitment campaign* is seeking to improve the image of the ECEC sector to attract skilled, imaginative, intelligent and competent individuals to the field – including men, ethnic minorities, older people, and people with disabilities. The campaign is complemented by new funding for training initiatives.

Box 3.10. **TEACH early childhood project in the US**

The goal of the TEACH (Teacher Education and Compensation Helps) project is to improve the training of ECEC workers, linking additional training to higher wages. TEACH is geared to all levels of practitioners already working in ECEC centres or family day care homes. The project ties lateral or vertical job mobility to courses and degrees. The director of the setting agrees to release time so that participants can attend courses, and participants agree to stay at the same setting for a year after completing their TEACH educational goals. The director pays the participant a higher salary, or a bonus, when the goal is completed. The educational goals are set by the participant, who may later set higher goals and enter the programme again. This scholarship programme can be used for entry-level training for assistants, or for higher-level graduate degrees for teachers or directors. By compensating ECEC workers for receiving more training and education, the programme works to retain staff and improve the quality of the workforce. TEACH was started in North Carolina by Day Care Services Association (a non-profit service, research and advocacy group) and has been adopted by other states, including New York, Pennsylvania, Georgia, Florida, Illinois, Colorado and Indiana. Both employers and employees pay a portion of the training costs, and the remaining funds come from federal, state, and private (business and philanthropic) sources. The project has built-in data collection and evaluation components.

Career opportunities in the field are limited for some

Opportunities for horizontal and vertical career mobility enhance the attractiveness of the early childhood profession. Policymakers are faced with a dilemma: how to meet the need for a well-prepared workforce while at the same time maintain the tradition of broad access to the sector for those with lower-skills? In most countries, there are two completely separate systems for care and education, representing different areas of expertise and training. Not surprisingly, training routes are fairly inflexible across this divide, and there is little career opportunity for lower-skilled workers to move into high-skilled and better paid positions.

Various approaches are being developed toward creating a more flexible, modular career structure, so that it is possible to acquire necessary training in a variety of ways, speeds, and to access routes and to exit at various stages of the training process. These strategies (including part-time training and distance education) are being adopted to ensure that women with less formal training, but with valuable skills and experience, are not excluded from the field, particularly as more rigorous and higher level training become the norm. Denmark, for example, takes a relatively mature intake of students and places weight on prior work experience, giving opportunities for those who did not excel at school. The diversification of routes into the profession also can be a useful step toward increasing training opportunities and career mobility. In Sweden, there are conceptual and practical links between the vocational and tertiary training for ECEC staff, which enable trained childcare assistants to enrol in university training for pre-school teachers and receive credit for prior experience. Such strategies are particularly important for countries that have recently raised qualifications (*e.g.*, Italy, Portugal) and are seeking to reconcile tensions between those in the field with a lower-level of training and their newly entering university-educated counterparts.

The challenges of attracting a diverse workforce

As the population of children in ECEC settings becomes more diverse, recruiting employees to match this diversity has become a priority in many countries. Countries face the challenge that as the requirements for formal qualifications to work in ECEC increase, the diversity of backgrounds of staff decreases. Data from the US, for example, indicate that family day care providers match the children they serve in terms of ethnic and linguistic background, out-of-school provision is more diversely staffed than ECEC centres, and centres are more diverse than public schools. Again, this supports the need for open entry to the field supported by a flexible, modular career structure.

There are several innovative approaches to support open entry of diverse workers to the field. A basic tenet of the Head Start programme is to employ parents and volunteers from the local community. Many complete the Child Development Associate (CDA) qualification[46] and work in centres after their children have "graduated." Several countries (*e.g.*, Australia, Denmark, Norway, Sweden, UK) recruit staff of immigrant backgrounds, some of whom are trained teachers from their home countries, to work in ECEC as bilingual assistants to help maintain children's home languages and facilitate communication with parents. In the Netherlands and Belgium (Flemish and French Communities), paraprofessional, ethnic minority parents have been employed to take part in early childhood programmes as bridge staff with the local community. There are some concerns that the involvement of paraprofessionals, who by definition have lower training than regular staff members, can lower the status of the work and jeopardise quality of provision. If well-supported through in-service training and mentoring, this strategy can enrich the lives of all young children, improve women's self-esteem and provide opportunities for them to pursue other training or employment. The trade-off is the turnover that results as women leave for higher-paid, better status positions.

Another strategy is to recruit diverse students into ECEC training programmes. In Australia, it has been a great challenge to recruit and train staff from indigenous backgrounds to the early childhood field, because of the geographic isolation of many of the students. The Bachelor Institute of Indigenous Tertiary Education (Northern Territory) has played a very important role in developing and delivering early childhood courses to Aboriginal students and in providing community development support for local communities wishing to develop ECEC programmes. Distance education courses using ICT may also help reach isolated students. Across countries, it seems that if training for diverse students and diverse communities is to be successful and relevant it needs to acknowledge the particular context of each community, as well as appreciate variations in cultural values and skills involving children and child rearing practices.

---

46. The Child Development Associate (CDA) is a national competency-based credential that was developed in 1971 for Head Start workers and has become known and accessible to workers in licensed centres and family day care. The CDA represents about half a two-year degree and may be applied toward post-secondary degree programmes in some states.

Gender issues

In all countries, ECEC work is highly gender segregated, beginning with student intakes. Why are there so many women and so few men working in early childhood? In some countries, the low levels of training, status, and pay of ECEC staff, particularly those working with infants and toddlers, may be reinforced by public views that ECEC is "women's work" rather than a skilled occupation. Yet, the issue of recruiting men is not only linked to low pay and conditions, since there are very few men even in countries with relatively higher pay and conditions. Some countries view this feminisation of the sector as a concern, while others fear that opening up the ECEC profession to men may threaten an area of employment where women traditionally have had more influence. Given the expansion of services and need for qualified staff, it should be possible to increase male involvement in the field without jeopardising women's employment opportunities. A further concern relates to child abuse, with many parents preferring not to have men in direct contact with very young children.

Why are there so few men in ECEC?

A few countries have sought to challenge traditional gender roles and patterns of employment in ECEC, with some success. For example, Denmark has worked to recruit men into the profession in recent years, and, 25% of Danish *paedagog* students are now male. In Norway, where currently 5% of trained staff and 7% of all staff are men, the government set a target to attain 20% male staff in ECEC by 2000 (see Box 3.11). As part of the Ministry of Children and Family Affairs plan to seek a more gender-mixed workforce, a regulation on positive discrimination in favour of male applicants for ECEC positions has been introduced. Recently, the UK has set a target of 6% of the workforce being male by 2004, from a base of 2% in 1998. The public commitment found in Denmark and Norway reflects a political view that men need to take an increased role with children for two reasons: gender equality (with men needing to assume more responsibility for children as women take a fuller part in the labour market) and the right of children to have both men and women in their lives. This relates to a wider Nordic discussion of "gender pedagogy," that is, the need to keep the gender composition of the group in mind when offering activities to children (Jensen, 1996).

A few countries have developed strategies to recruit men.

In many countries, however, despite intentions to recruit men to the field, the discourse has focused more on concerns about child abuse than on the consequences for children, parents, early childhood workers, and society of having men as carers. Clearly, the risk of child maltreatment and abuse is not to be taken lightly. Most countries require police records for all staff working with young children, and some regulations require that a woman be present when a male worker changes a child. Owen *et al.* (1998) have argued that the issues around abuse should be tackled separately from discussion about the roles of men as carers. In societies today, a male presence in a child's life can no longer be taken for granted. An increasing number of homes have no resident father, and both ECEC and the school have also become feminised environments. Yet, in their early years, children benefit from having male and female role models. In ECEC settings, the presence of men can bring in more diverse forms of caring and pedagogy (*e.g.*, men tend to organise many outdoor activities that are important for children's health and development). There are other related and unresolved issues in this debate, in particular the need for ECEC to reflect the current world, not only the mix of male and female, but also the multicultural balance of our societies. Finally, no matter how imaginative recruitment policies may be, it is unlikely that they will

---

Box 3.11 **Men as workers in ECEC in Norway**

During the 1990s, the Norwegian Government committed itself to recruit more men into the early childhood field. Various measures were taken to support the commitment, including conferences, the development of a network of male workers and the preparation of documents and videos to stimulate discussion. The Norwegian Ministry of Children and Family Affairs, responsible for ECEC policy in Norway, made a report, *Men in barnehager (kindergartens) and male care* that gives a summary of available research on the topic. In 1997, it published its programme of action: *The Barnehage: A Place in Which to Work for Men and Women – the Ministry's Initiatives, 1997-2000.* The goal of the programme was to have 20% of male workers in early childhood services by the year 2000. Most recently, in July 1998, it was agreed that within the Gender Equality Act, positive action could be applied to the recruitment of men in ECEC, the first time that positive action had been applied to men. The Ministry is working on a new plan for 2001-2003 to stabilise and recruit enough educated adults of both genders to work in ECEC.

For a number of reasons – including unresolved issues of pay, status and overall recruitment to early childhood teaching – the programme of action has not yet reached its goal. However by its commitment and work, Norway has made the issue of gender in early childhood visible a matter of discussion. It has approached it from the perspective of the child's need for both men and women, and with a desire to avoid the stereotyping of child rearing as "women's work":

Children need to associate with both men and women in day care. Since the great majority of children in due course are likely to attend day care, it is worrying from a gender-equality perspective that the day care seem set to remain a women's environment. A broad awareness of this is needed, both on the part of staff and authorities (Ministry of Children and Family Affairs in Norway, 1998).

---

have much success in the long-term unless societies elevate the status of the profession.

Staffing issues in family day care

More attention is needed to the training and status of family day care providers.

The preceding discussion has focused on training for centre- and school-based staff, which is high on the agenda in most countries. In contrast, training for providers of family day care has received very little attention (Karlsson, 1995). The levels of education and training of family day care providers are well below those found among centre- and school-based staff. Most have no prior training to work with young children, although providing access to specialised training courses can help raise qualifications. Municipalities in Sweden offer a 50-100 hour introductory class for family day care providers. In 1998, 72% of family day care providers in Sweden were trained to work with children, meaning they had completed either this class or a family day care certificate. In many nations, family day care providers are exempt from all pre-service training/education requirements, but this may vary according to the extent to which providers are employed within organised and publicly-funded schemes or networks (*e.g.*, Belgium, Denmark, Finland, Norway, the Netherlands, Portugal, Sweden) or operate as independent and self-employed providers (*e.g.*, UK, US). In some countries, there are incentives for self-employed providers to complete training, as in the UK where most publicly-funded family day care providers (childminders) are required to complete a pre-service vocational qualification. When workers are linked to a scheme, they are more likely to receive continuous training, technical assistance, and financial support.

As part of quality assurance efforts, several countries have provided incentives to ensure that family day care is regulated and supervised. In the Netherlands, providers must be part of a licensed scheme in order for parents and employers to be eligible for tax benefits. In Belgium (Flemish and French Communities), registration is obligatory for all family day carers, regardless of whether or not they receive public subsidies, but parents only benefit from tax relief when they use providers who are registered and supervised by the public authorities. As a result of such incentives, few parents use unregistered and unmonitored private providers.

Another concern is the lack of career mobility for workers in family day care. Across countries, family day care providers have limited possibility of moving into other forms of early childhood work or into accredited training programmes. Despite the large numbers of children in home-based organised provision, family day care providers are not recognised as professionals with the same status, benefits, and rights to training as staff working in other forms of ECEC. This may change, however, as the family day care sector is under the same recruitment pressures as other forms of informal and formal ECEC, and there will be a need to create incentives for workers to enter the field. Many countries already report difficulties in finding and retaining providers. Finally, it is surprising that supervisors tend to be either social workers or pre-school teachers and rarely have personal experience in the job. This raises the issue of whether training needs of family day care providers are similar to workers in other ECEC services, or whether their circumstances and ways of working are fundamentally different.

3.6. Developing appropriate pedagogical frameworks for young children

---

Key points

Developing appropriate pedagogical frameworks – general goals and guidelines – for work with young children is fundamental to raising and maintaining quality across an ECEC system. Most European countries have developed national curricula or frameworks, which state the general objectives and specific aims for children. These national frameworks may cover provision for children over 3 (Flemish and French Communities of Belgium; Czech Republic, Italy; Portugal; UK), infant-toddler provision (Flemish and French Communities of Belgium) or all provision for children under compulsory school age (Finland[47], Norway, Sweden). In Denmark and the Netherlands, frameworks are articulated at municipal or programme level, and in Australia and the US, several curricula guidelines for ECEC have been developed at the state and territory level:

- Most countries in the review have developed national pedagogical frameworks to promote an even level of quality across age groups and provision, help guide and support professional staff in their practice, and facilitate communication between staff, parents, and children.
- There is a trend toward frameworks which cover a broad age span and diverse forms of settings to support continuity in children's learning.
- For the most part, these frameworks focus broadly on children's holistic development and well-being, rather than on narrow literacy and numeracy objectives.
- Flexible curricula developed in co-operation with staff, parents, and children, allow practitioners to experiment with different methodological and pedagogical approaches and adapt overall goals for ECEC to local needs and circumstances.
- Successful implementation of frameworks requires investment for staff support, including in-service training and pedagogical guidance, as well as favourable structural conditions (*e.g.*, ratios, group size, etc.).

---

47. In Finland, there are two new documents: a curriculum for the 6-year-olds and guidelines (under development) for children under 6. The main goals for ECEC have been included in the Act on Day Care since 1983.

The utility of pedagogical frameworks in guiding early childhood practice

Frameworks promote an even level of quality across age groups and forms of provision.

Viewed from the perspective of ministerial authorities, pedagogical frameworks are important, even in the very early years when developmental aims are foremost. With trends toward decentralisation and diversification of policy and provision, there is more likely to be variation in programming at the local level. A common framework can help ensure an even level of quality across different forms of provision and for different groups of children, while allowing for adaptation to local needs and circumstances. In several countries [*e.g.*, Belgium (Flemish and French Communities), Italy, Portugal] frameworks have been developed, in part, to harmonise the general educational opportunities offered across public and private networks. A clear view and articulation of goals, whether in the health, nutrition, or the education field, can help foster programmes that will promote the well-being of young children and that will respond adequately to children with disabilities or special educational needs. The interests of younger children are served too by well-defined educational projects of the ECEC settings that they attend. In infant-toddler settings with a weak pedagogical emphasis or in which the educational level of staff is low, young children may miss out on the stimulating environments that are so important in the early years.

They can guide and support staff in their work with children...

At the programme level, guidelines for practice in the form of a pedagogical or curriculum framework help staff to clarify their pedagogical aims, to keep progression in mind, to provide a structure for the child's day and to help focus observation on the most important aspects of child development. When educators have only a broad statement of national goals to guide them, they normally seek out more detailed texts as a framework for their monthly, weekly and daily planning. In Norway, the co-ordinating committee of staff, parents, and providers, decides the "annual plan" for each institution, based on the national framework plan. In the French Community of Belgium, the *conseil de participation* with representatives of staff, parents, and the school administration develop and evaluate the local school project. In Denmark and the Netherlands, where there is no national curriculum framework, municipalities, parents, and staff develop their own programmes.[48] In many countries, ECEC staff consult or use curricula and manuals in publication.

... and facilitate communication and co-operation with parents.

For early childhood staff, the curriculum also can be an indicator of belonging to a professional group that has recognised responsibility for the foundation stage of lifelong learning. Signs of professionalisation are particularly important for personnel looking after the younger children as they are easily perceived by parents as being unskilled. Codified pedagogical frameworks may not only strengthen the educational emphasis of the programme, but also improve the status of early childhood workers. Particularly when staff have been directly involved in the development of frameworks (see Box 3.12), guidelines may legitimise good practice and encourage further reflection and improvement, though there is a need to provide staff with ongoing training and professional development opportunities. A curriculum framework can provide opportunities for staff to communicate with parents in order to articulate and discuss the goals and methods of activities taking place in the ECEC setting. Guided by common goals, staff and parents can work together to support the development and learning of individual children.

48. In Denmark, the Social Services Act states the broad purposes of ECEC facilities, and a guide from the Ministry of Social Affairs provides a more detailed description of the goals and purposes of these settings for children.

Box 3.12 **Providing curricular guidance in Portugal**

In order to address the isolation of many pre-school teachers, their lack of in-service training and the sharp divide between early childhood services and the primary school, the Department for Basic Education decided to introduce a curriculum framework to raise the pedagogical quality of the *jardim de infância* for 3- to 6-year-olds. After preliminary consultations with a range of stakeholders, it was decided that the new curriculum would take as a premise that ECEC should be seen as the first phase of lifelong learning. Viewed as such, the curriculum guidelines would focus on learning, and attempt to incorporate innovative approaches in the pedagogical activities of the settings. The curriculum would have to strike a balance between expert knowledge and existing professional capacity; between adult responsibilities and a statement of outcomes for children; between having a common reference point for all pre-school teachers and their freedom to adopt diverse educational programmes.

The official publication of the *Curricular Guidelines for Pre-School Education* in 1996 was preceded by a long discussion process involving the preparation of three drafts. The first draft was analysed by "institutional partners" *i.e.* Regional Directorates for Education, Inspector-General of Education, Initial Teacher Training Schools, Teachers' Association, Teachers' Union, Association of Private Education Providers (Private Sector, IPSS, Misericórdias) and Parent Associations. A second draft was produced based on comments received from the institutional partners and was distributed among groups of pre-school teachers for trialing and comment. Some groups met informally to discuss the guidelines, while other groups participated in study groups as a type of continuous training aimed at preparing teachers to question and introduce change in their professional approaches. Comments from teachers were incorporated in the draft and the final version of the Curricular Guidelines was prepared.

The Curricular Guidelines are intended to support pre-school teachers' decisions and activities, rather than to be a set of learning objectives to be achieved by children. They call on pre-school teachers, however, to observe certain fundamental principles or practices, such as:

– Children's development and learning are closely intertwined;
– Children are the *subjects* of the educational process; their knowledge should be valued and serve as the starting point for new learning;
– Different areas of learning should be approached in a global and integrated way;
– To respond to all children requires differentiated learning processes and children's co-operation where each child benefits from the educational processes developed in the group.

Based on these principles, curriculum development should take into account: 1) The overall aims stated in the Framework Law of Pre-School Education; 2) The organisation of the educational environment, including the classroom, the setting, and the community; 3) A focus on certain learning areas as a broad framework for teachers' planning and evaluation: *personal and social development*; *expression and communication*; *knowledge of the world*.

The planning of each centre's educational programme is a joint activity of the staff team with the participation of the children, parents and the community. The evaluation of the programme and its implementation is encouraged to take place regularly through self- and team-evaluations by staff, supported by government inspection teams and the pre-school board.

What age group should pedagogical frameworks cover?

In education systems in the past, it was assumed that pedagogical aims applied only to the age group 3 to 6 years. Contemporary research on early learning would question this assumption. Learning occurs, and can be supported, from the earliest age, as affirmed by the statement from the Jomtiem World Conference of Education For All, 1990, "learning begins at birth." What was seen almost exclusively as a care period is now recognised as an important moment in the human life cycle for brain, cognitive and social development (Lindsey, 1998). The period is gradually becoming a focus for education in the broad sense, as the realisation grows that from birth, children have entered the foundation stage of lifelong learning. How early childhood services for the younger children are organised and conducted has become therefore an important public policy issue, especially as research suggests that low-quality early childhood services are actually harmful for young children (Vandell and Wolfe, 2000).

A trend toward treating early childhood as an integrated learning period from birth.

For these reasons, many countries are moving toward establishing pedagogical frameworks that include children under 3. In the French Community of Belgium, for example, ONE (National Office for Children) has developed the official *Quality Code for care and its implementation* (*Le Code de qualité de l'accueil et son application*) described by the Minister as being "like the frame that holds the artist's canvas, a support through which every setting should develop its own project". The ONE has also put into place an intensive system of external quality assurance to support the framework. As a group, younger children need this attention most, as those who attend ECEC centres receive less care and interaction than children over 3 (Bühler Institute, 1994). A pedagogical framework can improve the educational focus of ECEC settings for this age group. Indeed, the practice in many countries (*e.g.*, Finland, Norway, Sweden) is to support an integrated pedagogical approach for all children under compulsory school age. As explored next, the policy trend is toward establishing links with other stages of education to provide pedagogical continuity for children.

How do frameworks ensure pedagogical continuity from ECEC to school?

In addition to broadening the focus of pedagogical frameworks to include children under 3, many countries are making efforts to strengthen the conceptual links across age groups and settings. Particular attention has been accorded to promote continuity in children's learning when they make the transition from ECEC to primary school. For example:

– The French Community of Belgium has organised early schooling around three "cycles of learning," the first two covering the age ranges from 2.5 to 5 and from 5 to 7. These cycles reinforce the structural and pedagogical links between pre-school and primary education and enable the staff team to better adapt their methods to the rhythm and progress of each child. One of the goals is to assure that all children have access to the *socles de compétences* (basic competencies) necessary for their social integration and for the pursuit of their further education. Developmental goals as well as competency goals related to numeracy, scientific enquiry and language are integrated into the curriculum.

– In Australia, a number of states and territories are developing curricular strategies to improve children's transitions. As an example, the new *South Australian Curriculum Standards and Accountability* (SACSA) Framework covers children from birth to 18 across diverse school and non-school settings. With regard to children in the early years, the framework is divided into age ranges of birth to 3, 3 to 5, and 5 to 8. The goal is to build a seamless system of learning in terms of curriculum but also in terms of services. Transitions and continuity are key themes throughout the SACSA Framework.

– Sweden has developed three curricula for pre-school, compulsory school, and upper-secondary school that are conceptually linked by a coherent view of knowledge, development and learning.[49] The goal is to promote an educational continuum for children *from birth through the first 20 years of lifelong learning*, guided by the same fundamental values: democracy, the inviolability of human life, individual freedom and integrity, the equal value of all people, gender equality, solidarity with the weak and vulnerable, and respect for the environment. Goals and objectives for children under 6 are specified, but pre-school and school staff are responsible for fostering the conditions and opportunities for children's learning.

Most recently, Finland has produced a framework to bridge children's learning from the last year of ECEC to the first years of primary school, and one for children under 6 is also under development. All these approaches help improve the conceptual and pedagogical links between ECEC and schools and promote increased continuity for children over the years. There is some concern about the dangers of a "downward push" from formal schooling when early childhood frameworks are linked with curricula for older age groups. On the other hand, as pre-school and primary school staff increasingly collaborate around curricular issues, they may develop new ways of understanding children's learning across a wide age span. This process can contribute to a synergy of cultures: schools can foster a more child-centred perspective and ECEC services have the chance to work more collaboratively with the schools to strengthen children's continuum of learning.

What are the goals and approaches in existing early childhood frameworks?

In all countries, governments responsible for early childhood institutions (at national, regional, or local level) define very *general goals or outcomes* that early childhood services must ensure for young children. According to EURO-STAT (2000), these goals are fairly similar in all countries: development, autonomy, responsibility, well-being, self-confidence, citizenship, preparation for school life and future education. Most official documents make at least some reference to the importance of facilitating children's transitions and the need for collaboration between ECEC and the schools. Co-operation with families is another common goal. In all countries, *goals in specific developmental areas* are also proposed in the official documents: *e.g.* physical development; socio-emotional development; the development of cognitive skills; the development of aesthetics and creativity; a positive relationship toward the environment. Many countries identify skills to be acquired by children in these domains.

Most countries define similar general goals or outcomes...

Several countries propose, in addition, *subject and learning areas*, in which ECEC is expected to foster the acquisition of knowledge, *e.g.* written and oral language; mathematics; introduction to art; introduction to science, technology and/or the environment, physical education; etc. In only a few countries (*e.g.*, Czech Republic, Denmark, Sweden), the official documents do not pro-

...and some provide more specific subject and learning areas for children.

---

49. The three curricula cover: 1) centre-based pre-schools (*förskola*) for children from birth to 6; 2) compulsory schooling [grades 1-9], the voluntary pre-school class (*förskoleklass*) for 6-year-olds, and leisure-time centres (*fritidshem*) for children from 6 to 12; and 3) upper secondary school [grades 10-12]. The National Agency for Education is working on guidelines, based on the same values, for other forms of ECEC (*e.g.*, family day care).

vide any information on these subject areas. Several countries [e.g., Belgium (Flemish and French Communities), Italy, UK, US] also define skills that children, in theory, should have mastered prior to beginning compulsory schooling. Cognitive skills (comparing, sorting, matching, sequencing, counting, letter/word recognition, etc.) predominate and knowledge items related to subject areas can also be included. Many countries also include values education, related to religion (e.g., Finland, Italy, Norway) or to civic democracy (e.g., the Czech Republic, Sweden) or both.

The pedagogical approaches used in ECEC vary across countries.

Beyond these broad goals and learning areas, significant differences exist between countries – and within countries – in terms of how ECEC is conceptualised, and hence, in the approaches adopted for working with children. The need to adapt to the individual needs of the child, taking into account each child's rhythm and individual differences, and the importance of providing continuity from ECEC to primary schooling are often mentioned in official documents. In Italy, for example, although programmes are highly-oriented toward learning, the recommended approach emphasises the autonomy and self-direction of children. Similarly, in the Czech Republic, Denmark, Finland, Norway, the Netherlands, Portugal, and Sweden, emphasis is placed on holistic child development, on providing a caring and stimulating environment, on children's learning through play, theme activities and social-emotional outcomes. The motivation to improve later school outcomes exists, but a reading of the Norwegian *National Framework Plan* for ECEC underlines that the rationale for public funding of services stems as much from the wider needs of children and the overall project of Norwegian society, as from the desire to ensure an easy transition for children from *barnehage* to primary school.[50]

In several other countries [Belgium (Flemish and French Communities), the UK, and the US] school-based ECEC is considered as part of the initial stage of the educational system, as well as the beginning of organised instruction. These programmes are seen primarily as instruments to provide equality of educational opportunities for children and to improve the effectiveness of the education system. Pedagogical approaches tend to be more formal – even if frameworks encourage otherwise – with children frequently placed in grouped according to age, with relatively high child-staff ratios. As the daily routine is fairly structured, and teachers spend a great deal of time preparing, selecting and organising activities, there is less emphasis on children's self-initiative. Quality control through regulation, inspection, and curriculum is customary. In order to prepare children for school, subject-based knowledge is stressed toward the end of the cycle. Most of these programmes are staffed by early childhood specialists, so there also is a focus on children's social and emotional development and on relations with families and the wider community.

How do countries approach early literacy and numeracy?

Most countries have adopted an emergent literacy approach.

Countries also have developed different approaches to the issue of setting goals in the areas of early literacy and numeracy. Most countries in the review have adopted an emergent literacy approach. The emergent literacy approach encourages (play-) reading, (play-) writing, counting, scientific theory and numbers as they arise naturally from the normal interests of children.

---

50. There are some basic differences between curricula in the Nordic countries. See for example, Alvestad and Pramling (2000).

The child's environment is enriched by symbols and literacy materials – drawings, photos, signs, books, writing materials, communication resources, etc. – but little attempt is made before the year immediately preceding entry to primary school to approach literacy or numeracy in a formal manner or to evaluate children's progress in these areas. This conception of literacy is found, for example, in the *Orientamenti*, or official guidelines governing the *scuola materna* system for 3-6 year-olds in Italy, in which the domains of reading, writing and measuring are incorporated into the broader perspective of communication and symbol systems. This is also the dominant approach in Australia, the Czech Republic, Denmark, Finland, Norway, the Netherlands, Portugal, and Sweden.

A second approach – most common in Belgium (Flemish and French Communities), the UK, and the US – places more emphasis on literacy and numeracy in the early years to ensure that children will develop mastery of these important skills at the beginning of primary schooling. In England, for example, the new Foundation Stage includes children from the age of 3 to the end of their reception year (around age 5). The accompanying guidelines for practitioners cover the development of children's personal, social and emotional skills, as well as more subject based areas of learning. *Early Learning Goals* set out what *most* children should be able to do by the end of the reception year and include quite detailed outcomes, for example, in the areas of literacy: to name and sound the letters of the alphabet; to read a range of familiar and common words and simple sentences independently; to begin to form simple sentences using punctuation; use their knowledge of phonics to write simple regular words. Goals for literacy and numeracy may be pursued using informal play-based approaches, but often more formal academic approaches are found, particularly among staff with inappropriate training.

A few countries emphasise more formal instruction and assessment of literacy and numeracy skills.

In the US, there is a strong focus on literacy and numeracy, particularly in programmes targeting children deemed at-risk of school failure.[51] Research shows the importance of children starting school motivated to read and with strong language and early literacy skills, yet many ECEC settings, especially those serving children from low-income families, do not provide environments that support early language and literacy development (Snow *et al.*, 1998). In this context of concern, the goals and curriculum of the federally-funded Head Start programmes, for example, are framed by "performance standards" which endorse a comprehensive approach to fostering child development and school readiness, including physical health, cognitive development, social and emotional development, language development, emerging literacy and numeracy development, and creative arts. Recent legislation mandates more explicit attention to tracking and fostering children's progress on specific indicators of language and literacy development (*e.g.* recognising ten letters of the alphabet). At the state level, many of the pre-kindergarten initiatives also prioritise the development of literacy and numeracy skills to ensure that children are prepared for primary school, and may use the Head Start performance standards.

---

51. According to US research, children who are likely to have difficulties learning to read when they begin school include: children from poor neighbourhoods, children with limited proficiency in English, children who attend elementary schools with low-achievement, children with hearing impairments, children with early language impairments or cognitive deficiencies, and children whose parents had difficulties learning to read (Snow *et al.*, 1998).

Whilst in practice these two approaches seem to have much in common, they do highlight an important, and unresolved, debate about appropriate ways for early childhood services to strengthen lifelong learning.

What are the keys to successful implementation of pedagogical frameworks?

Contemporary research suggests that flexible curricula, built on inputs from children, teachers and parents, are more suitable in early childhood than detailed, expert-driven curricula. These findings show that curriculum for ECEC should be: broad and holistic with a greater emphasis on developmental goals rather than on subject outcomes (Bredekamp and Copple, 1997); more process-related and co-constructive (EC Childcare Network, 1996a); defined by the vital interests and needs of the children, families and community (Carr and May, 2000); and more in tune with socio-cultural contexts (Woodhead, 1999). This supports the development of flexible frameworks that give freedom for adaptation, experimentation, and cultural inputs.

Most frameworks allow for adaptation to local needs and circumstances.

For the most part, pedagogical frameworks adopted by national, state, or local governments provide the main values base and pedagogical orientations for early childhood centres, but do not enter into detail as to how goals should be achieved. The well-being of children and their holistic development, guided by the values set by society, also emerge as major concerns. Ministries and municipalities normally rely on the staff and parents of each centre to work out their own educational vision, objectives, pedagogical methods and daily routines, guided by the national framework, and the curriculum or directives of the local authority. This allows for individual settings and practitioners to experiment with a range of pedagogical approaches or curriculum models (*e.g.*, Experiential Education, High/Scope, Montessori, Modern School Movement). A few countries [*e.g.*, Belgium (Flemish and French Communities), UK, US] focus more explicitly on areas or competencies that children should acquire prior to entering school, and subject categories are presented in detail with examples of activities. In practice, however, significant autonomy is often left to ECEC staff to adapt frameworks to the specific needs and circumstances of children and families in their communities. Indeed, a more proactive policy to encourage staff to adapt the curriculum to children's needs might lead to greater creativity and child initiative.

There is a need for ongoing guidance, training, and opportunities for staff reflection.

While local adaptation and variation are welcome, there are risks that without guidance and careful monitoring the intentions of the goals may be misinterpreted, particularly by staff with low levels of initial training. One concern is that practitioners with limited training about early literacy often revert to very formal approaches which do not connect with children's own experiences (David *et al.*, 2000). There is a risk that a model which is "too formal, too soon" will be adopted, which can be particularly difficult for those outside cultural norms and for those with special educational needs who can quickly acquire notions of failure. Another risk is that staff without appropriate training will avoid (and fail to make provision for) any kind of literacy engagement, which can mean that children from families with lower socio-economic backgrounds are again disadvantaged.

In-service training provides a valuable opportunity for staff to become familiar with frameworks and guidelines and with approaches to successfully use them in their groups or classrooms. There is also a need for professional development and non-contact time to support staff in the ongoing planning and evaluation of their work. What is needed most of all, perhaps, is to improve structural aspects such as initial training and professional development, staff-child ratios, and access to pedagogical advice for staff wishing to provide favourable conditions for children's learning and development. Moreover, as governments move toward a more consumer-oriented approach to policymaking, greater statutory participation of parents in setting the vision and curriculum of each centre can also promote settings that meet the needs of children and families within the broad framework of national or local goals.

3.7. Engaging parents, families, and communities

Key points

The arguments for engaging parents and families in early childhood education and care are strong. Parents are the first and primary educators of children, and despite some decline in both nuclear and extended family forms, their formative influence on young children's personal, social and cognitive development remains central. Supporting young children's early development and learning requires ECEC staff to form a partnership with parents, which implies a two-way process of knowledge and information flowing freely both ways (ECEF, 1998). After children themselves, parents are the first experts on their children and can assist programme staff to tailor programmes to the needs of particular children or particular groups. This section will explore why countries are supporting parent engagement and provide some examples of how policies and practices foster strong engagement in the countries in the review. Although mostly focusing on parents, some attention is devoted to opportunities to engage other members of families and the wider community in children's early development and learning:

- Parent engagement seeks to: a) build on parents' unique knowledge about their children, fostering continuity with learning in the home; b) promote positive attitudes and behaviour toward children's learning; c) provide parents with information and referrals to other services; d) support parent and community empowerment.
- Patterns of parent, family and community engagement in ECEC differ from country to country. Several formal and informal mechanisms may be used to foster full participatory and managerial engagement.
- Some of the challenges to active engagement of parents include, cultural, attitudinal, linguistic, and logistical barriers (i.e., lack of time). It is particularly difficult to ensure equitable representation and participation across families from diverse backgrounds.

What is the rationale for engaging parents in ECEC?

Parental engagement is not an attempt to teach parents to be "involved" (they already are) or to hold them solely responsible for difficulties a child may have. In democratic ECEC institutions, the approach of professionals is to share responsibility for young children with parents, and learn from the unique knowledge that parents from diverse backgrounds can contribute. Traditionally, parents have played a key role not only in providing important information about their children to staff, but also in sharing their families' cultural knowledge and traditions. In these ways, strong staff-parent relations can foster continuity in children's learning and experiences between ECEC and the home. Moreover, parent engage-ment in ECEC can help ensure that ECEC programmes cater to children's individual needs, strengths, and interests. Close co-operation between staff and parents ensure that the activities in ECEC take the home and living conditions of the children into consideration, helping to

Parent engagement builds on parents' unique knowledge about their children...

identify and assist children in need of special health, educational, or social welfare support. To build on parents' knowledge and expertise, public policy in most countries requires ECEC provision – school-based, centre-based and family day care – to welcome the participation of parents of young children. As discussed below, in some countries, parents have a statutory right to be involved in planning and evaluation activities, and even in the direct management of services.

... promotes positive attitudes among parents toward children's learning...

Countries participating in the review also have recognised the important role of ECEC settings in supporting parents in their childrearing responsibilities and in promoting positive attitudes and actions among parents toward their children's development and learning. Home-visiting programmes in the Netherlands, the UK, and the US encourage parents to read with their children and to become involved in learning tasks for which children need support. These programmes are found also to be effective in raising the participation rates of children from disadvantaged groups in formal ECEC and in heightening awareness among parents of how important their support and involvement is for their children's learning. In particular, collaboration between professionals and parents of children with special needs enhances programme planning, and reinforces the energy and optimism needed to conduct the intensive, individual learning programmes that children with special needs require. To that end, new legislation in the US has improved parental engagement in their children's special education by giving parents the right to be included in eligibility and placement decisions about their children, as well as in discussions about their children's individualised educational plan (IEP) or individualised family services plan (IFSP) (see Box 3.1).

...and supports parent and community empowerment.

Early childhood settings can support families by providing links to parenting education, continuing education and adult literacy courses, which may allow parents to resume their own education or develop new creative or social interests. ECEC programmes can provide parents and families with formal and informal opportunities to develop social support networks and ties with other families and members of the community (see Box 3.13). They may play a role in community-building by bringing members of a neighbourhood together toward the goal of meeting the needs of young children and their families. ECEC may engage community members in programmes in a variety of ways (*e.g.*, as teachers, volunteers, fund-raisers) and provide a public space where community members can gather. ECEC settings also may provide direct services to community members or act as a hub for referrals, as in the Early Excellence Centres in the UK. Community involvement linked to ECEC can contribute to the empowering process, leading to change in other areas, such as health, environment, or employment, as in initiatives involving immigrant communities *e.g.*, in Belgium (French Community), the Netherlands (see Box 3.14), and Sweden. In this way, ECEC can strengthen social cohesion that benefits individual families and society as a whole. In recognition of the important role of families and communities in building and providing social support, as well as the value of developing "social coalitions" among families, communities, governments, and the corporate sector, Australia recently launched the *Stronger Families and Communities Strategy*, which will expand parenting development programmes and playgroups in rural areas and help families with children with special needs access ECEC.

In sum, strong parent engagement benefits both parents and their children. Research in New Zealand has found that parents involved in early childhood programmes experience enhanced relationships with their chil-

Box 3.13 **Family and community engagement in two Italian municipalities**

Pistoia: long interested in the relationship between the needs of young children and the community as a whole, Pistoia has now expanded its ECEC provision beyond the *scuola dell'infanzia* and *asilo nido* to include a network of psycho-educational services. In 1987, the municipal government initiated this system of services in the form of special places for children with and without their parents as a part of a larger set of resources for children of all ages. A major rationale for the resulting *area bambini* [children's centres] is to provide a form of child and family support for those families not in need of full-time child care. Grandparents and parents can attend various enrichment activities with and without their young children, such that the centres serve as a form of community meeting place for adults as well as a source of play and experimentation for children. Researchers in Pistoia have focused on spatial and environmental influences on infants and toddlers and on fostering early child-child interaction. These children's centres also serve as after-school environments for school-age children and educational resource centres for teachers of Pistoia's elementary schools and the state and municipal *scuole materne*.

Milano: another form of *nuove tipologie* [new typology services] can be found in Milano. Milano's first *Tempo per la famiglia* [Time for the Family] was opened in 1986, and the city now has 12 such family-child centres. Distinct in purpose from that of the *nido*, the *Tempo per la famiglia* was designed as a flexible and informal service revolving around the needs of families with children 3 years and under, offering both children and their parents a caring environment that supports social experiences as well as learning opportunities. These municipal services were developed for several purposes particular to the changing demographics of Milan. As an alternative to the traditional *nido*, it includes the provision of a space where parents and professionals can interact around the care and development of the young child. Another equally important goal in Milano is that of connecting families of young children with one another, particularly those whose parents are young, culturally or linguistically diverse and/or socially isolated. Like Pistoia's *area bambini*, Milano's system of *Tempo per la famiglia* represent only one type of service in addition to the municipally supported *asilo nido* and *scuola materna*.

dren, alleviation of maternal stress, upgrading of education or training credentials, and improved employment status (Wylie, 1994). Studies in Ireland and Turkey show that parents, especially from minority and low-income backgrounds, report improved self-confidence and better relationships with their children, when they are involved as valued partners in ECEC (Kagitcibasi and Bekman, 1991; O'Flaherty, 1995). For these reasons, policy and practice in all countries in the thematic review attempt to strengthen the relationships between staff, families, and members of the community. In fact, as discussed in Section 3.2, parental satisfaction is often viewed as a measure of quality of early childhood services. In the Czech Republic, for example, attitudes are changing throughout the education system – including the kindergartens – toward becoming more welcoming of parents. Parent involvement as partners in their children's education is considered a high priority and an essential element toward rebuilding educational institutions as more open and democratic settings.

Ambiguities about the role of parents sometimes arise when parents are obliged to take the lead in providing voluntary services – *e.g.*, organising out-of-school provision for children – because public services are either absent or insufficient (ENSAC, 1994). Effective parental engagement does not mean that parents should substitute for professionals or professional services. In parent-sponsored ECEC in Norway and Sweden, for example, parents may volunteer their time and expertise in various ways. These services, however, must meet the same requirements as public institutions in terms of staffing, programme planning, evaluation, and fees. A second ambiguity stems from the perception

Parents and professionals have different, complementary roles in ECEC.

Box 3.14 **The Capabel Project: supporting families in an immigrant neighbourhood**

The Capabel Project, begun in 1991, is situated in the "Bos en Lommer" district in Amsterdam, an immigrant neighbourhood with over 32 000 inhabitants. Capabel is a networking organisation that aims to mobilise and co-ordinate the work of existing organisations in the neighbourhood, and draw the attention of the district services to the actual needs of the target groups. Needs are broad ranging, with employment, education and youth issues being particularly important. An important educational aim for the project is to minimise the number of children entering schools with developmental delays. To achieve this aim, Capabel seeks *to improve the links between families and the local agencies* through both practical supports and information exchanges. As an example, the project supports improvements to the housing stock, facilities and environments for families, while setting up contact points and networks to bring parents closer to schools, health, police, welfare work, relief, recreation. The many networks mutually strengthen each other and always aim to strengthen the participation of parents.

Capabel does not itself run early childhood or parent education programmes, but has *introduced innovative programmes for neighbourhood families* including: playgroups; a mother-child home instruction programme to prepare immigrant children of 2-4 for successful entry into the *basisschool*; programmes to support the learning of 5-7 year olds in primary schools, particularly during the key transition to reading and writing, etc. In addition, a crèche is provided so that mothers from linguistic minority groups can learn to speak the Dutch language, take part in activities with older children and also attend seminars where they learn to use play materials provided by the project. The tutors are also from the linguistic minority groups (mainly Turkish and Moroccan) and the seminars are conducted in the group members' first language. At the same time, parents are encouraged to help their children use Dutch, both for the sake of the children's education and for their own.

Capabel organises *social and political support at the level of the district and the city* and has established a number of mechanisms to maintain its consultative profile. It invites politicians, local civil servants and subsidising authorities into the project through its quarterly Policy Group meetings. The partners in the project are the Municipality of Amsterdam and the local district council. A central government official, from the Social Policy Department, is a member of the project's Steering Committee.

Capabel is also a significant *action research programme*. Research is conducted by the University of Amsterdam. Over an 18-year period, the university will supply the project with factual data and findings that will, in turn, be transformed by project leaders into hypotheses and guidelines for further action. In turn, the project provides the Dutch research community with extremely important data *e.g.*, developmental, social, and educational outcomes of young ethnic minority children, the employment of ethnic minority parents (especially mothers), crime and delinquency, and living conditions of families.

that almost anybody can substitute for a parent or professional in looking after young children. Ministries may see "childcare" as an opportunity to develop social employment schemes in which lowly-educated persons are employed, at a low cost, to work directly with young children. Social employment schemes can contribute to the ECEC sector, if untrained personnel are hired to perform non-contact tasks or if training is offered to persons who wish to work directly with young children. In several schemes in the Netherlands, for example, staff from immigrant backgrounds, who are trained and fairly paid to work alongside the other ECEC professionals, help facilitate communication and understanding among children, families, and other staff members.

How can ECEC policy contribute to strong parent engagement?

Parent engagement patterns vary across countries:

Traditionally, parents have formed the foundation of many types of ECEC provision, from parent co-operatives to playgroups to family day care. More professional, organised ECEC programmes have developed from these roots

– settings which complement learning in the home and build on close working relationships between staff and parents. Across countries, the reality is that the role of parents in ECEC is expanding and becoming more formalised, as illustrated in the diverse efforts described below. While policies with regard to parent involvement are present in all countries, patterns of engagement may vary, as follows:

Marginal engagement occurs when policy concerning parent involvement is considered unimportant, and official regulations, which exist in all participating countries, are observed only minimally. In such circumstances, centres may turn to selected parents as a source of extra funding or of help in extra-curricular activities, but no great effort is made by early childhood institutions to engage in regular dialogue with parents.

Marginal engagement.

Formal engagement is undertaken in compliance with official directives or regulations. Organised by the ECEC setting, formal engagement may take the form of regular staff-parent meetings and even home visits from teachers (*e.g.*, the Netherlands, US), to inform parents of their child's progress and about the goals and objectives of the programme. During these occasions, parents also have the opportunity to inform staff about the particular strengths and needs of their children. In the participating countries, there are many different instruments to promote formal engagement including school boards, pedagogical councils, class councils, parent-teacher associations, etc. Formal engagement may also involve regular consultation of parent organisations. In the Netherlands and Portugal, for example, parent associations are among the privileged partners in the consultation process leading to the formulation of national educational policies, including those concerning ECEC. The efficacy of formal engagement depends greatly on the comprehensiveness of the regulations and on the importance accorded to dialogue with parents, their representatives and professional staff. A challenge in almost all countries is that middle-class parents tend to predominate on school boards or other formal bodies, while families from more modest backgrounds are under-represented.

Formal engagement.

Formal engagement can also include mechanisms to provide regular information to parents on available ECEC options and to support them in their roles as consumers. In the US, there are over 600 Child Care Resource and Referral Agencies (CCR&Rs), which are important agencies for making the market visible for consumers, by maintaining a data bank on ECEC services in the region. They focus mainly on external dimensions of the various programmes (opening hours, child-staff ratios, etc.) and do not to make value judgements about provision. Other core services of the CCR&Rs include parent education about available ECEC facilities, provider training, local networking and advocacy, work with employers, and efforts to build the supply of provision. The UK Childcare Information Services (CIS) – local information centres linked to a national network – are available for free consultation by parents in supermarkets and other outputs in the UK. The Australian Childcare Access Hotline – a toll free number to parents to call when they need information on Commonwealth-funded childcare services in their area – is a similar initiative. In many countries, government departments, parent associations, and individual programmes prepare and disseminate (often multilingual) brochures, newsletters, and other publications to inform parents on the different ECEC options in a given community, parental rights and responsibilities, and other policy and programme developments. In Flanders, for example, the Ministry of Education, produces a *Manual for Parents* which offers a clear and accessible account of the rights and duties of children and their parents in the educational system. The editions of K*lasse*, a series of magazines and a website, also provide a democratic forum for communication within the pre-school and school community.

Informal, organised engagement.

Informal, organised engagement is frequent, varied and planned. Typically, informal consultations between parents and staff take place at the morning reception of the child or at the evening pick-up, when parents are welcomed and time is provided in the programme for parents to play with the children and to talk with staff. In these sessions, teachers inform parents about the child's experiences in the ECEC setting and listen to the expectations and concerns of parents. Informal morning and evening activities are organised jointly, so that ideas of both parties contribute to the vision and work of the setting. Research conducted in Australia and Norway suggests that "informal" briefing chats or sessions by staff are much welcomed by parents. While the frequency of contact through formal channels such as staff meetings, parents' meetings and thematic meetings appears to have just a small effect on the parents' general level of satisfaction, ongoing verbal information on their own children has a much stronger positive impact. These informal opportunities to communicate with parents are especially important as many parents are working and have little time to devote to meetings. Informal opportunities also may help engage and empower parents who are relatively inarticulate and unaccustomed to the protocol of meetings.

Policies in support of informal, organised engagement aim to foster strong parent-child-staff relationships. This can be particularly important during transitions from home to ECEC and from ECEC to primary school. As an example, many Italian labour laws, as well as regional and local policies now mandate parental leave to assist children and families during the delicate transition (*l'inserimento*) from the home to out-of-home ECEC setting. Diverse interpretations range from inviting parents to accompany the child during his or her initial transition into out-of-home provision to having parents stay with their child in the centre for as long as it takes for both to feel at ease in the new setting. Similarly, in Sweden when children begin pre-school, there is a two-week adjustment period when parents spend time with their children in the centre, which not only eases the transition for the child, but helps establish a positive relationship between the parent and the ECEC setting. Informal opportunities to take part in ECEC can be supported by flexible working hours and arrangements that exist in several other countries [*e.g.*, Belgium (Flemish and French Communities) Denmark, Finland, the Netherlands, Norway – see Section 2.1].

Participatory engagement.

Participatory engagement occurs when parents of different ethnic, cultural, linguistic, and religious backgrounds, as well as other members of the community, are invited, on a regular basis, to interact with staff and children and take an active part in the programmes of the setting. As a matter of course, parents are consulted as a group on all matters of concern to the programme. Efforts are made to have as wide a range of parents as possible to contribute to the life of the institutions – by participating in activities, assisting directly with young children, or leading activities in which they excel. In participatory engagement, parents may take part in outside trips, help with the upkeep and renovation of facilities and grounds, and contribute to cultural activities around national holidays and celebrations, linguistic or religious matters. Participatory engagement may be formalised, *e.g.* through centre-home contracts and agreements as in Italy or Finland (see Box 3.15), or may be a requirement to access special funding, *e.g.* the *Zorgverbreding* in the Flemish Community of Belgium, or *Sure Start* in the UK. The US Head Start programme mandates the

---

Box 3.15 **Parent engagement in Finland**

In Finland, as the ECEC system has developed, a shift has taken place from an emphasis on the professional autonomy of staff to closer co-operation with families. Parents are seen as important partners in designing the operation of ECEC provision, and have a right to express their opinions and be heard. ECEC centres aim to combine both the expertise of parents concerning their child and the expertise of staff developed through training and work experience. This shift toward greater appreciation of the knowledge and needs of parents has led to a number of initiatives:

Written care and development contracts: several municipalities use a care and development agreement made in joint consultation between the ECEC-centre staff and parents. The purpose of the agreement is to increase dialogue about educational objectives and attitudes, thus improving the parents' opportunities to influence the activities and ways of working in the setting. In addition, *parents' councils* also play a role in discussing or deciding the objectives and principles of the ECEC centre's activities and financial management within the framework set by the municipal budget.

Individual plans or growth portfolios: the growth portfolio is a record of each child's life and growth at the centre, and is often the basis for assessment discussions with parents during and at the end of each year. In addition to teacher comments and records, the child also contributes to the portfolio by entering photos, drawing and memories of significant moments. Through the portfolio, programme aims are explained to parents with the objective of mobilising parental follow-up and of achieving a shared understanding of education. Children can take their portfolio with them when they change to a new centre or school, which helps smooth their transition from one setting to the other. By law, *individual rehabilitation plans* to support and monitor the growth and learning of children with special needs must be prepared, in co-operation with parents, for children in need of special care and education.

Regular inquiry questionnaires seeking feedback from parents. In Helsinki, an inquiry questionnaire has been used in all parts of the municipality since 1989. It seeks to establish whether there has been an appropriate "contract" between centres and parents, and the parents' degree of satisfaction with it. It also provides an open-ended section for responses on specific good or bad points about the centre. In other municipalities, groups of parents have designed surveys evaluating the quality of municipal day care and expressed their opinions on day-care issues. Finally, *informal daily talks* when dropping off and collecting children are also important opportunities to discuss parent views on the quality of the centre and their children's development and learning.

---

development of volunteer programmes to support services. The participation of volunteers – parents, local residents, and members of the larger community – has been an effective way of mobilising community resources to strengthen services. Volunteers help lower adult-child ratios, meet the need for bilingual adults for non-English speaking children and parents, and support children with disabilities. Moreover, about a third of paid staff are parents of current or former Head Start children.

Managerial engagement goes beyond *formal engagement* discussed above, in its intensity of relationship and the responsibility given to parents for decision-making. Managerial engagement is found in many countries, as in Norway, Sweden, and the UK, in parent-run co-operatives and playgroups where parents are engaged in the programme focus, operation, employment, and budgetary decisions concerning the settings. Parents may be expected to spend several weeks per year actively engaged in a range of activities. In Denmark, parents constitute a majority on councils in kindergartens and family day care, and legislation gives parent boards in municipal centre-based ECEC the right to influence principles governing the work of the ECEC setting, the use of the budget, and to make recommendations to the local authority

Managerial engagement.

concerning the employment of staff. In family day care, parents have the right to influence on the principles governing the work of providers, as well as the use of the budget. In centres in Norway, not only must every child centre have a *parents' council* to promote the shared interests of all the parents at management level, but also a *co-ordinating committee of parents, staff, and owners* to act as an advisory body and to ensure good relations between the *barnehage* and the local community. In the Netherlands, a parent body for "co-steering" is required in subsidised ECEC and primary schooling so that parents have a voice in policies. In the US, federal legislation for Head Start mandates the right of parents to participate in programme decisions. A Parent Committee and a Policy Group formed of parents and community representatives assist in decisions about the planning and operation of the Head Start programme. Thus, managerial engagement promotes parent leadership and empowerment and may be a vehicle for bringing members of the community together in the context of meeting children's comprehensive needs.

Challenges to strong engagement

Cultural, attitudinal, linguistic, and practical barriers can challenge effective engagement.

Despite the range of possibilities, staff working in ECEC in many countries still find it difficult to move beyond marginal engagement of parents. Time seems to be one the largest barriers. When both parents are working or studying, it is often difficult for them to contribute effectively to the life of the early childhood setting, especially if they are coping with other life stresses. Parent engagement can be even more challenging for lone parents who carry the full burden of both work and caring responsibilities. Yet, governments and employers can support parents in their roles as partners in their children's ECEC, for example, by allowing workers paid time off to visit, monitor, and participate in ECEC programmes. Logistical barriers – difficulties securing transportation, linguistic differences, and the length of the family's stay in the local area – may also prevent the development of strong relationships with parents. Attitudinal and cultural differences between staff and parents can also be obstacles *e.g.*, different child rearing perspectives and communication patterns. In particular, negative experiences from parents' own schooling may dissuade some parents from expressing their points of view on the organisation or content of the ECEC programme. These barriers disproportionately affect parents with modest educational levels and low socio-economic backgrounds, who are already among the least empowered groups in society.

Training can support staff in building trusting, collaborative relationships with parents.

Parent engagement may take different forms and operate on different levels. Not all parents can or want to be involved in the same way. The frequency or time spent on activities may matter less than the quality of the staff-parent relationships and the trust and mutual respect that are built into these relationships. Staff need to continuously strive to engage parents in ways appropriate to their needs, strengths, interests, and availability. It is critical for staff to be trained to work with parents, as it cannot be assumed that training in child development will translate into an ability to collaborate and communicate effectively with parents and other family members, especially those from diverse backgrounds. However, in spite of these real challenges, the many interesting and innovative responses adopted by countries suggest that staff and parents can work together in flexible and creative ways that support the engagement of parents in their children's development and learning.

Chapter 4

Policy Lessons from the Thematic Review

Introduction: A broader contextual framework for ECEC policy

As a result of recent demographic, economic, and social developments, childhoods are changing in OECD countries. An increasing proportion of children are growing up in lone-parent households, and many hail from linguistically, culturally, and ethnically diverse families. In some cases, they are living in poverty and deprivation, at risk of social exclusion. Perhaps the most significant change in modern childhoods is that children no longer spend the first five years of their lives at home with their mothers. Increasingly, they are living a greater part of their early childhood in out-of-home settings, and often, in multiple settings with multiple caregivers. If these ECEC experiences are of sufficient quality, they will help strengthen children's dispositions to be lifelong learners and to take an active part in society. Governments need to acknowledge these societal changes and seek to better understand the implications for children, families, and society. A more contextually-sensitive approach will help policy and provision respond in a holistic and integrated manner to the needs of children and families.

Given that policies for young children and families are shaped by these dynamic contexts, and that, in turn, childhoods are shaped by these policies, ECEC policy needs to be understood and addressed within the framework of wider initiatives to meet the broad goals of democratic societies. A part of any strategy to improve outcomes through interventions early in life must be to reduce child poverty by ensuring sufficient income support to prevent deprivation and by pursuing measures to increase employability of parents. Policy-makers also need to recognise the interface between the needs of children, parents, and the labour market. Improved access to affordable and quality ECEC, paid and job-protected parental leave, and greater flexibility in work arrangements are all important to facilitating a better balance of work and family responsibilities. These supports can provide the key to better employment opportunities for young parents, particularly lone-parents. Shared family and employment roles increase the potential labour force, promote a better utilisation of human capital, enhance gender equity and improve quality of life. Greater participation in ECEC has implications for education policy as well, as quality ECEC experiences cannot produce lasting benefits if they are followed by poor school experiences. In sum, efforts to improve ECEC policy should form part of wider efforts to reduce child poverty, promote gender equity, improve education systems, value diversity, and enhance the well-being of children and parents.

Drawing on the background reports, country notes, and other materials collected during the review process, this final chapter identifies and discusses eight elements of successful ECEC policy. These are *key elements of policy that are likely to promote equitable access to quality* ECEC. The elements presented below are intended to be broad and inclusive so that they can be considered in the light of unique and diverse country contexts, circumstances, values and beliefs. They are interrelated elements and should be considered as a totality. They do not offer a prescriptive and standardised approach, but allow room for diversity among individual systems and services to interpret them in different ways. After discussing the key elements, the chapter proposes several areas for further cross-national work.

4.1. Key elements of successful ECEC policy

Key points

The eight key elements of successful ECEC policy that have emerged from the review are:

- A *systemic and integrated approach to policy development and implementation* calls for a clear vision for children, from birth to 8, underlying ECEC policy, and co-ordinated policy frameworks at centralised and decentralised levels. A lead ministry that works in co-operation with other departments and sectors can foster coherent and participatory policy development to cater for the needs of diverse children and families. Strong links across services, professionals, and parents also promote coherence for children.

- A *strong and equal partnership with the education system* supports a lifelong learning approach from birth, encourages smooth transitions for children, and recognises ECEC as an important part of the education process. Strong partnerships with the education system provide the opportunity to bring together the diverse perspectives and methods of both ECEC and schools, focusing on the strengths of both approaches.

- A *universal approach to access, with particular attention to children in need of special support*: while access to ECEC is close to universal for children from age 3, more attention to policy (including parental leave) and provision for infants and toddlers is necessary. It is important to ensure *equitable access*, such that all children have equal opportunities to attend quality ECEC, regardless of family income, parental employment status, special educational needs or ethnic/language background.

- *Substantial public investment in services and the infrastructure*: while ECEC may be funded by a combination of sources, there is a need for substantial government investment to support a sustainable system of quality, accessible services. Governments need to develop clear and consistent strategies for efficiently allocating scarce resources, including investment in an infrastructure for long-term planning and quality enhancement efforts.

- A *participatory approach to quality improvement and assurance*: defining, ensuring, and monitoring quality should be a participatory and democratic process that engages staff, parents, and children. There is a need for regulatory standards for all forms of provision supported by co-ordinated investment. Pedagogical frameworks focusing on children's holistic development across the age group can support quality practice.

- *Appropriate training and working conditions for staff in all forms of provision*: quality ECEC depends on strong staff training and fair working conditions across the sector. Initial and in-service training might be broadened to take into account the growing educational and social responsibilities of the profession. There is a critical need to develop strategies to recruit and retain a qualified and diverse, mixed-gender workforce and to ensure that a career in ECEC is satisfying, respected and financially viable.

- *Systematic attention to monitoring and data collection* requires coherent procedures to collect and analyse data on the status of young children, ECEC provision, and the early childhood workforce. International efforts are necessary to identify and address the existing data gaps in the field and the immediate priorities for data collection and monitoring.

- A *stable framework and long-term agenda for research and evaluation*: as part of a continuous improvement process, there needs to be sustained investment to support research on key policy goals. The research agenda also could be expanded to include disciplines and methods that are currently underrepresented. A range of strategies to disseminate research findings to diverse audiences should be explored.

A *systemic and integrated approach to policy development and implementation*

Countries are more likely to provide quality, accessible services when they take a systemic and co-ordinated approach to ECEC policy, including careful attention to the structural requirements – clear policy frameworks, effective governance and monitoring processes, supporting and training professional staff, and adequate funding and financing mechanisms. These countries tend to formulate a *clear vision* for childhood which underlies policy development for ECEC. It is important for countries to foster integrated and co-ordinated policy making for children from birth to compulsory school age, with attention to the links with the school system and other allied sectors such as employment, family, health, social welfare, etc. Most countries have acknowledged that quality ECEC provision can fulfil many policy objectives, including raising educational standards and increasing the labour market participation of parents. However, countries that have developed strong ECEC systems have recognised the importance of focusing on *children as a social group with rights*, and not just as dependents on parents or as primarily in need of childcare to enable their parents' employment.

A clear vision underlying policy, with a focus on children as a social group.

A systemic approach entails developing a common policy framework with consistent goals across the system (*e.g.*, with regard to staffing, financing, programmes, etc.) and clearly-defined roles and responsibilities at both central and decentralised levels of governance. Decentralisation can help ensure that national priorities reflect, and can be adapted to, local needs and circumstances. The success of these decentralisation efforts depends to a large extent on the degree to which a wide range of stakeholders are involved in discussing and negotiating local standards and patterns of provision. Government needs to balance decentralisation, with the need to foster consensus about national goals and targets, and develop the capacity to monitor fair access to ECEC and maintain quality across regions and forms of provision. The limited role of central government in some countries has led to fragmented policy and provision, including unacceptable variation in levels of quality and access.

Co-ordinated policy frameworks at centralised and decentralised levels.

Coherence and co-ordination is facilitated by integrated administrative responsibility at both national and local levels. Although there may be several ministries interested in, and committed to, ECEC policy, there is a need for one ministry to take national responsibility for all services for young children below compulsory school age. It seems to matter less whether the lead ministry is education, social welfare, or family affairs, as long as the education, care and social functions of early childhood services from birth to 8 years are acknowledged in an integrated, holistic policy approach. Countries that have developed systems under unified administrative auspices at the national level tend to address both the care and education of young children more holistically and coherently, with an integrated approach to staffing, financing, monitoring, etc. In countries where responsibility is divided according to the age of the child or according to whether policy is considered to have an education or social welfare orientation, policy and provision tend to be more disjointed. However, in both approaches, co-ordinating mechanisms across the ministries or local departments can help to form common goals and overcome this fragmentation. Another advantage of administrative and conceptual integration of ECEC policy is that it includes children under the age of 3. In most countries, the interests and needs of this age group have not been given the policy priority necessary to ensure adequate quality and access.

A lead ministry that works in co-operation with other ministries, departments and sectors.

A collaborative and participatory approach to reform.

Another policy lesson points to the need for a collaborative and participatory approach to reform in the field. While government should play a large leadership role, regional and local authorities, business representatives, organised civil society, and community groups should be involved in the formulation and implementation of a strong and comprehensive ECEC policy agenda. This inclusive and participatory approach will help ensure broad public support for ECEC and ensure that multiple perspectives contribute to decision making. In particular, parents need to be considered as valuable partners in policy and programme development in the field. All countries in the review acknowledge that mothers and fathers have the main responsibility for their children and that the home environment is extremely important to their children's well-being. At the same time, it is recognised that quality ECEC can support children's early development and learning, as well as their long-term social and economic welfare. A partnership approach reinforces the shared public and private responsibility for ECEC.

Strong links across services, professionals, and parents in a given community.

At the services level, strong partnerships among different forms of early childhood provision, with families, and across other services for young children (*e.g.*, schools, health, special education) can promote coherence. Integrated services can help meet the full range of children's learning and developmental needs in different settings on a given day and in learning institutions over time. This entails building stronger staff-parent partnerships based on trust and respect. Co-ordination can reinforce children's learning, identify and solve problems at an early stage, and ensure an efficient use of resources. In many countries, the links between pre-school, school, and out-of-school provision need to be strengthened to smooth children's transitions. Finally, a coherent educational approach can support the informal learning of children that takes place within families and communities, from the early childhood years to school and beyond. The development of flexible integrated services to meet the needs of working and non-working parents will support and build on these informal learning opportunities.

A strong and equal partnership with the education system

Supporting a lifelong learning approach from birth.

There is a welcome trend toward increased co-operation between ECEC and the school system in terms of both policy and practice. The moves toward integrated policy making for ECEC under education auspices in Sweden and the UK (also Spain and New Zealand), and more recently in Italy, raise important issues about the relationship between early childhood provision and the school system. Integration under education auspices may strengthen the conceptual and structural links between ECEC and primary schools by recognising ECEC as an important part of the education process. This strategy acknowledges that early childhood services are a public good, like the compulsory schools, and that all children should have the right to access quality ECEC before starting school. In all countries, attention to children's transitions from ECEC to schools has led to a greater policy focus on building bridges across administrative departments, staff training, regulations, and curricula. Closer co-operation with the education system supports a lifelong learning approach which recognises early childhood – from birth to 8 – as an important phase for developing important dispositions and attitudes toward learning. A lifelong learning approach recognises the importance of fostering coherence for children across the different phases of the education system along with learning that takes place outside of formal institutions.

Strong partnerships with the education system provide the opportunity to bring together the diverse perspectives and methods of both ECEC and schools, focusing on the strengths of both approaches, such as the emphasis on parental involvement and children's social development in ECEC and the focus on educational goals and outcomes in schools. Much could be done to further meld policy and practice, so that ECEC and primary education could benefit from the knowledge and experience of young children accumulated in each sector, and in the process help children and families negotiate the transition from ECEC to school. Some countries are moving toward integrated initial training across the age span, so that teachers at all levels of the education system share a common theoretical base. Curriculum frameworks that bridge pre-school and primary education (as well as out-of-school provision) help strengthen pedagogical continuity, and joint in-service training for early childhood and primary school staff could reinforce links. The needs of young children are wide, however, and there is a risk that increased co-operation between schools and ECEC could lead to a school-like approach to the organisation of early childhood provision. Downward pressure on ECEC to adopt the content and methods of the primary school has a detrimental effect on young children's learning. Therefore, it is important that early childhood is viewed not only as a preparation for the next stage of education (or even adulthood), but also as a distinctive period where children live out their lives. Stronger co-operation with schools is a positive development as long as the specific character and traditions of quality early childhood practice are preserved.

Building on the strengths of both ECEC and schools.

A universal approach to access, with particular attention to children in need of special support

Most countries have recognised the role of government in expanding provision toward full coverage of the 3- to 6-year-old age group. These services are acknowledged as important to children's early development and learning, independent of their parents' employment status. While the trend is toward universal access and full coverage for children over 3, there is still significant variation in access to and quality of infant-toddler provision and out-of-school arrangements. Unlike services for children over 3, there has not been sufficient emphasis on improvement and expansion for these two forms of provision, which suggests the need for a more universal approach. A universal approach does not necessarily entail achieving full coverage, as particularly for very young children, there will be variation in need and demand for ECEC. It does mean ensuring a quality place at an affordable cost for all children who need it. There is also a need to address unmet demand in rural and remote areas, as well as in some lower-income communities. In addition, *paid and job-protected maternity and parental leave schemes* of about a year should be considered as part of any comprehensive strategy to support working parents with very young children. Generous leave benefits for mothers and fathers may help reduce the need and demand for investment in costly infant provision and facilitate more equitable sharing of work and family responsibilities. To address the needs of children and working parents, a coherent approach includes the expansion of out-of-school provision to cover the working day, as well as strong administrative and conceptual links between these activities, ECEC and the schools.

More attention to policy and provision for the under 3s, including parental leave.

An *inclusive and flexible approach to diversity, without compromising quality or access.*

It is important not only to expand provision, but to ensure *equitable access*, such that all children have equal opportunities to attend quality ECEC, regardless of family income, parental employment status, special educational needs or ethnic/language background. The role of government is to set targets for equitable access and develop strategies for meeting these targets. Equal opportunity means that all children have the chance to benefit from the full range of learning strategies offered in quality ECEC. To that end, most countries take a universal approach to access, according special attention and resources to children who need them and linking with supportive services in allied fields. An inclusive approach means mainstreaming children with special educational needs, whenever this is deemed in the best interest of the child. When inclusion is not feasible, more targeted programmes and projects can be developed to provide equality of educational opportunity and promote social integration for children living in disadvantaged communities. While targeting resources and services to certain populations can help address inequities, there is a danger that services for disadvantaged children and families will become stigmatised and lower quality. Many countries have recognised the importance of developing services that are flexible in terms of setting, hours, and programme options to meet the diverse needs of children and parents, both working and not. There also is a call for strategies to ensure that ECEC provision responds to the needs and rights of diverse populations by providing resources for staff training, culturally appropriate educational materials (*e.g.*, books, music), language support, and outreach to parents and communities. Diversity and flexibility in approach, however, should not compromise quality or access.

Substantial public investment in services and the infrastructure

Recognising ECEC *as a public service requires government support.*

Although the financing of ECEC services may be shared by a range of different funding sources – public, private, business, parents – it is clear that *public* investment by national, regional and local government is necessary to support a sustainable system of quality, accessible services. If ECEC is to be treated as a vital public service – like primary schools – it cannot be funded largely by the parents who use it. Limited public investment leads to a shortage of good quality programmes, unequal access, and segregation of children according to income. In several countries, current approaches to funding and financing do not assure that all families who wish to enrol their children in quality ECEC can afford to do so. In particular, the fact that children from low-income and immigrant backgrounds, and children with special educational needs are less represented in ECEC provision in several countries raises serious equity concerns. Fee levels and structures within countries need to be closely examined to assess the impact on access for these children. The role of the private (for-profit and non-profit) sector raises issues as well. Without adequate resources from parents or elsewhere, these services may be forced to cut costs, usually through staff salaries and benefits, which may jeopardise the quality of children in these settings. To avoid the development of a two-tiered system, countries should consider allocating public funding to private services, as long as they meet or exceed the standards set for public provision. In terms of financing mechanisms, it seems that without government regulation and planning, demand-side subsidies are insufficient to ensure equitable access and an even supply of quality services across regions and across income groups.

Country evidence suggests that a coherent *system* of ECEC requires secure funding for services, including substantial (direct or indirect) public funding, as well as ongoing public investment in the infrastructure which supports them – in-service training, planning, research, monitoring. In many countries, there has been a focus on expanding and running direct services, without adequate attention to developing durable structures and the capacity for sustained long-term planning and quality enhancement efforts across various forms of provision. In order to maximise limited funds and avoid duplicative efforts, a rational use of resources entails new ways of *co-ordinating* financial planning and allocation. Governments need to develop clear and consistent funding and financing strategies for efficiently allocating and using scarce resources. In general, there is a need for better monitoring of the levels of public and private funding at different levels of government and across different departments and programmes, as well as the consequences of these funding levels and financing approaches for supply, demand, enrolment, and quality. Achieving universal access will require additional resources in some countries to ensure that all families who wish to enrol their children in a quality programme can afford to do so. Raising quality carries cost implications as well, especially if it includes improving staff training, professional development opportunities, pay and working conditions.

A well-funded system of services supported by an infrastructure for quality assurance.

A *participatory approach to quality improvement and assurance*

While there are national and local differences in how quality is understood, most countries recognise the importance of developing broad goals to guide the system toward early childhood experiences that foster children's holistic development and learning. In addition, creating and consistently enforcing standards at different levels of the system set a minimum guarantee that the safety and health of children is ensured. These standards tend to focus on structural and process features of quality. One major difference in policy is the degree to which private (for-profit and non-profit) provision is covered in legislation. This is of particular concern as in many countries, the majority of children under 3 attend settings in the private sector or are in informal arrangements. Equal access to quality services assumes that quality control, support, monitoring, availability, and cost will be addressed similarly in both public and private services. For equity reasons, regulations need to apply to all settings, whether they are publicly or privately operated and should cover infant-toddler, pre-school, and out-of-school provision, recognising that different settings and age groups may require different standards. In order to meet standards, provision will need to be supported by a strong infrastructure of co-ordinated national, state, and local mechanisms for assuring adequate financing at a level to attract and retain highly-trained early childhood staff.

The application of regulatory standards for all forms of provision supported by co-ordinated investment.

Equal access to quality provision depends on government at national, regional, and local levels assuming major responsibility in funding, and supporting the development of services – whether publicly- or privately-provided. Government needs to support and encourage local initiatives. Across countries, there is a need to balance setting standards that ensure even levels of quality across regions and forms of provision, and the need to respond to the widely differing needs of communities. Policy and provision should strive to exceed standards and continuously improve the quality and coherence of children's early experiences. Beyond these minimum standards,

Participatory and democratic process to define and assure quality.

131

defining and assuring quality should be participatory and democratic, involving different groups including children, parents, families and professionals who work with children. The way in which quality is developed and the priorities and perspectives which are emphasised may vary between or across countries. While countries have developed different approaches to working with young children, most recognise the importance of adapting practices to the needs of the child, taking into account individual strengths and differences.

A *pedagogical framework focusing on children's holistic development to support quality practice.*

A pedagogical framework may guide practice and ensure consistent standards across different forms of early childhood services. It can provide the basis on which to engage in a discussion about what is quality and how to achieve it. A framework also can promote continuity in children's learning and bridge children's transition to compulsory school. These frameworks seem to work best when they focus broadly on children's holistic development and well-being, rather than on narrow literacy and numeracy objectives, and when they are flexible enough to allow staff to experiment with different methodological and pedagogical approaches. Whether they are produced at the national, local, or programme level, frameworks should be co-constructed through consultation with a wide range of stakeholders including staff, parents, and other members of the community. Successful implementation of curriculum guidelines can be supported through ongoing training and pedagogical guidance.

Monitoring that supports and engages staff, parents, and children.

Quality inspection and monitoring can ensure that services are meeting standards consistently across regions and sectors. A quality assurance system includes both inspection and monitoring to enforce compliance of rules and regulations *and* mechanisms to provide pedagogical guidance and support. Some countries have developed quantitative measures of quality which focus on the environmental, organisational, and process features of provision. These evaluations could be complemented by processes to support services and enable them to change, grow, and develop. Many countries encourage externally-validated self-evaluation methods and ongoing reflective practice by staff members, parents, and children as important elements of quality assurance and improvement efforts.

Appropriate training and working conditions for staff in all forms of provision

Quality ECEC *depends on strong staff training and fair working conditions across the sector.*

The review has shown that most staff working with 3- to 6-year-olds in publicly-funded early childhood settings are trained at a high level, with at least three years of post-secondary education. However, the situation is not uniform for different types of workers in different forms of provision. In split systems, staff working with children under 3 in the welfare sector tend to have lower levels of training, compensation, and poorer working conditions than education staff. This has serious consequences for the quality of provision for children in these settings. In more integrated systems, there is a unified training system for staff, with high levels of training and adequate pay and working conditions across age groups and forms of provision. In-service training and professional development opportunities are uneven in many countries, and there needs to be more attention to developing a career structure that crosses care and education boundaries. In most countries, training and working conditions for workers in family day care and in out-of-school provision also need to be reconsidered and improved so that they are recognised and supported as qualified professionals. Auxiliary workers also perform important roles and tasks in ECEC, and attention needs to be paid to their training and working conditions.

The demand for more flexible services to accommodate diverse children and families points to the need for reconceptualising the roles of ECEC workers to encompass a wide-range of educational and social responsibilities, which goes beyond the focus of basic training in most countries. This suggests that the training of staff should balance the specific content and methods necessary to work with young children with a broader focus on how the sector connects with, and contributes, to social integration and lifelong learning objectives. This includes a heightened focus on how to communicate and collaborate with parents from diverse backgrounds and provide flexible opportunities for them to engage in their children's ECEC. It also means that more efforts are needed to train and employ staff who reflect the diversity of the local community. Therefore, it is important to ensure that a career lattice makes it possible for a wide range of trainees from different ethnic and social groups to enter the system. Another challenge is to help practitioners understand and build on the rich diversity of cultures in their everyday work with children and families by integrating a multi-cultural dimension into all components of initial and ongoing training.

Expanding initial and in-service training to reflect a wide range of educational and social responsibilities.

Recruiting and retaining a qualified workforce is one of the major challenges for the future. There are several national strategies to address this concern, but it is unclear whether they will be successful in the long-run. There is a critical need to address the working conditions of staff across the workforce – including family day care – to ensure that a career in ECEC is satisfying, respected, and financially viable. The cost implications are real and demand increased public investment, which cannot be expected to be covered through higher parental fees or in savings in other areas of service delivery. Finally, the feminisation of the sector has had negative consequences for the economic and social status of the workforce, yet few countries have developed strategies to recruit more men to the profession. With very few exceptions, countries have not addressed the larger issue of the role of men as carers in both home and out-of-home settings and the implications for staff, children, parents, and society. Nonetheless, raising the training, status and compensation of *all* early childhood workers – and ensuring access to professional development – would help address some of the difficulties of recruiting and retaining qualified women *and* men from diverse backgrounds to the profession.

Developing strategies to recruit and retain a qualified and diverse, mixed-gender workforce.

Systematic attention to monitoring and data collection

Given the trends toward increased decentralisation to local authorities and institutions, well-funded mechanisms for monitoring ECEC systems are important to support quality improvement in the field. Systematic data collection and development on the supply, utilisation, and unmet need for services, levels and training of staff, and other aspects of service delivery are necessary to support national and local policymakers in making informed decisions concerning ECEC.[52] Although considerable research data are available at national

Coherent procedures to collect and analyse data on the status of young children.

52. This section draws on a paper prepared by Rostgaard (2000) for the Thematic Review.

levels, different methods of collecting information operate in the various sectors of health, education and the social services and across the different providers. There is a need for a systematic procedure to collect and provide consistent and comparable information on ECEC within a given country, as well as across countries. Establishing on-going national data collection on the status of young children, the programmes they attend, and the staff who work with them is fast becoming an imperative for national leadership and responsibility.

Identifying and addressing data gaps in the field through international efforts.

The thematic review has identified several *data gaps* that lead to barriers in national and cross-national comparisons. Specifically, current approaches to data collection tend to focus on educational services for children over 3. There is a need for national efforts to collect data on fully-private, centre-based provision and family day care, as these arrangements often accommodate children under 3. Future data collection efforts would need to cover the whole age group birth to 8 and include all forms of provision, regardless of administrative responsibility (education, welfare), funding source (public, private) or setting (centre, school, home). Leave schemes need to be evaluated according to accessibility, length and payment, and comparable figures on take-up collected. Background indicators (*e.g.*, demographic, employment, and social data) can shed light on variations in need and demand. The availability of informal arrangements should also be documented. Indicators on quality need to include both quantitative and qualitative data. Indicators on availability and access might look at the objectives of services, the age groups served, affordability (including fee variation), and the number of children attending. In the future, using full-time equivalencies to convert part-time into full-time and term-time into full-year would facilitate comparisons within and across countries. It may be necessary to create an international network to identify the data gaps, priorities, and comparable collection methodologies for the ECEC field.

A *stable framework and long-term agenda for research and evaluation*

Research on areas concerning key policy goals and the links between research, policy, and practice.

Research on the key policy areas of ECEC is an essential element of a continuous improvement process. Setting up a strong, sustained national research infrastructure demands a long-term government funding commitment combined with a planned research agenda and generous training opportunities. Creating a stable research framework would help inform effective policy-making and raise the overall quality of ECEC. As in other areas of social and educational policy, the field is changing rapidly and there is a need for up-to-date research and evaluation information to strengthen the connections between research, policy, and practice. The body of international research in the early childhood field is growing, though much of it is dominated by the English-speaking world, which represents one particular paradigm. Increased investment in research and development in the field is needed in all participating countries.

Expanding the research agenda to include areas and disciplines that are underrepresented.

The research agenda might be expanded to include areas and disciplines that have not been accorded much attention in the past. The concerns and methodologies of developmental psychology have traditionally played a dominant role in much of ECEC research. While this perspective is important, there is a need for a stronger research focus on other disciplines including anthropology, sociology, public policy, and learning theory. For example, the *sociology of childhood* could provide a focus on the very different conditions under which children grow up, on children's views of the world and their experiences in ECEC. Descriptions of children's daily routines would help to deepen adults' perceptions and views of children and their social networks. Studies focusing on process quality in different *learning environments* would provide valuable data and help policymakers gauge priorities when setting up and raising the quality of services. How can very young children best be helped to develop life-coping and school-coping competencies? What balance is needed between child-initiated and adult-led activities? How do practitioners best assess if they are achieving the goals they set? How do different approaches towards language and literacy development influence children's proficiency? There is also a need for research to explore the *structural parameters* of a quality ECEC system (*e.g.*, regulation, governance, training, funding, etc.), as well as the research on the *infrastructure* and its relationship to quality. Finally, *longitudinal research* studies of the short-term and long-term impact of ECEC for children, families, and society are needed.

There also is a need to develop a range of research and evaluation instruments. Developing research instruments and evaluation procedures that are sensitive to the complex dynamics of early childhood environments, to the interdependence between the beliefs and practices of families and a centre's response, would be an important step towards deepening understanding in these areas. Research based on self-evaluation procedures and action research would support critical reflection and team development and complement external evaluation. Cost-benefit analyses of different approaches and initiatives which are underway in some countries should be supported more widely. Finally, there is a need for strategies to disseminate research findings and examples of good practice to diverse audiences. Governments should support innovative community-based initiatives to make them durable and to disseminate lessons from these experiences within and across countries. National or international early childhood observatories or institutes, networks and technical working groups, as well as regular meetings and opportunities for cross-national dialogue and research could help monitor the impact of different policy initiatives and contribute to the improvement of policy development.

Supporting a range of methods and dissemination strategies to inform diverse audiences.

4.2. Future directions of work

Countries that have adopted some or all of these elements of successful policy share a strong public commitment to young children and their families. They have assumed responsibility for the education and care of their youngest citizens in close partnership with families. In different ways, these countries have made efforts to ensure access for all children, and have initiated special efforts for those in need of special support. Quality is high on the agenda as a means to ensure that children not only have equal opportunities to participate in ECEC but also to benefit from these experiences in ways that promote their development and learning. *These countries have given young children high priority among the many concerns that compete for attention on the policy agenda.* They have recognised that strong national and local policies are needed to support children in the early years. ECEC is understood not only as preparation for later formal schooling, but also as an opportunity to foster healthy physical, social, and emotional development, and lifelong dispositions to learn. However, policy alterations alone cannot make universal access to high quality ECEC a reality. This report has highlighted that there is an inextricable link between

The key elements of successful policy need to be discussed in light of the social constructions of childhood.

135|

social context and the nature of policy and provision for young children and their families. Perhaps the time is ripe to open and fuel a wider debate about the place of government, children and families in different countries and, in particular, about the current and future needs of young children and families in the post-industrial, knowledge society. Creating a forum for democratic discussion about the social constructions of childhood, the goals of ECEC policy and provision, and the roles of different stakeholders would be an important starting point toward developing a shared vision for the future.

The review has identified several remaining issues and challenges for future cross-national work.

One of the main lessons from the review is that the diverse approaches to addressing issues of quality and access in different countries can help inform policy makers in all countries about the relative merits of different policy options. There would be value in further cross-national work, focusing on some of the critical issues and challenges in the field. Based on the findings from the thematic review, future policy work in the field may focus on questions such as:

- How are childhoods changing? What is a good childhood? What are the purposes of early childhood institutions? How do they protect the best interests of children? How do societies understand learning, care, knowledge? How do societies co-construct childhoods? What is the impact of different constructions of childhood within a society and how does the dominant construction affect different sub-groups? How do the demands of ICT, the knowledge economy, multiculturalism, globalisation affect ECEC?

- Which policy approaches should be developed to assist children with limited access to quality, affordable ECEC – children under 3, children from low-income families, children with special needs, children from ethnic minority backgrounds, children living in rural areas?

- What is the rationale for different ways of organising ECEC policy and provision? How can countries move toward integrated early childhood systems? What are the implications and challenges for policy and practice? How can policy and practice foster strong and equal partnerships between ECEC and schools, which build on the strengths of both sectors?

- How much additional investment is needed to improve quality and access? Who should fund the system? What are the returns on the investment? What are the advantages and disadvantages of various financing mechanisms? How should governments allocate resources? What should be the balance of investments between parental leave schemes and infant-toddler provision?

- How do we want to structure the early childhood workforce? Why are there so few men working in the field? What are the consequences for children, parents, workers, and society? Is a mixed-gender and ethnically-diverse workforce desirable, and if so, why? What are the most promising strategies to achieve it?

- How will our societies respond to staff shortages? Will countries recruit low-qualified workers, drawing on the pool of low-skilled women from immigrant backgrounds or welfare recipients? Will they revalue the profession to compete better for potential workers?

- How can policy help parents balance work and family life? How can government, employers, and early childhood staff promote parent engagement in ECEC given the current working hours and patterns? What does workplace flexibility mean in practice? How can gender equity be safeguarded? What are the implications of different work-family options for men, women, and children? What are some future scenarios for combining care, work, and lifelong learning?

– How can countries address the information gaps identified by the review? What types of data, indicators and research are needed to inform policy development in the early childhood field? What are the immediate data priorities? What information should be routinely collected, at national and international levels? What mechanisms should be used?

Early childhood is firmly on the agenda of the countries that have participated in the review. This report, like the other policy analyses produced for this OECD project, has demonstrated that all 12 countries should be pleased with their accomplishments over the past decade. Some countries have made dramatic progress, especially in light of the low base from which they started. Other countries, with a longer history of involvement in the field, have worked to further strengthen and update their policy and practice. Children and families are likely to benefit from the efforts to expand provision, improve quality, and promote coherence. Governments have improved training of staff, worked to engage parents and families, and developed closer co-operation with the school system and other allied sectors. While significant challenges remain, the developments and achievements in recent years are impressive. It is hoped that this OECD project and future activities will contribute to further policy improvements in the field.

References

Items cited below are those directly referred to in the text. The OECD background reports and country notes contain extensive reference lists of country sources.

ALVESTAD, M. and PRAMLING, I. (2000),
"A Comparison of the National Pre-school Curricula in Norway and Sweden", *Early Childhood Research and Practice*, Vol. 1(2).

AMERICAN EDUCATIONAL RESEARCH ASSOCIATION, AMERICAN PSYCHOLOGICAL ASSOCIATION, NATIONAL COUNCIL ON MEASUREMENTS IN EDUCATION (1999),
Standards for Educational and Psychological Testing, American Educational Research Association, Washington, DC.

BARNETT, W. S. (1995),
"Long-term Effects of Early Childhood Programs on Cognitive and School Outcomes", *The Future of Children: Long-term outcomes of early childhood programs*, Vol. 5(3), pp. 25-50.

BARNETT, S. and MASSE, L. (2000),
"Funding Issues for Early Care and Education in the United States", in US Department of Education (Ed.), US *Background Report for the* OECD *Thematic Review*, Office of Educational Research and Improvement, Washington, DC.

BOOCOCK, S. S. (1995, Winter),
"Early Childhood Programs in Other Nations: Goals and outcomes", *The Future of Children: Long-term Outcomes of Early Childhood Programs*, Vol. 5(3), pp. 94-114.

BOWMAN, B., DONOVAN, M. S. and BURNS, M. S. (Eds.) (2000),
Eager to Learn: Educating our preschoolers, National Academy Press, Washington, DC.

BREDEKAMP, S. and COPPLE, C. (Eds.) (1997),
Developmentally Appropriate Practice in Early Childhood Programs, Revised Edition, National Association for the Education of Young Children, Washington, DC.

BÜHLER INSTITUTE (1994),
A *Survey of the Childcare Environment: The conditions that foster or hamper development*, Part 1, Vienna.

BUSH, J. and PHILLIPS, D. A. (1996),
"International Approaches to Defining Quality", in S. L. Kagan and N. E. Cohen (Eds.), *Reinventing Early Care and Education: A vision for a quality system*, Jossey-Bass, San Francisco, CA, pp. 65-80.

CARR, M. and MAY, H. (2000),
"Te Whāriki: curriculum voices", in H. Penn (Ed.), *Early Childhood Services: Theory, policy and practice*, Open University Press, Milton Keynes, Buckingham (U.K.) and Philadelphia, pp. 53-73.

CASPER, L. M. (1995),
"What Does it Cost to Mind our Preschoolers?", *Current Population Reports: Household Economic Studies*, P70-52, US Department of Commerce, Washington, DC.

CHRISTOPHERSON, S. (1997),
"Childcare and Elderly Care: What occupational opportunities for women?", Labour Market and Social Policy Occasional Papers No. 27, OECD, Paris.

CLEVERLEY, J. and PHILLIPS, D.C. (1986),
Visions of Childhood: Influential models from Locke to Spock, Revised Edition, Teachers College Press, New York.

COCHRAN, M. (1993),
> "Public Child Care, Culture and Society: Crosscutting themes", in M. Cochran (Ed.), *International Handbook of Child Care Policies and Programs*, Greenwood Press, Westport, CT, pp. 627-658.

COST, QUALITY, AND CHILD OUTCOMES [CQCO] Study Team (1995),
> *Cost, Quality, and Child Outcomes in Child Care Centers*, Department of Economics, University of Colorado at Denver, Denver, CO.

COST, QUALITY, AND CHILD OUTCOMES [CQCO] Study Team (1999),
> *The Children of the Cost, Quality, and Outcomes Study Go To School: Executive summary*, Frank Porter Graham Child Development Center, Chapel Hill, NC.

DAHLBERG, G., MOSS, P. and PENCE, A. (1999),
> *Beyond Quality in Early Childhood Education and Care: Postmodern perspectives*, Falmer Press, London.

DAVID, T., RABAN, B., URE, C., GOOUCH, K., JAGO, M., BARRIÈRE, I., LAMBIRTH, A. (2000),
> *Making Sense of Early Literacy: A practitioner's perspective*, Trentham Books, Stoke-on-Trent.

DUNCAN, G. J. and BROOKS-GUNN, J. (Eds.) (1997),
> *Consequences of Growing Up Poor*, Russell Sage Foundation, New York.

EARLY CHILDHOOD EDUCATION FORUM (ECEF) AND NATIONAL CHILDREN'S BUREAU (1998),
> *Quality in Diversity in Early Learning: A framework for early childhood practitioners*, National Children's Bureau Enterprises Ltd., London.

EDWARDS, C., GANDINI, L. and FORMAN G. (Eds.) (1993),
> *The Hundred Languages of Children*, Ablex, Norwood NJ.

EUROPEAN COMMISSION CHILDCARE NETWORK (1996*a*),
> *Quality Targets in Services for Young Children*, Brussels, Belgium.

EUROPEAN COMMISSION CHILDCARE NETWORK (1996*b*),
> *A Review of Services for Young Children in the European Union* 1990-1995, Brussels, Belgium.

EUROPEAN NETWORK FOR SCHOOL-AGE CHILDCARE – ENSAC (1994),
> *Empowering the Parents: Report of 5th International Congress*, VBJK, Gent.

EUROSTAT (2000),
> *Key Data on Education in Europe*, 1999-2000, European Commission, Luxembourg.

EVANS, J. M. (2001),
> "Firms' Contribution to the Reconciliation between Work and Family Life", Labour Market and Social Policy Occasional Papers No. 48, OECD, Paris, http://www.oecd.org/els/employment/docs.htm.

FAGNANI, J. (1999),
> "Parental Leave in France", in P. Moss and F. Deven (Eds.), *Parental Leave: Progress or Pitfall? Research and policy issues in Europe*, NIDI/CBGS Publications, Brussels, pp. 69-81.

FÖRSTER, M. F. (2000),
> "Trends and Driving Factors in Income Distribution and Poverty in the OECD Area", Labour Market and Social Policy Occasional Papers No. 42, OECD, Paris.

FULLER, B., KAGAN, S. L. *et al.* (2000),
> *Remember the Children: Mothers balance work and child care under welfare reform*, University of California, Berkeley and Yale University, PACE Growing Up in Poverty Project, Berkeley, CA and New Haven, CT.

GALINSKY, E., HOWES, C., KONTOS, S. and SHINN, M. (1994),
> *The Study of Children in Family Child Care and Relative Care*, Families and Work Institute, New York, NY.

GALLAGHER, J. and CLIFFORD, R. (2000, Spring),
> "The Missing Support Infrastructure in Early Childhood", *Early Childhood Research and Practice*, Vol. 2(1).

GREENSPAN, S. I. and WIEDER, S. (1998),
> *The Child with Special Needs: Encouraging intellectual and emotional growth*, Perseus Books, Reading, MA.

GREGG, P., HARKNESS, S. and MACHIN, S. (1999),
> *Child Development and Family Income*, York Publishing Services for the Joseph Rowntree Foundation, York, UK.

GUNNARSSON, L., MARTIN KORPI, B. and NORDENSTAM, U. (1999),
Early Childhood Education and Care Policy in Sweden, Background Report prepared for the OECD Thematic Review of Early Childhood Education and Care Policy, Ministry of Education and Science in Sweden, Stockholm, Sweden.

HARMS, T., CLIFFORD, R. and CRYER, D. (1998),
Early Childhood Environment Rating Scale, Revised Edition, Teachers College Press, New York.

HARMS, T., CRYER D. and CLIFFORD, R. (1990),
Infant/Toddler Environment Rating Scale, Teachers College Press, New York.

HODGKIN, R. and NEWELL, P. (1996),
Effective Government Structures for Children: Report of a Gulbenkian Foundation inquiry, Gulbenkian Foundation, London.

JAMES, A. and PROUT, A. (Eds.) (1990),
Constructing and Deconstructing Childhood: Contemporary issues in the sociological study of childhood, Falmer Press, Brighton.

JAMES, A., JENKS, C. and PROUT, A. (1998),
Theorizing Childhood, Polity Press, Oxford, UK.

JAROUSSE, J. P., MINGAT, A. and RICHARD, M. (1992, April-June),
"La scolarisation maternelle à deux ans : effects pédagogiques et sociaux", Education et Formation, Ministère de l'Education nationale et de la Culture, Paris.

JENSEN, J. J. (1996),
Men as Workers in Childcare Services. A discussion paper, European Commission Childcare Network, Brussels.

JOSEPH ROWNTREE FOUNDATION (1995, November),
Findings: Meeting the needs of refugee families and their children, Social Policy Research No. 86, York, UK.

KAGAN, J. (1999),
Three Seductive Ideas, Harvard University Press.

KAGAN, S. L. and COHEN, N. E. (1997),
Not by Chance. Creating an Early Care and Education System for America's Children, Full Report, The Quality 2000 Initiative, Bush Center in Child Development and Social Policy at Yale University, New Haven, CT.

KAGITCIBASI, C. and BEKMAN, S. (1991),
Cognitive Training Programme, Finans Vakýf Publications, Istanbul.

KAMERMAN, S. B. (2000a),
"Early Childhood Education and Care: An overview of developments in the OECD countries", International Journal of Educational Research, Vol. 33(1), pp. 7-29.

KAMERMAN, S. B. (2000b),
"Parental Leave Policies: An essential ingredient in early childhood education and care policies", Social Policy Report, Vol. 14(2), pp. 3-15.

KAMERMAN, S. B. and KAHN, A. J. (1994),
A Welcome for Every Child: Care, education, and family support for infants and toddlers in Europe, Zero to Three, National Center for Clinical Infant Programs, Arlington, VA.

KAMERMAN, S. B. and KAHN, A. J. (1997),
"Investing in Children: Government expenditure for children and their families in western industrialized countries", in G. A. Cornia and S. Danziger (Eds.), Child Poverty and Deprivation in the Industrialized Countries 1945-1995, Clarendon Press, Oxford, pp. 91-121.

KARLSSON, M. (1995),
Family Day Care in Europe, EC Childcare Network, Brussels.

KAROLY, L. A., GREENWOOD, P. W., EVERINGHAM, S. S., HOUBÉ, J., KILBURN, M. R., RYDELL, C. P., SANDERS, M., CHIESA, J. (1998),
Investing in Our Children: What we know and don't know about the costs and benefits of early childhood interventions, RAND, Santa Monica, CA.

KEMPSON, E. (1996),
Life on a Low Income, Joseph Rowntree Foundation, York.

LINDSEY, G. (1998),
   "Brain Research and Implications for Early Childhood Education", in *Childhood Education*, Vol. 75(2), pp. 97-101.

MEISELS, S. (1994),
   "Designing Meaningful Measurements for Early Childhood", in B. Mallory and R. New (Eds.), *Diversity and Developmentally Appropriate Practices: Challenges for early childhood education*, Teachers College Press, New York, pp. 202-222.

MEYERS, M. K. and GORNICK, J. C. (2000),
   Early Childhood Education and Care: Cross-national variation in service organization and financing, Paper prepared for a Consultative Meeting on International Developments in Early Childhood Education and Care, May 11-12, 2000, The Institute for Child and Family Policy at Columbia University, New York.

MINISTRY OF CHILDREN AND FAMILY AFFAIRS IN NORWAY (1996),
   Framework Plan for Day Care Institutions: A brief presentation, Oslo.

MINISTRY OF CHILDREN AND FAMILY AFFAIRS IN NORWAY (1998),
   Early Childhood Education and Care Policy in Norway, Background report prepared for the OECD Thematic Review of Early childhood education and care policy, Oslo.

MINISTRY OF EDUCATION IN PORTUGAL, DEPARTMENT OF BASIC EDUCATION (1998),
   "Early Childhood Education in Portugal" (includes translation of the *Framework Law on Basic Education 5/97* and the *Curriculum Guidelines Ruling 5220797*), Lisbon.

MINISTRY OF SOCIAL AFFAIRS IN DENMARK (1997),
   Social Policy in Denmark: Child and family policies, Copenhagen.

MINISTRY OF VWS/MINISTRY OF OCenW (2000),
   Early Childhood Education and Care Policy in the Netherlands, Background report to the OECD Thematic Review of Early Childhood Education and Care Policy, The Hague, The Netherlands.

MOSS, P. (2000),
   "Training of Early Childhood Education and Care Staff", *International Journal of Educational Research*, Vol. 33(1), pp. 31-54.

MOSS, P. and DEVEN, F. (Eds.) (1999),
   Parental Leave: Progress or Pitfall? Research and policy issues in Europe, NIDI/CBGS Publications, Brussels.

MOSS, P. and PENCE, A. (Eds.) (1994),
   Valuing Quality in Early Childhood Services: New approaches to defining quality, Paul Chapman, London.

NATIONAL EDUCATION GOALS PANEL (1997),
   The National Education Goals Panel Report: Building a nation of learners, 1997, US Government Printing Office, Washington DC.

NEW SOUTH WALES DEPARTMENT OF COMMUNITY SERVICES (2000, April),
   Draft of the Practice of Relationships: Essential provisions for children's services, NSW Curriculum Framework for Children's Services, Sydney, Australia.

NICHD – National Institute of Child Health and Human Development (1997),
   Mother-child Interaction and Cognitive Outcomes Associated with Early Child Care: Results of the NICHD study, Society for Research in Child Development meeting symposium, Washington, DC.

O'FLAHERTY, J. (1995),
   Intervention in the Early Years. An Evaluation of the High/Scope Curriculum, National Children's Bureau, London.

OBERHUEMER, P. and ULICH, M. (1997),
   Working with Young Children in Europe: Provision and staff training, Paul Chapman Publishing, London.

OECD (1991),
   Shaping Structural Change: The role of women, Report of a high-level group of experts to the OECD Secretary-General, Paris.

OECD (1996),
   Lifelong Learning for All: Meeting of the Education Committee at the Ministerial Level, 16-17 January 1996, Paris.

OECD (1998*a*),
> Co-ordinating Services for Children and Youth at Risk: A world view, Centre for Educational Research and Innovation, Paris.

OECD (1998*b*),
> Early Childhood Education and Care Policy: Proposal for a thematic review: Major issues, analytical framework, and operating procedures, DEELSA/ED (1998)2, Paris.

OECD (1999*a*),
> A Caring World: The new social policy agenda, Paris.

OECD (1999*b*),
> "Early Childhood Education and Care: Getting the most from the investment", Education Policy Analysis 1999, Paris, pp. 27-46.

OECD (1999*c*),
> "Training of Adult Workers in OECD Countries: Measurement and analysis", Employment Outlook 1999, Paris, pp. 133-175.

OECD (1999*d*),
> Inclusive Education at Work, Centre for Educational Research and Innovation, Paris.

OECD (2000*a*),
> Education at a Glance: OECD Indicators, Centre for Educational Research and Innovation, Paris.

OECD (2000*b*),
> Family-friendly Policies: The reconciliation of work and family life, DEELSA/ELSA/WP1/(2000)6, Paris.

OECD (2000*c*),
> OECD Social Expenditure Data Base 1980-1997, Paris.

OECD (2001*a*),
> Education at a Glance: OECD Indicators, Centre for Educational Research and Innovation, Paris.

OECD (2001*b*),
> Preliminary Synthesis of the First High Level Forum on Learning Sciences and Brain Research: Potential implications for education policies and practices. Brain mechanisms and early learning, Sackler Institute, New York City, US, 16-17 June 2000, Centre for Educational Research and Innovation, Paris.

OECD (2001*c*),
> "Work and Family Life: How do they balance out?", Employment Outlook, Paris.

OWEN, C., CAMERON, C. and MOSS, P. (Eds.) (1998),
> Men as Workers in Services for Young Children: Issues of a mixed gender workforce, Institute of Education University of London, London.

PASCAL, C. and BERTRAM, A.D. (1997),
> Effective Early Learning Project: Evaluating and developing quality in early childhood settings – A professional development programme, Centre for Research in Early Childhood, University College Worcester, Worcester, UK.

PENN, H. (2000) (Ed.),
> Early Childhood Services: Theory, policy and practice, Open University Press, Buckingham (U.K.) and Philadelphia.

PHILLIPS, D. A. (Ed.) (1995),
> Child Care for Low-income Families: Summary of two workshops, National Academy Press, Washington, DC.

PHILLIPSEN, L., BURCHINAL, M., HOWES, C. and CRYER, D. (1997),
> "The Prediction of Process Quality from Structural Features of Child Care", Early Childhood Research Quarterly, Vol. 12, pp. 281-303.

PRESS, F. and HAYES, A. (2000),
> OECD Thematic Review of Early Childhood Education and Care Policy: Australian background report, DETYA, Canberra, Australia.

PRITCHARD, E. (1996),
> "Training and Professional Development: International approaches", in S. L. Kagan and N. E. Cohen (Eds.), Reinventing Early Care and Education: A vision for a quality system, Jossey-Bass, San Francisco, CA, pp. 124-141.

ROSTGAARD, T. (2000),
Recommendations for Data and Indicator Development for ECEC Systems, Background paper prepared for the OECD Thematic Review of Early Childhood Education and Care Policy.

ROSTGAARD, T. and FRIDBERG, T. (1998),
Caring for Children and Older People: A comparison of European policies and practices, The Danish National Institute of Social Research, Copenhagen.

RUTTER, J. and HYDER, T. (1998),
Refugee Children in the Early Years: Issues for policy-makers and providers, The Refugee Council and Save the Children, London.

SCHULMAN, K., BLANK, H. and EWEN, D. (1999),
Seeds of Success. State Prekindergarten Initiatives 1998-1999, Children's Defense Fund, Washington, DC.

SCHWEINHART, L.J. BARNES, H.V. and LARNER, M. (1993),
Observing Young Children in Action to Assess Their Development, The High/Scope Child Observation Record Study in Educational and Psychological Measurement, Vol. 53, pp. 445-455.

SHEPARD, L., KAGAN, S. L. and WURZ, E. (Eds.) (1998),
Principles and Recommendations for Early Childhood Assessments, National Education Goals Panel, Washington, DC.

SHORE, R. (1997),
Rethinking the Brain: New insights into early development, Families and Work Institute, New York, NY.

SNOW, C., BURNS, M. S., GRIFFIN, P. (Eds.) (1998),
Preventing Reading Difficulties in Young Children, National Academy Press, Washington, DC.

STATISTICS NORWAY (1998),
Women and Men in Norway 1998, Oslo.

SYLVA, K. and WILTSHIRE, J. (1993),
"The Impact of Early Learning on Children's Later Development", European Early Childhood Education Research Journal, Vol. 1(1).

UNICEF (2000),
A League Table of Child Poverty in Rich Countries, UNICEF Innocenti Centre, Florence.

U.S. DEPARTMENT OF HEALTH AND HUMAN SERVICES (1999),
Access to Child Care for Low-income Working Families, Washington, DC.
http://www.acf.dhhs.gov/programs/ccb/reports/ccreport.htm

U.S. DEPARTMENT OF LABOR, BUREAU OF LABOR STATISTICS (December 1999),
1998 National Occupational Employment and Wage Estimates, Washington, DC.
http://stats.bls.gov/oes/national/oes_nat.htm

U.S. DEPARTMENT OF LABOR, BUREAU OF LABOR STATISTICS (2000),
Labor Force Statistics from the Current Population Survey, US Government Printing Office, Washington.

U.S. GENERAL ACCOUNTING OFFICE (1995),
Early Childhood Centers: Services to prepare children for school often limited, Washington, DC, pp. 95-121.

VANDELL, D. L. and WOLFE, B. (2000),
Child Care Quality: Does it matter and does it need to be improved?, US Department of Health and Human Services, Washington, DC. http://aspe.hhs.gov/hsp/ccquality00

VERRY, D. (2000),
"Some Economic Aspects of Early Childhood Education and Care", International Journal of Educational Research, Vol. 33(1), pp. 95-122.

WHITEBOOK, M. and SAKAI, L. (1995),
The Potential of Mentoring: An assessment of the California early childhood mentor teacher program, The National Center for the Early Childhood Workforce, Washington, DC.

WHITEBOOK, M., HOWES, C. and PHILLIPS, D. (1989),
Who Cares? Child care teachers and the quality of care in America: Final report of the National Child Care Staffing Study, Child Care Employee Project, Oakland, CA.

WHITEBOOK, M., HOWES, C. and PHILLIPS, D. (1998),
> *Worthy Work, Unlivable Wages: The National Child Care Staffing Study*, 1988-1997, Center for the Child Care Workforce, Washington, DC.

WOODHEAD, M. (1996),
> *In Search of the Rainbow: Pathways to quality in large-scale programmes for young disadvantaged children*, Bernard van Leer Foundation, The Hague.

WOODHEAD, M. (1999),
> "Toward a Global Paradigm for Research into Early Childhood Education", *European Early Childhood Education Research Journal*, Vol. 7(1), pp. 5-22.

WYLIE, C. (1994),
> *What Research on Early Childhood Education/care Outcomes Can, and Can't, Tell Policymakers*, New Zealand Council for Educational Research, Wellington.

Appendix 1

An Overview of ECEC Systems in the Participating Countries

1. Introduction

The aim of this appendix is to provide a comparative snapshot of ECEC in the countries that participated in the review. A common profile of each country is presented, using the following descriptors: auspices; developments; context; provision; staffing and training; and policy issues identified by the OECD review teams. These descriptors provide an insight into present country characteristics and, if read in conjunction with Chapter 3, give some indication of the qualities of each system. No doubt, further descriptors might have been added – regulatory policy and system monitoring, funding mechanisms, curriculum and programme characteristics, quality indicators and control, but space did not allow their inclusion. An overview of terms and organisation of the main forms of ECEC provision is provided in Table 3.1 and Figure 3.1.

The brief paragraph on *Auspices* indicates which ministries have competence in ECEC matters, and whether decentralisation of responsibilities has taken place. Apart from giving factual information as to who is in charge, auspices can also indicate whether unified policies for young children from birth to 6 years are the rule, or whether the traditional division between care and education is perpetuated through administrative structures. The main source for this section is the background report of each country.

The section on *Developments* describes advances made in the past five years by countries in the review, starting from very different bases and levels of provision. From the evidence presented, it is clear that countries have made remarkable efforts to expand and improve services in the ECEC field in recent years. Even countries that have enjoyed decades of extensive service provision have refocused their efforts and undertaken needed policy reforms. The main sources of information for national developments are the background reports and the visits carried out by the OECD review teams.

Context includes four elements that influence young children's experiences in their early years:

– ECEC *expenditure as a percentage of* GDP: although we received much information from ministries about various items of expenditure in the early childhood field, we have been obliged, for reasons of comparability, to use the 1998 ISCED Level 0 data, supplied to the OECD by ministries of education. The backgrounds reports of several countries (Australia, Czech Republic, Denmark, Finland, the Netherlands, Sweden and the United Kingdom) suggest that much additional funding is being invested in early childhood services, but the exact nature of this funding is not always clear. The use of ISCED Level 0 data cannot either be considered satisfactory. ISCED level 0 programmes are defined as *centre or school-based programmes that are designed to meet the educational and developmental needs of children at least 3 years of age, and that have staff that are adequately trained (i.e. qualified) to provide an educational programme for the children.* When these programmes are considered to be "pre-primary education", they are further defined as *the initial stage of organised instruction.* Such an understanding does not correspond to how early childhood programming is conceived in many countries. Further, an instructional agenda limits greatly the wider definition of ECEC provided in Chapter 1. Moreover, as the "instructional" or "educational" properties of programmes are difficult to assess directly, different proxy measures are utilised by countries to determine whether a programme should be classified at this level. Variation in these proxy measures undermine comparability. In sum, the design of data collection in the early childhood remains a real challenge in terms of scope, basic definitions and comparability. The question is further treated in Chapter 4.

– *The levels of female participation in the labour force*: although women still take up the greater proportion of part-time employment available, participation rates for women in the child-bearing years from 25-34 years show a remarkable progression in the last decade, and range from 63% in Italy to 81.6% in Denmark. In parallel, there is a growth in expectations that equality of opportunity in work should become a reality through equal wages, better early childhood services and recognition of paid parental leave, which is taken up almost exclusively by women. The percentage figures provided in the profiles are for 1999, and are taken from the OECD data base on labour force statistics.[53]

---

53. Except for Italy, the data for which is extracted from EUROSTAT sources.

- The *provision of maternity and parental leave*: though problematic in certain regards, a developed maternity and parental leave provision generally improves the quality of care provided to an infant in the crucial first year. Without it, parents are obliged, particularly in countries with under-developed ECEC provision for children 0-3 years, to have recourse to informal, unregulated arrangements. In contrast, countries that fund adequate parental leave seem to offer greater parental choice, to eliminate or reduce unregulated care and to achieve high participation of women in the labour market. The major sources of information on parental leave schemes are the national *background reports* and the recent publication *Parental Leave: progress or pitfall* (Moss and Deven, 1999). Further references to the issue are found in Chapters 2 and 3 of this report.

- A fourth element for analysis, outlined in Chapter 2 and running throughout the entire report, is one particularly important for ministries, viz. *Attention to children with special education needs before their entry into compulsory school*. Figures quoted are taken either from the background reports or in the case of child poverty, from *Child Poverty in Rich Nations*, (UNICEF, 2000). Most countries now pay attention to children with disabilities, sometimes under pressure from the courts. Close attention is given also by many to children from low-income families. Rates of household and child poverty are often in excess of 15%, even after redistribution mechanisms have come into effect, that is after fiscal transfers, child benefits and social assistance payments have been allocated to poor families.

- Children from low-income and immigrant families are most at risk of school failure. Analysis of education statistics show that between 15-25% of children in schools in the OECD countries experience some kind of learning difficulty or failure in their school careers. Major research projects have shown that quality ECEC services have a positive impact on children from disadvantaged backgrounds. Appropriate early childhood programmes can contribute greatly to improving the life chances of these children and to preparing them effectively for school. In addition, early services can play an important role in identifying and supporting, children with special learning needs.

Rates of coverage: countries are often evaluated by the percentages of children in each age cohort for whom they are able to provide either full-day or part-day services. The figures herein come from the country *background reports* or directly from government authorities. Without other information being supplied, such statistics may beg the question of the base from which a country is starting, tell little about the level of demand, and provide no indication of the quality of services. A pattern of coverage is seemingly emerging across the industrialised countries: a coverage rate ranging from 20-30% in year 1-2, and reaching over 80% coverage in full-time places, some time in the fourth year (see Chapter 3)[54]. Some countries do not approach this rate, especially for children aged 1-3 years. Many factors can influence demand, such as the attitudes of a society toward child-rearing, the presence of high quality services that parents can actually see in operation, affordability, and to a lesser extent, the rate of participation of mothers with young children in the labour market.

A final indicator chosen is *Staffing and training*, one of the more important issues of the review, which has been treated comprehensively in Chapters 3 and 4. Wide differences can be seen between countries in their recruitment and training of staff, ranging from countries with 98% of staff fully trained, to countries in which less than a third of contact staff have a recognised early childhood qualification. Yet, well-motivated, professional staff are perhaps the key to quality in a system. Early socialisation and the stimulation of children's learning in out-of-home environments is a complex task, ideally entrusted to well-trained, professional staff. The positioning of ECEC as the first phase of lifelong learning carries the implication that the staff of early childhood centres should also be pedagogues or educators. As children approach school age, the professionals should be able to ensure young children a smooth entry into primary school classes, which, in turn, should employ methodologies appropriate to the age of these children. The major source of information for this section is the *background report* of each country.

OECD *policy issues*: the country profiles are rounded off by a section outlining *policy issues*. These are issues or challenges that emerged in the course of the different country reviews, and were written up by each visiting review team. The issues vary from country to country and reflect the variety and the wide range of concerns that country-wide ECEC systems can present. Because of the nature of the profile format, the issues as presented here have had to be radically abbreviated, but a fuller and more adequate treatment can be found in each *country note*.

---

54. This report follows the conventions adopted by the EC Childcare Network (1996*b*) as illustrated by the following two examples: "children aged 0-3 years" covers children from birth up to 36 months, i.e. up to their third birthday, but does not include three-year-olds. "Children aged 3-6" covers children from 36 to 72 months *i.e.* up to their sixth birthday, but does not include 6-year-olds.

Table A.1. **Contextual table**

	Total area thousand sq. km.	Population (thousands) 1998	Population density (per sq. km.) 1998	GDP per capita USD (using current PPPs[1]) 1999	GDP per capita USD, OECD=100 (using current PPPs[1]) 1999	GDP per capita USD (using current exchange rates) 1999	Total tax receipts as a percentage of GDP 1997	Educational expenditure as a percentage of GDP 1997	Public social expenditure as a percentage of GDP 1997
Australia	7 687	18 751	2	24 400	110	20 700	29.8	5.6	17.4
Belgium	31	10 203	335	24 300	109	24 200	46.0	5.2 [2]	23.5
Czech Republic	79	10 295	131	13 100	59	5 200	38.6	5.2	19.4
Denmark	43	5 301	123	26 300	118	32 600	49.5	6.8	30.8
Finland	338	5 153	15	22 800	102	24 900	46.5	6.3	28.7
Italy	301	56 979	189	21 800	98	20 100	44.4	4.8	26.4
Netherlands	41	15 698	385	25 100	112	25 000	41.9	4.7	24.2
Norway	324	4 418	14	27 600	124	33 900	42.6	m	25.1
Portugal	92	9 979	108	16 500	74	11 100	34.2	5.8	18.2
Sweden	450	8 851	20	23 000	103	27 000	51.9	6.9	31.9
United Kingdom	245	59 237	242	22 300	100	23 900	35.4	m	21.1
United States	9 372	269 092	29	33 900	152	33 900	29.7	6.9	m
Austria	84	8 078	96	24 600	110	25 800	44.3	6.5	25.3
Canada	9 976	30 300	3	25 900	116	20 400	36.8	6.5	16.6
France	549	58 845	107	21 900	98	23 600	45.1	6.3	29.4
Germany	357	82 024	230	23 600	106	25 700	37.2	5.7	26.2
Greece	132	10 507	80	14 800	66	11 800	33.7	4.9	22.0
Hungary	93	10 114	109	10 900	49	4 800	39.4	5.2	m
Iceland	103	274	3	27 300	122	32 300	32.2	5.7	m
Ireland	70	3 705	53	25 200	113	24 200	32.8	5.0	17.6
Japan	378	126 486	335	24 500	110	34 500	28.8	4.8	m
Korea	99	46 430	467	15 900	71	8 800	21.4	7.4	4.8
Luxembourg	3	427	164	39 300	176	43 100	46.5	m	22.4
Mexico	1 996	95 675	48	8 100	36	4 900	m	5.5	7.9
New Zealand	269	3 792	14	18 000 [3]	81 [3]	14 100 [3]	36.4	m	m
Poland	313	38 666	124	8 100	36	3 900	41.2	m	24.5
Spain	505	39 371	78	18 100	81	15 000	33.7	5.7	19.9
Switzerland	41	7 106	172	27 500 [3]	123 [3]	36 000 [3]	33.8	6.0	m
Turkey	781	64 789	83	6 300 [3]	28 [3]	3 000 [3]	27.9	m	m

m: missing data.
1. Purchasing Power Parities (PPPs) are the rate of currency conversion which eliminates the differences in price levels between countries. They are used to compare the volume of GDP in different countries. PPPs are obtained by evaluating the costs of a basket of goods and services between countries for all components of GDP; PPPs are given in national currency units per US dollar.
2. Belgium (Flemish Community) only.
3. Countries still using the System of National Accounts (SNA) 1968.
Sources: OECD in Figures (2000); Education at a Glance - OECD Indicators 2000; OECD Social Expenditure Database (2000).

Australia

Auspices

In Australia, ECEC has separate and layered auspices, shared at central government level by the Department of Family and Community Services (FaCS) and the Department of Education, Training and Youth Affairs (DETYA), and in competency terms, by both Commonwealth and State Governments. Traditionally, day-care has been separate from education and seen as an issue of employment and family support, so responsibility for policy is held by the Commonwealth, represented by FaCS. States are responsible for minimum standards and licensing. Pre-school education, on the other hand, is considered the responsibility of the State Governments, although the Commonwealth Government, represented by DETYA, exerts a strong influence through national agenda setting, and provides supplementary funding for indigenous children and children with disabilities. Several inter-governmental committees exist at Commonwealth level. At State level, education, childcare and community services are sometimes unified in one department.

Developments

Starting from a low base, the Commonwealth Government committed itself to the expansion of ECEC provision and quality improvement, through fostering new investment and competition in the sector. Over the past decade, a gradual shift in emphasis has occurred from funding services directly to providing increased social support to families. The provision of fee relief to families using private centres in 1991 brought new investment into childcare from the private sector. More recently, the Child Care Benefit scheme, has increased fee subsidies for parents using approved services. With some exceptions, direct operational subsidies to community, non-profit services were removed in 1996 and 1998. Indigenous and other special services, family day care and occasional care still receive operational funding. Quality issues in long-day services (and soon family day-care) are being addressed through the *quality improvement and accreditation system* (QIAS) (see Box 3.4 in Chapter 3). In the education sector, a major emphasis is on learning outcomes, especially literacy and numeracy skills, which are seen as vital for equity reasons and for future labour market participation. The commitment of several States to improving quality can be seen from their support to curriculum development and quality standards. Both Commonwealth and State governments have at their disposal a rich resource of professional expertise in their various ministries and the research universities.

Context

Expenditure on ISCED Level 0 *institutions as a percentage of* GDP[55]: 0.1%.

Labour force rates: 67.9% of women aged 25-34 years participate in the labour force, of which almost 34.1% part-time. 47% participation of women with children below 3 years; 28% participation by lone mothers, of which 7% full-time.

Parental leave: workers have a minimum entitlement to 52 weeks unpaid, parental leave, after 12 months of continuous employment with the same employer. This leave can be shared between mother and father at any ratio, but periods of leave cannot overlap.

Attention to children with special educational needs before compulsory education begins: a) *Children with disabilities*: inclusion of children with disabilities into ECEC services is growing; b) *Children from low-income families*: the child poverty level in Australia is 12.6% after redistribution (the OECD average is 11.9%); c) *Ethnic and bilingual children*: poverty is particularly marked in the Indigenous communities (2% of population). 40% of the indigenous population is under 15 years and life expectancy is nearly twenty years less than for the white population. Significant Commonwealth investment is being channelled toward indigenous programmes. In addition, 38% of children in ECEC are from culturally diverse backgrounds (of which 4% indigenous).

---

55. See introduction to Appendix 1.

Provision

The Australian ECEC system is one of mixed public and private provision. Parental fees are subsidised by a comprehensive Child Care Benefit (CCB), paid for attendance at approved (formal) services both public and private (less benefit is paid if a parent uses a registered, informal service). Low-income families receive a higher rate of CCB, which can cover total costs.

0-1 year: parental and informal care predominate. About 4% of infants are enrolled in regulated services.

1-4 years: about 22% of children are enrolled in either full-day or part-day care, provided mainly by QIAS approved private-for-profit long day care centres (58%), QIAS approved community-based, non-profit, long day care centres (23%) and community-based, non-profit family day-care schemes (18%). Family day care is provided for children 0-12 years. Fee support is available to over 98% of parents using services (formal, approved and informal/registered) through the Child Care Benefit scheme.

4-6 years: early education services are provided through kindergartens or reception classes generally attached to schools, for 6-hours daily, during school term. Attendance in the year before compulsory schooling (at 6 years) ranges from 80.4% in Western Australia to 96.3% in Queensland.

Child-staff ratios: child-staff ratios in long day-care centres are: 5:1 for children 0-2 years; 8:1 for children 2-3 years, and 10:1 for children 3-6 years (variations occur across States). Staff are not necessarily qualified (see below). In general, long day care centres are required (depending on the State) to have one qualified staff for every 20-25 children.

Staffing and training

The staffing of ECEC varies according to the regulatory requirements of each state and territory. In general, non-school services employ a mix of trained (often two-year vocational) and untrained staff. In the case of family day-care, contact staff are not required to have a qualification, other than a First Aid diploma. In Long Day Care Centres, the need to minimise staff costs so as to limit fee increases has worked against the employment of qualified staff, whenever such staff are not a regulatory requirement (see child-staff ratios above). Although they may have longer hours, greater responsibility, fewer holiday and less planning time than teachers, the status and pay of staff in non-school services is low. Turnover rates are high and difficulties in recruiting staff are reported. Men are hardly represented in care services (3.3%) or pre-school (2.3%).

In pre-schools, a teaching qualification is required, but not necessarily with an early childhood specialisation. A teaching qualification requires normally a three- or four-year university degree. The Commonwealth and State governments fund a limited number of in-service hours for teachers and staff in the non-school sector, but day-care staff report a lack of opportunity for professional development, due to the difficulty of being released from their jobs.

OECD policy issues

Among the issues for policy attention identified by the OECD Review team for Australia were:

Understandings of childhood and early education: ECEC in Australia reveals a range of beliefs and policy directions depending on government philosophy, jurisdiction (the government department or administrative body in charge), type of setting and community perception. It was felt that a clearer vision (including a strategy framework) of Australian ECEC policy should be elaborated, drawing from the views and interests of children, families, communities, professionals and researchers across the states and territories.

System coherence and co-ordination: currently, real limitations on system coherence are imposed in Australia by the complexities of government in a federal state and the multi-layering of administration and regulation. Other difficulties arise from the vastness of the territory and the dispersion of populations.

Quality issues: it was felt that the low pay, low status and training levels of ECEC staff undermines quality, and may counterbalance the investments governments are making in the sector. In addition, attention was drawn to the poorer work conditions experienced by teachers and staff in the early childhood sector, compared to other education sectors.

Training and status of ECEC staff: the OECD team suggests that firmer regulations about the numbers of *trained* staff to be employed by long day centres and family day-care would help to improve the quality of their services, and that comprehensive in-service training at a range of levels for staff in this sector is a necessity.

Children with special educational needs: poverty and early education issues arise most acutely with regard to Indigenous children. The determined targeting of resources by recent governments towards Indigenous educational, economic, and health programmes is acknowledged. The key to the success of the new programmes will be their respectful approach to issues of self determination, cultural ownership, and for some, language.

Belgium – Flemish Community

Auspices

In the Flemish Community of Belgium, a clear division exists in responsibility for education and care. All child-care arrangements must be reported to *Kind & Gezin*, a governmental, public agency dependent on the Flemish Minister of Welfare, Health and Equal Opportunities. *Kind & Gezin* officially supervises the great majority of such arrangements and subsidises a significant number of them. In addition to providing day-care places, *Kind & Gezin* has responsibility for policy and inspection of out-of-school care. Local authorities and non-profit organisations also have a role in providing childcare, a role that is partly historical and, in some cases, partly in response to initiatives being developed by *Kind & Gezin*.

The Ministry of Education of the Flemish Community has competence for education matters in Flanders and sets the broad aims and objectives of education in the Community (the Federal Government sets the requirements for diplomas, the duration of compulsory schooling and pensions). In parallel, there is considerable autonomy to organise schools, a freedom originally established to guarantee confessional choice. Most schools and educational services fall under one of three main umbrella organisations or networks: *Official Community Education* that is, non-confessional, Flanders Community education, covering 13% of children; *Official Subsidised Education* organised by local authorities, covering 22% of children; and *Private Subsidised Education* covering 64% of pupils.

The Federal Government intervenes with regard to minimum requirements for diplomas, beginning and end of compulsory education, pensions, tax benefits for childcare costs, parental leave and career breaks, or with the regions, in employment policy.

Developments

Flemish society has become increasingly multicultural, and there is growing public awareness of immigrant issues, poverty and the need for equity. Child poverty levels have been reduced to a low level, and a main policy concern is to make regular care and early education accessible to all children who need it, irrespective of their family situation, their socio-economic background or their ethnic origin. Demand for childcare is growing rapidly, and legislation is before parliament to expand services by another 10 000 places over a period of four years. There emerges also a strong concern to improve quality in care, especially to make care settings more educational and stimulating for infants and toddlers. Much effort is being invested in professional development, especially in the subsidised sector.

In early education, a universal and well-organised system has been in place for decades. There is a firm determination to promote equity and quality across the system, and significant funds are being invested on behalf of low-income and immigrant children. Another important policy orientation is to bring pre-primary (the *kleuterschool*) and school closer together, so as to make basic education a cohesive unity. Goals are elaborated in the "Developmental Objectives" or minimum goals (knowledge, insights, skills and attitudes) considered desirable and attainable by children in primary and pre-primary classes. At the same time, there is widespread recognition that pre-primary has its own specificity, that of developing the total personality of the children. Many in-service training opportunities are offered to *kleuterschool* teachers, and new co-constructive approaches to inspection, quality improvement and control are being put into place. The research capacity of the universities and their ability to bring quality instruments and new pedagogies into the system is also another strength.

Context

Expenditure on ISCED *Level 0 institutions as a percentage of* GDP: 0.5% for Belgium as a whole.

Labour force rates: for all Belgium, 82.7% of women aged 25-34 years participate in the labour market, of which 31.5% are part-time.

Parental leave: universal paid maternity leave is 15 weeks, with partly paid parental leave to 3 months full-time or 6 months part-time before the age of 4 years.

*Attention to children with special educational needs before compulsory education begins a) Children with disabilities:*in Flanders, the tradition has been to support these children at home, but there is growing awareness of the benefits of including children with light handicaps in ECEC. Subsequent special education is well funded, though often separate from mainstream provision; *b) children from low-income families:* the child poverty level is 4.3% after redistribution; *c) Ethnic and bilingual children:* at least 5.5% of children are from immigrant backgrounds. The government makes significant investments in social exclusion and priority education programmes.

Provision

Both day-care and early education are characterised by mixed public and private provision, funded by the Flemish Government. Education from 2.5 years is free, with supplementary investments given to schools catering for low-income/ethnic areas and families. *Kleuterschool* are operated by the different networks (see above), each group being financed or subsidised by the government.

In the subsidised care sector, parents pay fees, according to income, on average, 28% of actual costs in day-care centres and 75.7% of costs in family day-care. In non-subsidised provision, parents pay the full costs. All parents are granted tax benefits to recuperate these costs, up to 80% or 450BF daily (year 2000 rates). Services are mostly used by working mothers in dual-income families, which weighs use toward middle-class parents, although statistics show that there is also a strong uptake by single-parent families.

0-1 year: in the first year, maternal and family care predominates. It is not unusual, however, for infants below the age of one year to have a place in day-care services. Because tax relief is offered to families that use care supervised by *Kind & Gezin,* the use of informal family day-care is not common.

1-3 years: 29.5% full- or half-day coverage of children in family day-care (18.4%) and day-care centres (11.1%). Normally, day-care centres are open 10-12 hours per day.

2.5-5 years: 85% coverage at 2.5 years in free pre-primary school. Almost 100% coverage at 3-4 years (at 98.4% in 1997-98). The pre-primary school opens daily (half-day Wednesday) from 8.30-15.30, with after-school care if needed.

Child-staff ratios: child-staff ratios in subsidised day-care centres are 7:1. In the *kleuterschool,* government investments to increase staff for the young children has reduced the maximum child-staff ratio to 18:1 (1997-98), but numbers can be greater or lesser depending on the time of the year.

Staffing and training: the division between care and education is reflected in the training and status of staff in each sector. Staff in subsidised day-care centres are generally trained childcare workers (*kinderverzorgster*), who have taken a vocational stream in education and are given one further year of specialisation in their field. Trainees do not receive a strong theoretical base for their future work. Family day-carers in subsidised provision are selected by interview, and receive an in-training of between four to sixty hours. Afterwards, though regularly visited and guided by *Kind & Gezin* supervisors, they benefit little from further in-training. In contrast, intensive in-training of childcare workers in the subsidised centres is provided within their contractual hours.

In the *kleuterschool*s, the *kleuteronderwijzers(essen)* (nursery school teachers) are trained at tertiary level for three years in teacher training colleges alongside primary and lower secondary teachers. In-service training is well developed in the education sector, and the Ministry of Education devolves substantial training budgets to the level of the school. The umbrella organisations are also required by the Quality Decree to engage in in-service training activities and quality inspection.

OECD policy issues

Among the issues for policy attention identified by the OECD Review team for the Flemish Community were:

Better child-staff ratios for the early years classes: traditionally in the *kleuterschool* (kindergarten), there has been no guarantee of favourable adult-child ratios or of group size for children of 30 months upwards. Since September 2000, schools have received instructions to increase the weighting of children from 2.5-3 years by 10%, and the intention is to improve this weighting further in the next years.

Co-ordination of care and education: there seems to be a need for greater co-ordination between the systems to promote coherent policy and provision. The co-operation that took place a result of the OECD visit has been a useful starting point for considering the issue.

Status and training of personnel: several issues arose in this field: a) the barriers that exist to hinder the movement of personnel from one system to another. Since September 2000, pre-primary schools can employ childcare workers; b) the relatively low status and pedagogical training of childcare workers and family day-care providers (considerably better in-service opportunities are offered to subsidised childcare centre staff); c) the scarcity of staff from ethnic origins, and the weakness of multicultural training at many levels.

Further action and research on inclusiveness: several innovative and publicly funded projects (MEQ, OVB and *Zorgverbreding*) to address the needs of immigrant children deserve to be developed and extended. Outcome targets and measures for the different groups might be also be considered, so as to measure the effectiveness of programmes.

153

Belgium – French Community

Auspices

In the French Community of Belgium, education and care are divided administratively, although brought together under the Minister of Childhood (Ministre de l'Enfance). The Minister has full competence for early care and basic education (the *école maternelle* and primary education) within the French Community. Some policy and funding responsibilities have been devolved to the two regions, Wallonie and Bruxelles-Capital.

For children from 0-3 years, the Minister relies on ONE (Office de la Naissance et de l'Enfance), a governmental, public agency responsible for mother and child health and protection, and for all aspects of childcare policy and provision. All settings, wishing to provide care to children under 6 years of age must declare themselves to the ONE, obtain its authorisation and bring their programme into conformity with the *Code de qualité de l'accueil*, decreed in May 1999.

The Minister of Childhood also designates the broad aims and objectives of basic education in the Community, which includes primary education and the *école maternelle* for children from 2.5-6 years. Most schools and educational services fall under one of three main umbrella organisations or networks: French Community Schools (non-confessional, covering 10% of children); the public network of Communal Schools, organised by local communes, covering 50% of children; and the Free or Private Schools (including the voluntary, state-aided Catholic system) covering 40% of pupils.

Developments

In the French Community, childcare and the *école maternelle* are seen as powerful tools against social exclusion, and a privileged means of integrating "at risk" children (including immigrant children) into the education system. At the same time, the *universal* right to early care and education is emphasised, and is implemented through the *école maternelle*, which is open to all children from the age of 2.5 years.

In the care sector, the wish to improve the quality of services has given rise to management reform, concertation and planning. A code of quality for child services was decreed in 1999, based on the UN Convention on the Rights of the Child, and European Union recommendations. Emphasis is placed too on training and professional development. There is high take-up of training opportunities, particularly in Brussels where the FRAJE, a training association attached to the region, has been very active (see Box 3.3 in Chapter 3). There are also efforts to create new municipal posts to co-ordinate early childhood services in different milieus.

At the *école maternelle*, the focus on quality has given rise to official guidelines (*Décret mission*), drawing attention to fundamental goals, such as developing the creativity of children, early learning, socialisation and citizenship, and the early diagnosis of disability or special need. Consultations are taking place to translate these guidelines into a curriculum that can be used by teachers in all *écoles maternelles*. In-service training is also seen as a privileged instrument to improve the understanding and professional practice of personnel. It is planned to bring together the different networks for common training sessions. The commitment of university researchers to the early childhood sector is great, and in collaboration with teachers and staff, they carry out many action-research projects on the ground. An important signal to the early childhood sector sent out by the government has been the recent decision to upgrade pre-school teacher salaries to a level equivalent to that of their primary school colleagues.

Context

Expenditure on ISCED Level 0 institutions as a percentage of GDP: 0.5% for Belgium as a whole.

Labour force rates: in Belgium, 82.7% of women aged 25-34 years participate in the labour market. 31.5% work part-time.

Parental leave: universal paid maternity leave is 15 weeks, with partly paid parental leave to 3 months full-time or 6 months part-time before the age of 4 years.

Attention to children with special educational needs before compulsory education begins: a) *Children with disabilities*: in Belgium, the tradition has been to support these children when young in the home, but there is growing awareness of the benefits of including children with light handicaps in ECEC. Special education is well funded, though often separate from mainstream provision; b) *Children from low-income families*: after redistribution mechanisms, the child poverty level for Belgium as a whole is 4.4%, but poverty can be more severe in low-income neighbourhoods in the large cities of the French Community; c) *Ethnic and bilingual children*: immigrant children constitute 12% of the basic school population, reaching 30% in Brussels. Strong government investment in social exclusion and priority education programmes exists.

Provision

In both care and education, the system is one of mixed public and private provision. Education from 2.5 years is free, with special supports for low-income/ethnic areas and families. In the care sector, parents pay fees to recognised services, according to income, from 17%-25% of actual costs. In turn, they are granted tax benefits to recuperate these costs, up to 80% or 345BF daily. In the care sector, provision is publicly subsidised and supervised when supplied by community services, and supervised only when provided by private bodies, *e.g.* private family day-care. In the education sector, *écoles maternelles* are operated by official, community and private networks – almost completely financed by the French Community Government.

0-1 year: parental care predominates, although many infants from three months are enrolled in the public crèches. Because of regulations and tax-credits paid to families for use of accredited services, there is little informal care except familial.

1-3 years: 21.5% full- or half-day coverage of children in day-care centres and a further 12% in family day-care. Further care is provided by drop-in services (*haltes-garderies*, etc.) and by informal, non-registered childminders. Normally, the registered services open 10-12 hours per day.

2.5-5 years: 85% half-day coverage from 30 months in free pre-school. Almost 100% of children are enrolled at 3-4 years. The pre-school is open daily (half-day Wednesday) from 8.30-15.30, with after-school care available if needed.

Child-staff ratios: in childcare, ratios are as follows: in centre-based day-care (*crèche*) 1 children's nurse (*puéricultrice*) for 7 children; in family day-care, 1 adult for 3 children. Crèches (18-48 places) must also employ a medical nurse and trained social worker, one of whom is generally the manager. In the *école maternelle*, the maximal child-staff ratio is 19 to 1, but in most cases, it is much less. *Puéricultrices* are often employed to assist teachers with the younger children.

Staffing and training

The division between care and education is reflected in the training and status of staff in each sector. The *puéricultrices* in the care sector have a secondary level, four-year general professional course, followed by two years (16-18 years) of child nursing, which comprises a number of paramedical courses and practical placements. Their salary level is low, about half that of a pre-school teacher. Personnel in family day-care or *maisons d'enfants* (children's centres) are required simply to have a "useful experience" although in the *maisons d'enfants*, many *puéricultrices* are found. Much in-service training is available, especially for personnel belonging to community services in Brussels. In the *école maternelle*, teachers are trained at tertiary level for three years in one of 14 higher education colleges. The Community devolves in-training budgets to the level of the school, which must organise eleven days training per year. The umbrella organisations are also required to engage in training activities and inspection of quality.

OECD policy issues

Among the issues for policy attention identified by the OECD Review team for the French Community were:

Understandings of gender roles, and the reconciliation of work and family life: there are ambiguities in the roles offered to women – in principle, equal opportunity to work, but in practice, an insufficient number of affordable childcare places, a low benefit parental leave scheme and little paternal participation in parental leave. Together, these conditions create an incentive for poorly educated mothers to leave the workforce and remain at home. Key issue here are: the level of parental leave benefit, the duration of leave, a more diversified supply of affordable services and more flexible work conditions that provide an opportunity for paternal time with children.

Understandings of childhood and early development: the construction of childhood in the French Community has been based on a clear division between care and education. Although services still remain apart, a more unified approach

155

is being adopted today, which could be further strengthened through greater co-ordination between the services, and the dissemination of a common psycho-pedagogical vision in the training of *puéricultrices* and teachers. In this regard, a unifying factor may be the Belgian tradition of the *école maternelle*, especially its understanding that early learning takes primarily through play, discovery and the child's own activity.

The coherent organisation of after-school provision: the situation on the ground is unsatisfactory for many young children, for whom after-school provision is not available or is little better than "supervision" on school premises. Both supply and quality need to be increased, the parents and networks consulted and supported, and a particular effort made to provide adequately for disadvantaged families and children.

The need to value the social role of the école maternelle: the *école maternelle* in Belgium often plays close attention to identifying and supporting children in need of special educational support. This tradition should be further strengthened as late diagnosis can lead to children "at risk" being placed in special classes in primary school, which may reinforce their sense of failure. The opening toward immigrant communities, practised in many *écoles maternelles*, should also be disseminated widely and encouraged.

Greater co-operation between the school networks and the local authorities so as to make transitions for children easier between family, care, school, or out-of-school hours.

Czech Republic

Auspices

Early education in the Czech Republic is almost entirely a public service. Kindergartens (*mateřská škola*) are part of the educational system, under the responsibility of the Ministry of Education, Youth, and Sport. Regional and municipal education authorities have increasing responsibilities, however, and centres enjoy a great deal of autonomy. Financing is drawn from multiple sources – the regional school authority (teachers' salaries, books and equipment), municipalities (running costs and capital investments) and from parental fees, while funds to improve material conditions or purchase equipment and toys are often generated through sponsoring contracts with private enterprises. Some private and church kindergartens are now in operation, though on a very small scale.

In practice, there is no longer an organised day-care system for children from 0-3 years. Only 67 crèches have survived from the previous regime, administered by the Ministry of Health. Former crèche buildings have been sold or allocated to other purposes.

Developments

Since the "velvet revolution" of 1989, the Czech Republic has renewed its links with its long tradition of early childhood education. There has been an impressive increase in diversification and pedagogical freedom. The understanding of education as conformity to accepted knowledge and social norms is giving away to a spirit of enquiry and innovation. There is a fresh appreciation of the child as a subject of rights, reflected both in the desire to lessen the pressures placed on children in pre-school institutions, and to integrate children with special needs. Pedagogical approaches and methods of work more suited to the young child's needs and mentality have been encouraged, and daily routines in kindergartens have been relaxed. Greater emphasis is placed on free play and creative expression. Innovative experiments with age-integrated classes are also current.

Decentralisation is taking place, and great efforts have been made to change the relationships between the education partners. Outreach to parents as equal partners has improved immeasurably, and men have been invited into the previously female world of kindergarten teaching (Army duty may be replaced by service as assistants in kindergartens and other institutions, bringing a young male presence – and alternative role models – to young children).

Work on the preparation of a framework curriculum for the kindergarten has begun. The new curriculum will orient kindergartens to offer systematic and appropriate programmes to young children, yet remain open enough to allow innovation and experimentation. The content of education will be worked out in five spheres: biological, psychological, interpersonal, socio-cultural and environmental. General competencies (personal, cognitive and operational) that children should acquire in the kindergarten will be set, linked with the behaviours and knowledge expected in the first cycle of primary school.

Context

Expenditure on ISCED *Level 0 institutions as a percentage of* GDP: 0.5% (the Czech background report provides a figure of 1.16% for all ECEC).

Labour force rates: in 1999, 70.1% of women aged 25-34 years participated in the labour market. 13.3% worked part-time.

Parental leave: universal paid maternity leave of 28 weeks (69% of earnings) with a flat-rate, parental leave of four years, taken almost exclusively by mothers.

157|

Attention to children with special educational needs before they enter compulsory school: a) Children with disabilities: there is growing inclusion of children with disabilities, though many special kindergartens and schools still exist, even for children with relatively light handicaps; *b) Children from low-income families:* the child poverty level is 5.9% after redistribution, and specific and means-tested benefits are available to families with young children; *c) Ethnic and bilingual children:* problems of poverty, social exclusion and education under-achievement are most acute among the Roma. Other ethnic groups, *e.g.* Polish, German, generally organise education in their own language. The settled Roma community constitutes 0.7% of the population, but according to estimates, numbers may rise to 2% of population if migrant Roma are included. High rates of unemployment are recorded among the group and levels of education are low compared to Czechs, 84% of whom complete upper secondary education. Since 1993, the government has invested in several pilot projects for Roma children, and preparatory classes for socially or culturally disadvantaged children of 6-7 years, whose entry into compulsory school had been delayed.

Provision

In early education, 3-6 years, the system is almost entirely public. It is now decentralised, with a great deal of autonomy given to each centre. Helped by falling fertility rates, sufficient numbers of places are available. Parental fees are capped at 30% of costs, and are reduced or waived for families in need. There are special supports for low-income/ethnic areas and families. Despite this, families considered to be most in need are least likely to enrol their children in pre-school settings.

0-3 years: children in this age group are cared almost exclusively by mothers and/or by informal caregivers.

3-6 years: 66.5% of children enter public fee-paying, full-day pre-school at 3 years, reaching 98% at 5-6 years. The average coverage rate for children aged 3-6 years is 86%. Children whose parents are on leave have right of access to the kindergarten for 3 days every month. Kindergartens remain open eight or more hours per day.

Child-staff ratios: child-staff ratios are 12:1, but classes will often have up to 25 children, looked after by more than one teacher for, at least, part of the day.

Staffing and training

More than 95% of teachers in the *mateřská škola* have completed four years of training (15 to 19 years) in one of the 18 training or secondary pedagogical schools in the country. Particular emphasis is placed on skills in art, music and sports, areas that traditionally have been deemed important for Czech pre-schools. All graduates are female, but increasingly fewer of them actually enter the profession. Wages are low, only 76% of a primary teacher's salary, which itself is 103% of the national average wage. Further accreditation through in-service courses has not yet been organised.

OECD policy issues

Among the issues for policy attention identified by the OECD Review team for the Czech Republic were:

An informed public discussion of gender issues and policy for children under 3: given the drastic shift in policy in recent years, it seems timely to bring together different stakeholder groups, including parents, to engage in a broad public discussion about the needs of very young children, women, and parents in modern Czech society. It seems that if this issue is not carefully addressed, the Czech Republic might face a critical shortage of ECEC provision for the coming generation of parents and children, with potential effects on women's access to the labour force and on birth rates.

Improving access to kindergartens, especially for children and families in need of special support: despite marked improvements in outreach to parents and families, socially or culturally weak groups still have serious difficulties in trusting the municipal kindergartens or entering into close relationships with kindergarten staff. As a result, children from these groups are underrepresented in kindergartens. The practice found in preparatory classes of employing bridge staff from the Romany community might be extended to the kindergartens as a promising initiative to welcome Romany children and parents into educational settings. In-service training for teachers to work with low-income and ethnic minority families also needs to be strengthened. In addition, co-ordination between local and national authorities governing health, social services and education is particularly important to serve children and families in need of special support in a comprehensive and holistic manner.

Addressing work conditions and the initial and in-service training of staff: an important area for policy attention concerns the recruitment and retention of staff, *e.g.* the ageing of present staff, and the reluctance of many young women who have completed pre-school teacher training to embark upon kindergarten teaching as a career. There is a need to improve the wages, but also the low status of the profession. Another challenge concerns the lack of men working in the profession. Some of these workforce issues may be addressed by shifting initial training to the tertiary level, although care should be taken to preserve the focus on practical skills that is a strong part of the current training. If training requirements for new staff are raised, mechanisms need also to be identified to upgrade the training of teachers who are already working in the field. There also seems to be a need for additional in-service training to work with parents in order to foster stronger co-operation between kindergartens and the home.

The need for more national research: in the light of future social and economic trends, more national research on the needs of families and children in the Czech Republic is needed to provide policy makers with reliable information. It also will be important to identify present data gaps and future needs of the early childhood field and to support ongoing data collection on public and private ECEC settings. The Ministry of Education may wish to consider building up the early childhood research capacity by financing the development of a national framework to support research and evaluation in the field.

Denmark

Auspices

In Denmark, services for children aged 0-6 years have traditionally been considered as an integral part of the social welfare system. A major aim is to support, in collaboration with parents, the development of young children and provide caring and learning environments for them while their parents are at work. The Ministry of Social Affairs has the primary responsibility for national early childhood policy, but many policy and operational matters have for long been decentralised to local authorities. The Ministry of Education has policy responsibility for pre-school classes (5/6-7 years) and SFOs (school-based, leisure-time) facilities. Within the overall aims of the Act on Social Service and the Act on the *Folkeskole* (covering primary and lower secondary education), local authorities determine the objectives and the framework for work carried out in day-care facilities and schools, and are responsible for funding and supervision. Frequently, they establish unified departments, bringing together care and education.

Developments

Despite the high coverage rates achieved by Danish ECEC services, demand continues to rise. The law requires that a place should be provided to parent(s) for each child within three months[56] of demand, but waiting lists exist in some ten municipalities. New investments by local authorities are meeting the challenge, and it is expected that places for all children will soon be available. Attention is also being focused on providing places and appropriate programmes for children at risk, *i.e.* children with low socio-economic status, immigrant children, children from dysfunctional families. A Danish language stimulation programme is available to bilingual children and families in the years prior to compulsory school.

Qualitative developments are also taking place. The traditional division in Denmark between primary education and the kindergarten is now being questioned, and seen as a challenge to be overcome through discussion and partnership. The debate is focused on the need to develop a common set of values and aims for the later years of kindergarten and the first stages of primary education. ECEC is seen to include structured "learning activities in a caring environment", as well as play, informal learning and social development. The non-compulsory kindergarten class at the start of the *Folkeskole* (the basic school) is to a large extent characterised by this approach. Co-operation and cohesion between the day-care system (*i.e.* the kindergartens) the school system and leisure-time activities are given special attention in the project *Folkeskole* 2000. With the help of their pedagogical advisors, some municipalities are pushing ahead with plans to make of their kindergartens and schools, active *learning centres* which will develop their own learning plans. In addition, the Ministry of Social Affairs, in collaboration with the National Association of Local Authorities in Denmark created a working group in 1996 to improve quality, and develop new methods for educational work in kindergartens. Other initiatives are being considered, which include reforms in staff training and curriculum guidelines.

Context

Expenditure on ISCED Level 0 institutions as a percentage of GDP: 1.1% (the Danish background report provides a figure of 2.37% for all ECEC).

Labour force rates: in 1999, 81.6% of women aged 25-34 years participated in the labour market. 24.4% worked part-time.

Parental leave: universal paid maternity leave of 28 weeks for mothers + 2 weeks paternity leave paid at 100% salary level (public sector employees and increasingly private sector). Possibility of another 26 weeks at 60% of unemployment benefit. In many municipalities, parents returning to work after 26 weeks have the guarantee of an immediate childcare place for their child, but difficulties are often experienced by parents at this stage.

---

56. After parental leave, within four weeks, provided that parents have requested a place within the time framework set by the municipality.

Attention to children with special educational needs before they enter compulsory school: a) *Children with disabilities*: inclusion of children with disabilities in all early services and schools is customary; b) *Children from low-income families*: the child poverty level is 5.1% after redistribution; c) *Ethnic and bilingual children*: immigrants form 4.1% of the Danish population, and it is estimated that bilingual children will constitute 9% of pupils this year. In February 2000, the government published an overall action plan for the improved integration of these children. It is now mandatory for local authorities to offer language-stimulation activities to bilingual children from 4-5/6 years. Language activities mostly take the form of intensified Danish language coaching in kindergarten and in the first years of primary education. When children are not in the kindergarten system, 15 hours per week of Danish language contact may be offered to families in their own home.

Provision

The system is predominantly a public service, supervised by local authorities and funded from local taxes and central government grants. Fees are capped for parents at 30-33% of running costs, with poorer families using services free of charge or at reduced rates. Major forms of provision are:

i) Day-care facilities (*dagtilbud*) for children from 6 months to 6 years, which are divided into family day-care (*kommunal dagplaje*), centre-based day-care (crèche, age-integrated centres and kindergartens) and independent day-care facilities. 70% of day-care facilities are operated by public, community services. They are supplemented by independent facilities and networks (30%) that offer parents further choice. To receive municipal grants independent providers must work in conjunction with the local authority and observe local authority regulations and operating guidelines.

ii) Kindergarten classes (*bornehaveklasse*) for children 5/6-7 years (7 is the compulsory school age). The kindergarten class, led principally by a pedagogue, takes place in the primary school (*Folkeskole*) and is free. Teaching in the kindergarten class must be developmental and play-based. Approximately half of all public schools run a programme called "integrated school start" where pupils from pre-school classes and 1st and 2nd classes may be taught in age integrated groups. In recent years, emergent literacy approaches have been gaining ground in the kindergarten class.

iii) Leisure time centres and school-based, leisure time facilities (*fritidshjem and* SFO facilities). Out-of-school provision is fee paying, but is massively enrolled, with 81% of 6-9 years.

0-1 year: parental care predominates, but from the age of six months or so, just over 22% of parents use the services of a registered family day-care, and 3% of babies are in crèches. Informal care outside the family is little used.

1-3 years: 68% of children are enrolled in day-care facilities in this period; family day-care predominates (45%) especially in rural areas, with age-integrated facilities (14%) and *creche* (12%) having next preference.

3-5 years: on average 88.5% of 4-year-old children are enrolled, 58% of children in kindergartens and 33% in age-integrated centres. Furthermore, there are 15 hour-programmes for bilingual children who are not attending the day care system.

5/6-7 years: 98% enrolment in free pre-school class in *Folkeskole*, with wrap around care provided for them in fee-paying, integrated services or leisure-time facilities.

Child-staff ratios: child-staff ratios in 1999 per full-time adult were as follows: *crèche* (0-3 year olds) 3:1; *kindergarten* (3-7 years) 6 or 7 children to 1 trained adult; *age-integrated facility* (0-7 years) 6:1; *special day-care* 3 children to 2 trained adults; *out-of-school care* 9 or 10 children to 1 trained adult.

Staffing and training

With the exception of family day-care, all facilities have a manager and deputy-manager, both of whom must be qualified pedagogues. Pedagogues (social educators) – who are the lead personnel in all facilities, including kindergarten class – are trained for 3.5 years at tertiary level in Centres of Further Education. *Assistants* are now offered an adult education or vocational training course for 18 months. Much in-service training is available. There is no mandatory training for family day-carers, but all receive at least three weeks training, and have access to intensive supervision and in-service training. Men make up 8% of employees in day-care facilities for children aged 6 months to 6 years, and make up 25% of staff in out-of-school care. Work conditions/salaries of educators are considered satisfactory.

OECD policy issues

Among the issues for policy attention identified by the OECD Review team for Denmark were:

Differences in policy implementation across municipalities: policies and guidelines for children in Denmark are promoted at national level by several ministries. These policies and guidelines are then locally interpreted by the 275 different

161

municipalities, which establish their own ECEC goals. Independence leads, at times, to some diversity in approach, provision and quality. Guidance may be needed from the ministries as to what are the national objectives for early childhood development and education, and how the achievement of these goals are to be monitored in a systematic way.

The traditional division between kindergarten and primary school, between "development" and "education": a consequence of the division is the lack of common goals for children, and of a shared learning theory and educational approach. Progress toward a more unified vision has been made in recent years with the new focus on the learning needs of young children. Teachers and pedagogues co-operate closely in the integrated school start programme, to provide "learning experiences in a caring environment". These efforts need to be reinforced, while respecting the rhythms of children and their fundamental need of companionship, play and self-determination.

Issues related to staffing and training: staff recruitment, initial and in-service training are well developed in Denmark, but concern was expressed about differences in working conditions and the difficulty of movement between the care and education sectors. A shared responsibility for both teaching and leisure hours may be a more effective use of financial resources and the different educational competencies of staff, while providing better continuity and flexibility for children across the different services.

Issues relating to access: two groups of children have limited access to early education and care, viz. infants between 6 and 9 months and the children of the New Danes or immigrants. For infants, an extension of universal parental leave to one year may be a solution to consider, while, in parallel, requiring municipalities to include the 6 to 12 months period among the guaranteed places. The second group with insufficient access are the children of immigrants, who frequently do not access services until the kindergarten class. The response of the public authorities has been to promote language courses, which may leave unanswered other important issues.

Finland

Auspices

Central responsibility for the education and care of young children 0-6 years falls to the Ministry of Social Affairs and Health, assisted by its research agency, STAKES. Early childhood policy is intended to support the development and learning of young children and enable them to become ethically responsible members of society. The National Agency for Education has chief responsibility for the curricular orientation of pre-school education for 6-year olds.

Developments

The ECEC system in Finland is a well-developed and stable system much appreciated by parents. It is characterised by a sensitivity to the rights of the child and an avowed concern for equality and fairness throughout the system. One of its most notable features is the subjective and unconditional right of every child to have a place during the years, 1 to 6, or from the end of parental leave to the beginning of primary school. This unconditional right also includes the right of parents to choose a home care allowance instead of municipal day-care for their child. Services are very affordable to parents. Free, pre-school education for the 6-year olds – based on the "educare" concept in which care, education and instruction are combined – has become a reality since August 2000. There is much commitment across the two involved ministries to the pre-school reform, and much effort has been invested by the National Board of Education in formulating a new curriculum to embrace the pre-school year and the first two years of primary school. In parallel, STAKES is about to develop a curriculum to guide the organisation and content of ECEC programmes. ECEC in Finland is also gaining a foothold as a teaching and research discipline in the universities and polytechnics. Kindergarten teachers are highly trained and graduate after three to four years as Bachelors of Early Childhood Education, some of them going on to Master's level. Municipalities encourage and fund research, bringing together university researchers and ECEC personnel in common research projects. A new focus for research and the early childhood centres is the broader community and family context of a child's life. Greater outreach to parents is being practised, seeing them as not only clients but as valued pedagogical partners.

Context

Expenditure on ISCED *Level 0 institutions as a percentage of* GDP: 0.4% (the Finnish background report provides a figure 1.43% of GDP for all ECEC).

Labour force rates: in 1999, 70% of women aged 25-34 years participated in the labour market. 13% worked part-time.

Parental and child care leave: universal 18 weeks maternity leave + 26 weeks parental leave paid at 60-70% of salary. A further paternity leave of three weeks maximum is also granted, which can be taken by fathers during maternity and/or parental leave time. In addition, for those parents opting not to enrol their children in municipal day-care, a flat-rate, three-year child care leave can be taken, or a six-year partial child care leave.

Attention to children with special educational needs before they enter compulsory school: a) Children with disabilities: the inclusion of children with disabilities is customary in all ECEC services, and they have priority admission to services; *b) Children from low-income groups*: the child poverty rate in Finland is 4.3% after redistribution; *c) Ethnic and bilingual children*: apart from the Swedish-speaking population (6%), there are no significant language or ethnic minorities in Finland. Much attention and investment is devoted to the small indigenous Sami population (only 121 children under 7). New immigrants from Somali and other countries have access to immersion programmes and special courses in schools, but to date, young children from such groups do not generally attend childcare centres, because of family custom or because the present municipal services are not attractive to them. The municipalities in which there is some small concentration of immigrants, for example, in Helsinki and the surrounding municipalities, have begun to make policy to support immigrant families and to create experimental programmes for them.

Provision

The ECEC system in Finland is predominantly public with some private provision. In general, municipalities provide services directly through municipal day-care centres (*päiväkoti*), family day-care homes/places or pre-school groups (the main forms of provision), but they may also outsource to private providers (about 5% of total provision) or support voluntary services, *e.g.* the play groups provided by the Lutheran Church. Play groups and family circles run by voluntary organisations and the Church are much in demand, as the 1973 Act on Children's Care did not especially mention afternoon care. The municipalities have the obligation to organise day-care (including afternoon care) for all children who need it, but only children under 7 years have an unconditional right to be taken in charge. Parents may also request a private childcare allowance (700FIM per month) to be paid by the municipality to the childminder or day-care centre of their choice.

Every child in Finland under compulsory school age (7 years) has an unconditional right to early care and education, to be provided by the local authority once parental leave comes to an end. This right is scrupulously respected in Finland, and problems of access are found most usually in isolated rural areas in which children may be very dispersed. Affordability is not an issue, as all together, client fees cover only 15% of costs, the rest being subsidised by state and local authority taxes. Parents pay eleven months only per annum, although their child's place is available during holidays also. No fee is charged for low-income families, while the highest fee cannot be more than FIM1 100 per month (c. $150). Pre-school hours for the 6 year olds are free.

0-1 year: almost all children are cared for by parents or through informal family care.

1-3 years: about 24% of children are in ECEC services during this period, of which 54% in family day-care and 46% in childcare centres. Services are open 10-12 hours daily, and almost all children take full-time places.

3-6 years: 54% of children from this age group attend, generally full-time in childcare centres, with another 12% in part-time provision.

6 year olds: 78% of children currently attend the pre-school class, either in the kindergarten (90%) or in schools (10%, but a growing trend). Forecasts predict that about 90% of the age group (60 000) will participate in the new pre-school amounting to 18-20 hours per week (700-760 hours annual), which began in August 2000.

Child-staff ratios: child-staff ratios are low in Finland: in full-time day-care centres, there should be at least 1 trained adult for every 4 children under 3, and 1 child nurse or kindergarten teacher for every 7 children over 3 years. In family day-care, the ratio is 4-5 children per day-care parent. In part-day services, the ratio is 13 children per one child nurse or kindergarten teacher.

Staffing and training

Lead educational staff in *päiväkoti* settings are trained as pedagogues (social educators) for over three years at tertiary level. Auxiliary staff have an upper-secondary qualification and are trained nursery assistants or paediatric nurses. Heads of centres generally receive further training. Family day-carers are not required to have a qualification, but they are well-protected with the same social benefits as other ECEC staff. At present, a vocational training qualification of 40 credits has just begun for them.

OECD policy issues

Among the issues for policy attention identified by the OECD Review team for Finland were:

The possible negative effects of the prolonged child home care allowance: many of the children, whom policy-makers would like to see come early into the system, remain at home. The position of their mothers in the labour market is weakened, and domestic stereotypes are reinforced.

The weakness of provision for children outside school hours: the unconditional entitlement of children to day-care did not include afternoon care. Consequently, the majority of municipalities excluded out-of-school care from their list of responsibilities. The parishes (with trained personnel) and voluntary organisations often provide afternoon care, but the leadership and funding of the municipalities is needed.

The variability of in-service training: access to in-service training opportunities depends essentially on the interest shown by municipalities. A more stable base for training needs to be found.

The effective co-operation forged during the recent curricular reforms between the Ministry of Social Affairs and Health /STAKES and the Education sector should be continued.

Further attention to the issue of monitoring the ECEC system and evaluating quality: the 1994 Local Government Act decentralised much responsibility for ECEC to the municipalities, generally with good effect. However, governmental and local authorities may wish to consider the need for a national steering system to orient municipal policy, monitor quality and remain in touch with the changing needs of Finnish children and families.

Italy

Auspices

Policy responsibility for ECEC in Italy is split between the Ministry of Education for the *scuola materna* (nursery school) catering for the 3-6 year olds, and the regions and municipalities for the *asili nidi* catering for infants and toddlers. A proposal has been made to give responsibility for the whole age group to the Ministry of Education, and is still under discussion in Parliament. For the moment, the Ministry of Education is responsible for educational orientation, quality inspection and evaluation of the *scuola materna* system, but its regulations are not necessarily applied in non-state *scuole materne*. At local level, in response to community demand, municipalities may provide and operate services, using part of their own funding. The region supplements municipal budgets, through the distribution of the employer's 1% contribution to social funds (devoted, in principle, to infants and toddlers). The region is also responsible for financing buildings and training.

Developments

Though reaching only 6% of children (figures from 1991 Census), several municipal ECEC programmes in Italy for children under 3 are recognised as outstanding. Because of divisions of competencies, these programmes are predominantly regional and local. A concerted effort has not yet been made to bring successful programmes to scale across Italy, although a significant proportion of the children in the age-group 1-3 years are looked after outside the home by relatives and informal childminders. Some important twinning initiatives between municipalities in the north and south of Italy have been launched, with the aim of sharing knowledge and expertise in creating and managing ECEC projects. A major national initiative is the current reform in staff training. In the future, co-ordinators of the *asili nidi* will have a university degree, and other contact staff will require a three-year tertiary diploma.

Developments for the 3-6 year olds are also far-reaching. Again, a staff-training reform is under way: in the *scuola materna* system, and teachers will have in the future a university degree. Enrolment rates in the *scuole materne* are climbing steadily higher, and achieve mass participation, over 90% of the 3-6 age group. The Ministry of Education, municipalities and the private providers are moving toward greater collaboration. A large number of *scuole materne* are now under State control (52%, but enrolling over 57% of children), and enjoy more autonomous management (Bassanini Law). Many *scuole materne*, funded initially through the ASCANIO project, have experimented with new interpretations of school organisation, curriculum methodologies and evaluation techniques.

Context

Expenditure on ISCED *Level 0 institutions as a percentage of* GDP: 0.4%.

Labour force rates: in 1999, 63% of women aged 25-34 years participated in the labour market. 17.1% worked part-time.

Parental leave: five months maternity leave at 100% earnings and 10 months parental leave at 30% earnings. Incentives are also offered to employers to provide opportunities for part-time or flexible work hours to parents of young children.

Attention to children with special educational needs before their entry into school: a) Children with disabilities: general inclusion of children with disabilities into ECEC and schools is the rule, with reduced group sizes and special needs teachers at their disposal; *b) Children from low-income families:* the child poverty level in Italy is 20.5% after redistribution (OECD average is 11.9%), but the national figure covers wide regional variations; *c) Ethnic and bilingual children:* The Ministry of Social Solidarity has increased investment and programmes for immigrant groups, estimated over one million, with many Moroccan, Albanian and Romany children at risk. It is reported that many immigrant children are on waiting lists – with Italian children – for entry into *scuole materne* in Rome and other large urban centres.

Provision

Three main types of provision are found in Italy:

i) The *asilo nido* for children under 3, which enrols about 6% of children (enrolments are, in fact, declining), and is open 8-12 hours daily. Most of the provision is sponsored and funded by municipalities, generally in the north of Italy, where levels of female work force participation and childcare provision reach northern European levels, *e.g.* the city of Bologna enrols 30% of the age-group 0-3 years. Fees differ according to municipality and the ability of parents to pay, and range from 90-460 Euros monthly, that is, on average, 12% of disposable income.

ii) The *scuola materna* for the 3- to 6-year olds which enrols in the year before entry into compulsory school (age 6) 95% of children. About 57% of *scuole materne* are now under the direct responsibility of the Ministry of Education. The private sector organises and operates 29% of *scuole materne*, most of which are confessional, and funded by parental fees and to some extent by the State and the regions. Municipalities fund and organise a further 14% of early education provision. The *scuola materna* offers a full day programme, from 8.30 a.m. to 16.30 p.m. from September to June, with municipal services generally offering summer programmes. Attendance at state and municipal *scuola materna* (combined, c.71% of provision) is free, except for meals. Modest fees are charged in the confessional *scuola materna* (18% of provision), as these services receive some regional funds. Other private providers (c. 11% of provision) may charge higher fees, but many private services are, in fact, non-profit.

iii) *Integrated municipal services*. Typically, these services combine care and education, and although they may remain institutionally divided, they are considered essentially as educational services for children 1-6. Among the best known are the municipal programmes of Reggio Emilia. Municipal services may also include new service typologies that are characterised by integrated, inter-generational approaches, with outreach to families and children who normally would not have opportunities to interact and socialise with others.

0-1 year: most care is parental, supplemented by informal family care.

1-3 years: children are looked after in the following ways: 27% home care; 48% relatives or informal care; 15% by a child-minder in the home; 6% in *asili nidi* (open full day for 11 months); and 2% each fathers and family care.

3-6 years: from 70%-90% of children (depending on region) attend *scuole materne* from 3 years, reaching a national coverage of over 96% in year 5-6.

Child-staff ratios: the established ratios are: 7:1 in the *nido*, 8:1 for complementary services outside the home, and 3:1 for services inside the home. Ratios are higher in the *scuola materna*: 20-28 children per teacher.

Staffing and training

At the moment, radical reforms are taking place, in the staff training field (see "Developments" above). In the *scuola materna*, teachers are currently paid at the same rates as primary teachers, and conditions of work are good. The State provides them with many opportunities for in-service training. Conditions for staff in the *nidi* are much less satisfactory. Although often as highly trained, these staff have less pay, longer working hours, less status and access to in-service training than teachers in the *scuola materna*. Limited opportunities for advancement can lead to high rates of turnover and little motivation to take on professional development courses.

OECD policy issues

Among the issues for policy attention identified by the OECD Review team for Italy were:

Understandings of childhood and ECEC: in terms of state intervention, the early childhood system in Italy has been focused most strongly on the 3-6 year olds. There is an urgent need for the State to take on greater responsibility to meet the needs of children under 3 and their parents. The recent extension of paid parental leave has been a significant step forward. Further support to municipalities to extend their integrated programmes would help to address the learning and socialisation needs of infants and toddlers, even when being cared for by a parent.

Co-ordination of administrations and services: fragmentation of responsibility has been a longstanding obstacle to the coherence of ECEC services in Italy. A need is perceived for increased co-ordination of policy formulation and planning both vertically (state, regional and municipal levels) and horizontally (across state, municipal and private providers). More collaborative projects between the different partners may be useful, *e.g.* the creation, both at national and regional levels, of a network of experts drawn from the different constituencies to guide the new teacher training or other initiatives.

The effectiveness of policy formulation and its actual outreach to the municipalities and regions: basic texts governing ECEC services are not necessarily applicable in parts of the private system. More effective monitoring of the system is needed. Standards need to be developed enabling internal evaluation and communication to the public as to how resources and services are managed. Integrated in-service training for administrators and teachers from the different networks is recommended.

After-school provision: the low provision of publicly-funded after-school and leisure-time care needs attention, particularly as in some parts of the country, non-state *scuole materne* and elementary schools are open only in the morning.

Dissemination of research and good practice: Italian early childhood educators have a wealth of knowledge about young children, and many Italian programmes are recognised world-wide for their high quality. To date, however, much of what has been learned in the various cities and schools in Italy has remained in those settings, to the benefit of small numbers of children and their families. In spite of the growing frequency of local, regional, and national conferences for teachers of the *asilo nido* and *scuola dell'infanzia*, there is still no nation-wide system for insuring that all Italian early childhood educators have access to the new understandings and innovations that have been developed in Italy.

Netherlands

Auspices

ECEC policy and provision in the Netherlands is a shared responsibility between national, provincial and local governments. The national government takes on those tasks that can be more efficiently organised at national level, *e.g.* legislation, rules and regulations, developing policy frameworks, formulating national standards and attainment targets, promoting innovations, national monitoring and evaluations of quality. At central government level, two ministries have major responsibility for young children. The Ministry of Health, Welfare and Sport (VWS), has responsibility for family support, socio-educational activities and the funding and supervision of out-of-home childcare. The Ministry of Education, Culture and Science (OCenW) is responsible for children in primary education from 4-6 years (compulsory schooling begins at 5 years but children remain in the early years cycle up to 6 years). In addition to the different levels of local government, other major bodies are expected to play a role in decision making and implementing early childhood policy, viz. the employers, unions, parent, youth and other professional organisations.

Developments

After a period of decentralisation, the Dutch Government is moving toward an integrated framework of services for young children from 0-6 years, crossing traditional education, social welfare and preventive youth healthcare lines, and achieving consensus with local authorities about ECEC policy goals. Much work has been done to tighten up regulatory frameworks, training regimes and quality control. National standards and attainment targets are becoming better known. A special focus is given to children "at risk", including ethnic or bilingual children, toward whom increasing government and local authority investments are being made. Another striking feature of Dutch early childhood policy has been the use of an experimental phase to trial innovative programmes in ECEC. A number of such programmes are now being mainstreamed to the advantage of children both in school and outside. Dutch governments have also succeeded in involving employers in the ECEC sector as a major funder of childcare provision.

Context

Expenditure on ISCED *Level 0 institutions as a percentage of* GDP: 0.4%. The Dutch background report and further communications from the Ministries provide information of massive new investments in ECEC both by central government and municipalities, especially toward children "at risk".

Labour force rates: in 1999, 78.5% of women aged 25-34 years participated in the labour force. 55.7% worked part time.

Parental leave: 16 weeks maternity leave at 100% earnings + non-paid, partial leave (must work 50% of regular working hours per week) up to six months. Family-friendly work policies have been introduced and initiatives to bring flexibility into the length and timing of work hours.

Attention to children with special educational needs before their entry into compulsory school: a) Children with disabilities: with a growing awareness of the benefits of including children with light handicaps in ECEC, more children are being integrated into mainstream services. Subsequent special education is well funded, though often apart; *b) Children from low-income families:* the child poverty rate is 7.7% after redistribution; *c) Ethnic and bilingual children:* the immigrant population is significant in the Netherlands: 13% of children between 0-5 years are from ethnic or bilingual backgrounds, mainly concentrated in the large cities. Government and local authorities make important investments in social integration and targeted educational programmes.

Provision

Three "circles of provision" have been created around the child and family i) *General provision* for young children aged 0-6 years; ii) *Interventions* toward families and children who need special attention, and iii) *Specialised or intensive forms of help for children with special education needs* (SEN).

General provision includes childcare in *childcare centres* for 0-4 years (generally full-day or half-day), *family day-care* (for the youngest children) and *out-of-school care* for the 4-12 year olds. Each type of provision has its own aim, background, funding system and governing structure. Childcare for 0-4 years is used by about 20% of children, out-of-school care is used by 5.3% of children; and places in family day-care amount to about 10% of the total volume of childcare for 0-12 year olds. There are also *playgroups* (used by over 50% of 2-4 year olds) and *pre-primary education* for 4-6 year olds which takes place in the *basisschool* and is the first stage (though non-compulsory) of primary education (100% enrolment). Primary education is free. Two-thirds of schools are privately managed, but all are fully publicly funded.

Childcare provision is private (both for-profit and non-profit) but publicly co-funded. Though the parental share of total costs is high (over 40%), childcare costs are subsidised by government and employers. Employers are an important stakeholder, either setting up their own childcare services or, more usually, purchasing or renting "company places" in childcare centres. These places represented about 50% of all childcare places for 0-4 year olds in 1998. Cost ceilings are calculated by the Ministry of Health, Welfare and Sport. Depending on income, costs to parents range from 6%-21% of net family income for a full-time place in childcare. Parental fees are related to the actual use of childcare, and some costs can be deducted from income tax. The aim of government is to fund childcare equally through (local) government, employers and parental fees.

Childcare provision mainly targets families with two working parents, resulting in a marked tendency for middle- and high-income parents to use services more than low-income families. Despite a fourfold increase in places in the nineties, the demand for day-care places still outstrips supply in the Netherlands.

Playgroups are the most popular form of provision for 2-4 year olds in the Netherlands, usually established by private bodies with the legal status of foundations. Many of these foundations are independent; others are part of a larger co-operative structure, frequently a childcare organisation or general welfare foundation. Children usually visit the playgroups twice a week (2-3 hours per visit) to play with their peers or participate in an intervention programme. Almost all playgroup provision is subsidised by local government, but parental contributions are also demanded, often income-related. Special efforts are directed to children at risk (children from low-income families and from ethnic minorities) in both playgroups and primary schools. In addition to the *Law On Funding Education Disadvantage*, further significant investments are planned – 100 million guilders each by central and local governments – in the effort to expand playgroups and provide more intensive programmes in schools and outside school.

Child-staff ratios: child-staff ratios in childcare are set for each age cohort. One qualified group leader (either MBO or HBO level, see below) must be assigned to every 4 children, ages 0-1; to 5 children, ages 1-2; to 6 children, ages 2-3; to 8 children, ages 3-4; and to 10 children, ages 4-12. Staff ratios in the early years of the basic school are higher, but have been reduced recently to 1:20. As large investments are being made to improve general quality and to integrate more effectively children at risk, it is probable that class sizes may be reduced further.

Staff training and ratios

The status of staff, almost wholly female, has traditionally been low, particularly in the day-care and playgroup sector. Acute recruitment problems and staff shortages are now imminent but efforts are being made to address the issue through raising wages and improving secondary labour conditions. ECEC workers in contact with children must have, in principle, a higher professional qualification, either a HBO (four-year tertiary, non-university qualification) or an MBO (a senior secondary level, vocational education qualification of two-three years). Quality regulations with regard to childcare also apply to the out-of-school care and to play-groups, including staff qualifications. In the education sector, teaching staff are trained for four years in the PABOs or primary teaching training colleges (HBO), as polyvalent teachers who can work in the entire 4-12 year age range. They take, however, a specialisation for either the age group 4-8 years or 5-12 years. Regardless of what class they teach, all teachers are now paid at equal rates.

OECD policy issues

Among the issues for policy attention identified by the OECD Review team for the Netherlands were:

Coherence and co-ordination of services: during the early years of decentralisation, the co-ordination and coherence of the system was often stretched in terms of management, training and categorisation of personnel, equitable access and quality control.

Understandings of childhood and early education: during the early 90s, ECEC was mainly seen from a protection and care angle. Progress is being made, particularly in playgroup and early primary school provision, where a number of improved educational programme are coming on stream. However, the institutional division between care and education still remains, leading to quite separate treatment of infant/toddlers and pre-schoolers.

Greater support to parents: the funding of Dutch ECEC services relies heavily on parents in terms of fees, opportunity costs and daily time devoted to children, a contribution borne in particular by mothers. The review team recommends further attention to gender issues. A reduction of costs to parents may also be necessary, particularly to encourage greater use of services by low-income parents. The parental contribution to child-rearing could further be supported by expanded maternity and parental leave and the provision of more out-of-school care.

Staffing and training: imminent staff shortages may be explained by a combination of factors, but within the care sector, relatively low status, uncertainty about career paths, poorer work conditions and wages, are issues that merit attention.

Norway

Auspices

In Norway, responsibility for ECEC policy lies with the Ministry of Children and Family Affairs (BFD), and within the ministry, to the Department of Family Affairs, Child Care and Gender Equality. BFD co-ordinates all matters on early childhood and has convened a cross-ministerial Committee for Child and Youth issues, which meets regularly at senior official level. The Ministry of Education, Research and Church Affairs has responsibility for schools, out-of-school care and the training of teachers in general. In recent years, much responsibility has been devolved to Norway's 19 counties and 435 *kommuner* or municipalities, which for the most part, have unified school and early childhood services into one department. The county governor administers the State grants to *familiebarnehager* (family day-care), *barnehager* (kindergarten), and *apen barnehager* (open kindergartens or drop-in centres for parent and child, led by a trained pre-school teacher). The county also informs and supports the different municipalities in the region on ECEC questions and policy. There is a national regulatory framework for *barnehager*, the Barnehager Act, 1995. An important *Framework Plan for Barnehager* was elaborated in 1996, which provides guidelines to *barnehager* concerning values and objectives, curricular aims, and pedagogical approaches.

Developments

In Norway, an integrated system of services for children from 0 to 6, with a well-established and quite extensive system of publicly-funded *barnehage* has existed for many years. Underpinning the system is a well articulated vision of children, both individually and as a social group, of their place in society and their relationship with the environment.

For 2001, the Norwegian Government has committed itself to increased funding of *barnehager*, so as to avoid excluding certain categories of children because of costs to parents. The government aims that by 2005, state grants will cover 50% of costs, municipalities will underwrite 30%, leaving a maximum 20% to parents. These measures have still to be agreed by the municipalities. In addition, as access had been variable across Norway, it is a political priority to achieve universal access for all children under 6 years. From figures supplied by the Ministry, full access (based on a coverage rate of 80% but not necessarily meeting full demand) for children over 3 has been reached this year, with full access for the younger children being postponed to 2003. Plans to recruit up to 20% male workers in the *barnehager* have also been renewed, but using present means, these goals may be difficult to achieve.

Quality issues are also being addressed in these new initiatives. A new, three-year programme has been announced to improve overall quality in the *barnehage*. Special attention will be paid to children with special educational needs, staff recruitment will be broadened and improved, while parents as consumers will be consulted more widely about their needs and expectations with regard to opening hours and programmes. The *barnehage* has an important role in terms of preventive child welfare, and supports will be provided to enable it to accompany effectively children with disabilities, children from low-income families and bilingual children.

Context

Expenditure on ISCED Level 0 *institutions as a percentage of* GDP: 0.6%.

Labour force rates: in 1999, 81.4% of women aged 25-34 years participated in the labour force. 37.3% worked part time.

Parental leave support: universal 52 weeks maternity leave at 80% earnings (or 42 weeks at 100%). A one month paternity leave is included in this quota. Time accounts are used to enable parents to combine partial parental leave with flexible work hours.

Attention to children with special educational needs before they enter compulsory schooling: a) *Children with disabilities*: general inclusion of children with disabilities, who have a priority right to services. In 1997, nearly 2% of children in *barnehager*

171

had a disability, and 3% received additional support; *b) Children from low-income families*: The child poverty rate in Norway is 3.9% after redistribution; *c) Ethnic and bilingual children*: Norway has an indigenous ethnic group, the Sami who constitute 1.7% of the population. Sami language kindergartens are funded generously whenever there is a concentration of Sami families. New immigrant groups constitute 3% of the population, with 28,000 children in primary schools (just less than 6% of school population) registered as non-native speaking children. Less than 40% of these children attend a *barnehager* in the larger towns. The government has funded the hiring of minority ethnic workers in *barnehager*, but largely as bilingual assistants rather then as pedagogical staff.

Provision

47% of *barnehager* are public (municipal) and cater for 58% of children using the service. Private *barnehager* are more numerous but smaller, and cater for 42% of children. Both receive subsidies from the government amounting to 32% (public) and 38% (private) for their costs. Municipalities also have the duty to provide funding to their own and private providers, but often fail to support adequately private providers. Costs to parents range – depending on the municipality, income and the type of care chosen – from 28%-45% of actual costs (see "Developments" above). In addition to family allowances and lone parent (22% of families) allowances, all parents are allowed tax deductions to cover care and kindergarten costs. Research shows that low-income parents pay proportionally higher for a place in a kindergarten (c. 19.5% of income) compared to middle- (11%) and high-income families (c. 8%). There is also a Cash Benefit scheme that provides a cash grant to a parent who looks after a child at home, or who places a child in an ECEC context that does not receive state grants (*e.g.* with a childminder). The amount of the grant is almost equivalent to the state subsidy per child paid to kindergartens, *i.e.* about $400 per month. In principle, there are sufficient places for all children over 3 years in grant maintained *barnehager*, as the lowering of the school age to 6 years freed many places. Provision rates are as follows:

0-1 year: care is predominantly home care by parents. Only 2% of children are in centre-based care.

1-4 years: over 48% of enrolment. Given the high participation of mothers in the work force, it may be presumed that many parents are choosing to use family and informal child-minding. The goal of the Ministry is to have full coverage (meeting demand) for children under 3 years by the year 2003.

4-6 years: currently, demand is considered fully met with enrolments of just 80% of the age group.

Child-staff ratios: for children 0-3 years, the ratio is 7-9 children per trained pre-school teacher. For children 3-6 years, the ratio is 14-18 children per trained pre-school teacher; and for children in family day-care, a trained pre-school teacher must be available for every 30 children. In addition, the 1995 Act also stipulates that the number and level of staff must be sufficient to carry out satisfactory educational activities based on the Framework Plan.

Staffing and training

Head teachers and teachers in kindergartens have 2-3 years tertiary level training at one of the state (17) or Christian (2) university colleges. About a third of trained staff in Norwegian *barnehager* are ECEC teachers, a relatively low proportion of lead personnel. Further, because of recruitment shortages linked to the expansion of the system, only 80% have a formal qualification. Their status, pay and working condition compare unfavourably to those of primary school teachers. Assistants who make up the bulk of the staff, have no particular qualification, but with the 1994 reform of upper secondary education, assistants in the future will have the secondary level diploma of "child and youth worker". Men make up 6.6% of total kindergarten staff. A ministerial plan 1997-2000 aimed to bring the proportion of men up to 20% by the end of 2000. Issues of status, pay and working conditions may need further consideration before the goal can be achieved.

OECD policy issues

Among the issues for policy attention identified by the OECD Review team for Norway were:

Issues of equity and access: despite the high level of subsidy and policy attention provided, inequalities exist both in access (provision varies with respect to areas and social groups) and funding (private *barnehager* receiving much less support from municipalities than public). The commitment to more government spending, achieving consensus with the municipalities about national ECEC goals, and greater attention to children in need of special support are important contributions to addressing these inequalities.

Issues of diversity: in recent decades, diversity issues have become a challenge for Norwegian society. An ECEC system in which multi-cultural recruitment and a greater emphasis in programmes on tolerance and anti-racist practice can be formative for young children, and give confidence to their families. A challenge is posed to provide a values framework that public and private *barnehager*, and minority and majority families, can accept.

Issues of staffing: although well-trained, only a third of staff in Norwegian *barnehager* are qualified teachers. Their status, pay and working conditions compare unfavourably to those of primary school teachers. Staffing in the SFOs (school-based, leisure-time activities), an expanding sector, a particular challenge, as staff have little or not training. The intent to pursue better gender balance in staffing is noteworthy, and shows an awareness of the child's need for both men and women as role models.

The possible negative effects of the Cash Benefit Scheme: the review team, while recognising the choice and equity arguments advanced in its favour, drew attention to possible downstream effects, such as the impact of the Scheme on equity and the quality of provision. Rather than encouraging more parental care of children, the CBS may become a financial incentive to some parents to continue working and place their children in unregulated, informal care. In parallel, according to some Norwegian surveys, the parents most likely to take the benefit *and* remain at home with their children are lone mothers, mothers with several young children and/or low-income, one salary families. In short, the positive results for children from this expensive measure may be meagre.

Issues of evaluation and monitoring: although the Ministry collects relevant statistics and indicators, and supports a range of research, the amount of government funding allocated to ECEC research, development and evaluation activities remains modest, compared to the size and importance of the sector. Data collection for the ECEC system at national level, and the responsibilities of the actors at different levels (state, region, municipalities) need to be further considered.

Portugal

Auspices

The national ECEC network in Portugal is public and private, and overall policy responsibility for both networks is shared between two ministries. The Ministry of Education is responsible for pedagogical quality in all settings, and for the funding of kindergarten educational contexts for the age group 3-6 years. The Ministry of Labour and Solidarity has charge of family support, provision of socio-educational activities and the funding and supervision of out-of-home childcare, for children aged 3 months and older. A move toward decentralisation has recently taken place, and several policy and organisation matters are now being decided by municipalities, the Regional Directorates of Education and the Regional Social Security Centres, which have the responsibility of enabling the implementation of national ECEC policies in their regions. To ensure co-ordination, a *Bureau for the Expansion and Development of Pre-school Education* was established in 1996, bringing together the major ECEC stakeholders, including the National Association of Municipalities and the larger non-profit or voluntary providers, such as the Private Institutions of Social Solidarity (IPSS). The 1997 National Framework Law provides the definitions, major policy aims, orientations and implementation strategies for pre-school (kindergarten) education. Although the Law perceives pre-school as the first stage of lifelong learning, co-operation with families is emphasised.

Developments

In recent years, Portugal has made notable progress in ECEC policy formulation and implementation. The whole sector has effectively been reformed, and the pre-school budget has more than doubled. A government *Programme for the Expansion and Development of Pre-school Education* was drafted in 1996, followed one year later by the 1997 *Framework Law* which co-ordinates the hitherto diverse provision for young children, and includes for the first time the 3- to 6-year-olds within the realm of Basic Education. The government programme intends that the expansion and development of pre-school provision should take place in co-ordination with municipal, private and social welfare institutions, with central government assuming a guiding and regulatory role. The increase in coverage has been remarkable, going in the pre-school sector from 57.5% coverage in 1995 to over 72% in 1999. Free access to a 5-hour session has now been accorded to 5-year olds, and is planned for 4-year olds in the near future. Much attention has been devoted to staff training and status, and Portuguese *educadores* are now required to have a four-year, higher education degree. Curriculum guidelines have been formulated and issued, and there is growing public interest in provision for 0-3 year old children.

Context

Expenditure on ISCED *Level 0 institutions as a percentage of* GDP: 0.2%.

Labour force rates: in 1999, 80.3% of women aged 25-34 years participated in the labour force. 7.8% worked part-time.

Parental leave: universal 18 weeks maternity leave paid 100% of earnings + 6 months unpaid parental leave for each parent.

Attention to children with special educational needs, before they enter compulsory school: a) *Children with disabilities*: in Portugal, there is growing inclusion of children with disabilities in all branches of education; b) *Child poverty rates* reach 24% after redistribution (OECD average is 11.9%); c) *Ethnic and bilingual children*: there are sizeable immigrant minorities, centred especially around Lisbon, Setúbal and Porto. Several social integration programmes with an educational component have been sponsored by the High Commission for Ethnic Minorities, government ministries and municipalities. Children at risk are given priority entrance into some services. Recent legislation has called attention to these children and provides for early intervention strategies to meet their needs.

Provision

Children from 3 months to 3 years can attend crèches (11% of children) or family day-care (either nannies or family crèches – together 1.5% of children). Children from 3-6 years generally attend kindergarten or *jardims de infância*. Average costs to parents for childcare amount to about 11% of an average aggregate family salary. In addition, the State through the Ministry of Labour heavily subsidises family support components such as meals, medical supervision, socio-cultural activities. Families also receive tax exemption for various educational expenses Pre-school education is free for 5-year olds and will become free to 4-year olds in the coming year.

0-3 years: almost 90% of children cared for by their families or in informal care arrangements; 12% in some form of full-day crèche or family day-care.

For the age group *3-6 years*, enrolment rates in *jardims de infância* are as follows: 3-4 *years:* 60% enrolled. 4-5 *years:* 75% and from 5-6 *years:* 90% are enrolled. Community centres and itinerant provision are available on a small scale in areas where it is difficult to maintain a *jardim de infância*. Children can also attend socio-educational activities when pre-school activities are over, if working parents need this extra time. *Jardims de infância* open from 5-6 hours daily (depending on auspices). The Ministry of Education has introduced curriculum guidelines to improve pedagogical method and content.

Child-staff ratios: child-staff ratios in *jardims* are:15:1 for 3-year olds, with 20-25 children to one trained teacher. In the crèches, ratios of up to 10 children per adult professional are practised.

Staffing and training

All settings should have a pedagogical director, and each class a qualified kindergarten teacher (*educador*). Crèches are staffed by *educadores* (see below), nurses and social workers, all of whom have tertiary-level, professional qualifications. They are assisted by auxiliary workers who are not required to have a particular qualification. In the *jardim de infância*, the *educadores* or kindergarten teachers are the lead staff. They are required to complete a four-year university degree as polyvalent educators. *Educadores* have the same pay conditions as primary school teachers, but their pay levels and conditions of work may be considerably reduced when they work in IPSS crèches in the social sector.

OECD policy issues

Among the issues for policy attention identified by the OECD Review team for Portugal were:

More attention to children from 0-3 years is needed: in a context where family networks are weakening, and informal care by neighbours coming under scrutiny, public intervention to support child-rearing needs to be organised, and seen as an education and social service of public interest. The necessary government support to the future expansion of crèche and family centres can include educational, family support and social integration components as well as labour market and gender equity objectives.

Coherence and co-ordination of services: in the early childhood field in Portugal, a tradition of multiple and over-lapping levels of decision-making has tended to diffuse accountability, and render national policy less effective. In recent years, the ministries have established clearer policy frameworks for the entire field. Agreement about the structural requirements of services, the interfaces between different services, and the strengthening of monitoring processes could further help to improve the coherence of the system.

The educational quality of early childhood services: in many instances, early childhood services in Portugal have tended to be loosely structured, play oriented and geared toward care and social aims, often according to the preferred aims of the providers. The new curriculum guidelines, new inspection approaches, and the improved training of staff are expected to improve learning focus and outcomes. The organisation of in-service training between the sectors and the different providers may also be helpful.

Accountability, self-evaluation and inspection: greater emphasis needs to be placed by ministries and local authorities on the contractual obligations that receiving subsidies brings, such as the presentation of verifiable evidence of value for money, target achievement, impact or outcome measures. Likewise, quality could be improved with more systematic and effective self-evaluation procedures for settings and staff, with the necessary external moderation, support and validation.

Children with special educational needs: although it has been part of the traditional role of the kindergarten in Portugal to support children with learning difficulties, their limited access to services has sometimes prevented the detection of special needs in children until their enrolment in primary school. The high rate of child poverty tends also to increase the incidence of special educational needs. The recently passed legislation on early intervention, and the trend toward universalisation of access will do much to remedy these weakness and strengthen preventive child welfare.

Sweden

Auspices

Auspices for young children 7 years are unified in Sweden. Responsibility for central policy, for the goals, guidelines and financial framework of ECEC lies solely with the Swedish Ministry of Education and Science. Distinctions between day-care and kindergarten were removed by the 1998 School Act, which defines all services for young children from 1-6 as "pre-school" and from 5/6-7 years as "pre-school class". Compulsory schooling begins at 7 years. Like the shifting of responsibility for the sector toward the Ministry of Education some years earlier, this Act signals – and reinforces – a major shift of understanding in Sweden with regard to early childhood services. The School Act also devolves major responsibilities to municipalities. Municipalities have the duty to provide sufficient numbers of pre-school and leisure-time centres and places, of monitoring the quality of ECEC services and of providing sufficient resources. The National Agency for Education is responsible for overall evaluation, data collection, development and supervision of ECEC at central and regional levels.

Developments

Several far-reaching developments have taken place in ECEC in Sweden over the last years. In addition to moving the sector into the sphere of education, the system has been much expanded and reformed. The right of every child to a place "within reasonable limit" (defined as not more than 3 months) has now been achieved in almost all municipalities. A government bill to make pre-school universal and free for 5-year olds has been drafted and, if a draft law before Parliament passes, will be extended to all 4-year olds. For children from bilingual backgrounds, a free three-hour session every morning is available from the age of 3. Fee variability across municipalities, which sometimes hindered low-income parents from using services, has also been countered in the draft law, which will introduce a low flat, parental fee for services. The municipalities will be compensated for loss of revenue by central government. Much effort has been invested also into improving quality, particularly for the older children. A *Curriculum for Pre-school* was elaborated in 1997-98, linking into the curricula for primary and secondary schools, and providing a common view of knowledge, development and learning. From the point of view of the Swedish State, it sets out the foundation values for the pre-school, and the tasks, goals and guidelines for pre-school activities. The means by which those goals should be attained are not prescribed. Co-operation between the pre-school class, the school and the after school care centre is emphasised. A new proposal would extend the pre-service training of *pedagogues*, the lead personnel in the pre-schools, by another six months (totalling three-and-a-half years) to allow a common psycho-pedagogical training with teachers and leisure time pedagogues.

Context

Expenditure on ISCED *Level 0 institutions as a percentage of* GDP: 0.6%. The Swedish background report provides a figure of 2% of GDP for expenditure on ECEC.

Labour force rates: in 1999, 81.5% of women aged 25-34 years participated in the labour force. 32.1% worked part-time.

Parental leave: 360 days paid 80% of earnings for a year and 60 SEK daily for 90 days. There is great flexibility about taking this leave full or part-time. A further pregnancy benefit of 80 % of earnings is paid for expectant mothers with employment who are unable to go on working from 60 to 11 days before birth. Fathers are allowed a 30 days non-transferable paternity leave, as well as ten days temporary parental benefit in connection with the birth of his child.

Attention to children with special educational need before they enter compulsory education: a) *Children with disabilities*: children with disabilities or psycho-social problems have a priority right to services and are well integrated; b) *Children from low-income families*: the child poverty rate after redistribution is 2.4%, the lowest in OECD countries; c) *Ethnic and bilin-*

gual children: Sweden has a growing immigrant population. An estimated 18 % of the population are first or second generation immigrants, *e.g.* 40 000 refugee children between 1-6 years were given asylum from 1990-95. Government has made funds available to provide daily, a free three-hour session of day-care for bilingual children from the age of 3.

Provision

By law, all children 1-12 years have a right to childcare, as long as both parents work or study. Most pre-school provision is provided directly by municipalities in day-care centres, but municipal provision in family day-care covers 12% of children, especially in rural areas. Private day-care provision by parent and personnel co-operatives, churches, corporations and other providers, also exists for 13% of children. Except for parental fees, private provision is funded by the municipalities and contractually, is expected to meet the basic standards of public childcare, although without the obligation to follow the *Pre-school Curriculum*. Currently, parents may pay between 2% and 20% of income for childcare, depending on their income and municipality fees. To reduce disparities between municipalities and provide greater support to families with young children, there is a proposal before Parliament to have free pre-school for all children from the age of 4 years. Further costs would be capped at 3%, 2% and 1% of income for the first, second and third child. Enrolment rates are as follows:

0-1 year: almost all children are looked after by a parent (generally, the mother) on parental leave at home. In general, children begin in day-care at about 15-18 months.

1-6 years: 64 % of children attend a full-day pre-school, with a further 11% in family day-care.

6-7 years: 91% of children attend the pre-school class, with another 7% already in compulsory school.

6-9 years: 65 % of children from 6-9 years are enrolled in leisure-time centres. In addition, there are also open pre-schools that offer a service to children and families (often low-income, immigrant) for a few hours every day. In rural areas, some of these drop-in centres are being transformed into family resource centres. The National Agency for Education has formulated guidelines for the conduct of these centres and family day-care.

Child-staff ratios: national statutory requirements for child-staff ratios do not exist, but monitoring of the actual ratios practised is compulsory and ongoing. In pre-school centres, the present ratio is 5.6 children per adult. In the pre-school class, the average ratio practised is 13 children per adult.

Staffing and training

98% of staff in Swedish pre-school centres are trained to work with children. Each centre must have a director, with a university teaching or pedagogue qualification. Educational pedagogues (pre-school teachers) make up 60% of the personnel in the pre-schools. Like leisure-time pedagogues, they require a three-year tertiary degree (soon to be extended to three-and-a-half years) from a higher level college or university. The pedagogues are assisted by child minders (38% of personnel) who currently, are given a senior secondary, three-year vocational formation in "Children and Leisure-time Activities". Some older staff have fewer formal qualifications, but the current career ladder has various points of entry for childminders to take up higher training leading to pedagogue status. Family day-care providers are not required to have a qualification, but 72% have either a child-minder certificate or have received 50-100 hours of mandatory training from their municipal employers. The National Agency for Education recommends that family day-carers should receive a training and certification equivalent to the child-minders in the pre-schools. Unlike many other countries, leisure-time staff in Sweden are also highly trained at university level. In-service training is well developed for centre-based day-carers and leisure-time staff, but less well for family day-carers. About 5% of pre-school personnel are men, 60% are pedagogues and 35% are certified child minders.

OECD policy issues

Among the issues for policy attention identified by the OECD Review team for Sweden were:

Access issues: all children 1-12 years have a right to childcare, *as long as their parents work or study*. This means in effect that the children both of unemployed parents (oftentimes, of immigrant origin) and of parents on parental leave may not have access to services. In 1997, 59 000 such children were not enrolled. As a result, criticism of the conditions of access has grown, seeing them as limiting the child's right to early education and care, and discriminating against children and families who perhaps most need social and educational services. Several measures to address potential inequities of access have been taken at both national and municipal levels, such as the government bill to provide free and universal half-day access to all pre-school services for 5- and 4-year-old age groups. The flat-rate fee for services will also do much to improve access for the children of low-income parents.

Quality issues: because of the high level of decentralisation in Sweden, municipalities have full control over their spending on ECEC. Most municipal councils see childhood services as a priority, but some have chosen to maintain

177

the less demanding quality levels with respect to staffing, diversity of services, fee reductions to low-income families, etc. This was especially the case during the economic crisis of the early 90s, when, for example, child-staff ratios rose, in-service training for ECEC staff was diminished, and many drop-in and multi-functional family centres closed. In sum, the "non-essential" services, which are often frequented by the less-involved families, were cut back. The National Board of Education is currently developing consensus among the municipalities about national early childhood aims, and will publish guidelines for the services not covered by the national curriculum, viz. family day-care, open pre-schools and open leisure activities.

Family day-care: family day-care caters for fully 12% of Swedish children. Though unable to offer children the range and quality of provision that highly trained staff in an urban pre-school can develop, family day-care should not be seen as solely an emergency, back-up service. It often provides an essential service for more traditional urban families and for isolated families in rural areas. In sum, family day-care networks are an integral part of the system, and need to be provided with adequate investment, supports, monitoring and training. Even in municipalities that invest in the service, the monitoring of family day-care and the training offered has not always been consistent.

Research issues: Sweden has a long tradition in research on early childhood. The OECD review team recommended further research on a number of issues, and in particular the dissemination of research that could be of use to the international community. Research on the continuity between the pre-school class and schools may be particularly relevant, as might information pertaining to school transformation, the use of space, and the relationship between ratios and quality. The conceptualisation and method of ECEC data collection was also another aspect of the Swedish system that may merit international interest and dissemination.

United Kingdom (England)[57]

Auspices

Historically, responsibility for ECEC policy in England has been shared between national and local government. Services for children from birth to age 3 were in the province of the Department of Health, while the Department for Education and Employment (DfEE) had responsibility for children 3-5 years. In an effort to have better articulation of policy, and to overcome the division between education and care, the responsibility for implementing policy and delivering planned outcomes was assigned to the Department for Education and Employment (DfEE). In addition, a new Children's Unit has recently been established at Cabinet level to co-ordinate the work of the major ministries in favour of children.

Developments

Since 1997, the government has launched an unprecedented effort to increase investment in families and young children, and to develop a wide-ranging plan of action that will expand and reform the early years system. In May 1998, a *National Childcare Strategy* was announced, to be implemented by locally based, *Early Years Development and Childcare Partnerships* working in concert with the local education and social services authorities (see Box 3.7 in Chapter 3). Special funding for disadvantaged areas has been allocated through the *Sure Start* initiative. A pilot *Early Excellence Centre* programme was established in 1997 to test integrated approaches to care and education. In the year 2000, *Curriculum Guidelines* for the Foundation Stage (3-5 years) were published, to help practitioners to plan how their work will contribute to early learning goals. A *Childcare Tax Credit* (CTC) for parents working a minimum of 16 hours per week, has also been instituted, targeted at low-income families.[58] The Office for Standards in Education (OFSTED) will formulate national standards to ensure that all children receive good quality service, and that providers are clear about the standards they must meet. Already, the accumulation of these initiatives is radically altering the picture of early years provision in England. It is estimated that 1.6 million new childcare places will have been created by 2004, and a further 80 000 childcare workers recruited. In addition, local education authorities are now required to provide an early education place (of two-and-a-half hours daily) for all 4-year olds by 2001 (target already reached), and for all 3-4 year olds by September 2004. It is anticipated that 80% of these new places will be provided by playgroups, voluntary and private providers.

Context

Expenditure on ISCED Level 0 institutions as a percentage of GDP: 0.4%.

Labour force rates: in 1999, 75.1% of women aged 25-34 years participated in the labour force. 35.8% worked part-time.

Parental leave: universal 18 weeks paid maternity leave, plus an entitlement to a further unpaid 22 weeks and to an unpaid four weeks annual leave over for three years, until a child reaches 5 years. A further extension of parental leave is being considered.

Attention to children with special educational needs before their entry into compulsory schooling: a) Children with disabilities: the growing awareness of the benefits of mainstreaming children with disabilities is leading to their increased inclusion in ECEC services. Recently, the government has announced a significant increase in investment for these children; *b) Children from low-income families*: for the United Kingdom, the child poverty rate after redistribution is 19.8% (OECD

---

57. The OECD review focused on England, but the review team also visited Scotland which has taken a slightly different approach to ECEC policy. Please see the UK country note for more details on Northern Ireland, Scotland, and Wales.

58. The CTC can be worth £70 per week (c. $100) or meet up to a maximum of 70% the costs of registered childcare.

average: 11.9%). About 23% of children under 6 years are being raised by a lone parent; *c) Ethnic and bilingual children*: 6% of the British population is composed of ethnic minorities (esp. London, West Midlands where the proportion may rise to 15%). As research indicates that immigrant children are seriously underachieving in education, policies to prevent discrimination and racism have been strengthened, and very significant investment made in the Sure Start programme for disadvantaged families and their children from 0-4 years.

Provision

Compared to most other European countries, ECEC provision in the UK is starting from a low base. In general, children 0-3 of working parents are cared for by private childminders, playgroups and day nurseries. Until the recent Childcare Tax Credit, children in these services were not eligible for public funding, unless they qualified for special services or were considered to be seriously at risk. From 3-4 years, almost all children tend to join playgroups or nursery schools, moving toward reception class as they come to 4 years. All 4-year-olds are in state-funded primary school reception classes (the majority) or in nursery school provision, operated mostly by local authorities. All 5-year olds are in primary and reception classes. Provision patterns are as follows:

0-1 year: almost all children are cared for by parents or, informally, by relatives and childminders.

1-3 years: care provision is mostly private, *e.g.* childminders or day nurseries. Provision statistics on a full-time equivalence basis are not available. 20% of 2-year olds attend a playgroup, two-thirds of which are run by church or voluntary associations, and one-third by private persons or agencies.

3-4 years: c. 90% of children participate in some form of early education programme. 55% of 3-year olds attend a playgroup and 29% of the age group are in nursery school or nursery class, generally for two-and-a-half hours per day.

4-5 years (compulsory education begins at 5 years): all children have a guaranteed early education place. Local education authorities currently provide 59% of early education places for 3- and 4- year olds mainly through nursery schools and nursery classes (2.5 hours daily during school terms), and reception classes for 4-year olds of 6.5 hours daily, from 9 a.m. to 3.30 p.m., during school term. The private sector (generally companies or trusts) provides about 30% of places in independent, fee-charging schools, while community and voluntary agencies provide a further, non-profit 9%.

Child-staff ratios: the regulation ratios are: 4:1 in opportunity groups and special schools; 4:1 and over in local authority nurseries, depending on the age of the child; 8:1 in private day nurseries, playgroups and nursery schools; 10:1 in nursery schools with trained teachers and nurses; 13:1 in nursery classes and early years units; 30:1 in reception classes (but in practice, much less).

Staffing and training

A significant divide in training levels exists between early care (0-4 years) and early education (4-5 years) personnel. Only 20% of care personnel, mostly in opportunity groups and day nurseries, have a university or tertiary qualification. In fact, the majority of childcare workers – and many classroom assistants in the reception classes – do not have formal training, except for some hours required by a few local authorities. On the whole, childcare staff have poor conditions of work, are paid much less than the average wage and do long hours with little access to training or support. The government has recognised these concerns: it has introduced a national, minimum wage which improved the wage situation, and is attempting to bring coherence to the patchwork of recruitment approaches and training schemes. Teachers in the education sector are better paid and protected. They have a four-year university or teacher training qualification, some with a specialisation in early years education.

OECD policy issues

Among the issues for policy attention identified by the OECD Review team for the UK were:

Progress requires continued funding: provision in the UK has begun from a very low base. It is now benefiting from significant funding and a radical reform of policy, co-ordination and planning. These reforms will require continued strong funding over the coming years if progress is to be maintained and a stable, national ECEC system established.

Co-ordination issues: the 1998 *National Childcare Strategy* and the creation of the locally based, *Early Years Development and Childcare* (EYDC) *Partnerships* have already improved co-ordination significantly. A key to further movement is continuing government support to the EYDC Partnerships, who have the capacity to bring together different services and constituencies at local level, and overcome the institutional divide between care and education.

Expanding toward full-time access for children: present access to early education for children under 4 years is part-time, that is, 2.5 hours daily, and there is a need to re-examine whether the time available is sufficient to address the social, emotional and language needs of children, especially ethnic minority and children from low-income families. Pilot projects are being set up which will deliver part-time education with wraparound care. These pilots, alongside the *Early Excellence Centre* programme and other local initiatives will help to inform thinking about approaches to full-day provision.

Staff recruitment, training and status: careful recruitment and training of personnel is a pre-condition to establishing an acceptable early education and care system. Levels of recruitment and training need to be reviewed across the care system and, in the interests of retention, improvements in salary levels and conditions of work considered. Recruitment of staff from ethnic backgrounds remains a priority.

Creation of a quality assurance and inspection regime that will respect diversity: The difficulties faced by children – many from low-income backgrounds – to conform quite so young to national academic demands have not always been recognised. Greater attention is now being given to this concern. It is generally agreed that realistic outcomes and competencies can be defined only after consideration is given to the context, developmental stage and needs of young children.

A *need to increase work-family supports*, *e.g.* parental leave, flexible work scheduling. As mentioned above, serious investments are being made in poorer families, to provide them with support to find work and with early childhood services. A further extension of parental leave is also envisaged. These policies – along with more family friendly work practices – are to be encouraged, with a particular concern that they should serve equality of opportunity for women in the workplace.

United States

Auspices

Because of its constitutional history, size and diversity, the US has no single, comprehensive national child or family policy. Public education is primarily a state responsibility. The Federal Government plays an important role, however, through Congress, which formulates ECEC policies and goals, focusing primarily on funding services to children considered "at risk". Most funding for social services (including the Head Start programme, which is also educational) is managed by the U.S. Department of Health and Human Services (DHHS), while the U.S. Department of Education (DOE) funds compensatory and special education for disadvantaged 3- to 5-year olds. As part of "welfare reform" through the Personal Responsibility and Work Opportunity Reconciliation Act (PRWORA) of 1996, the government has provided additional funding to the states to expand provision of childcare, as an incentive to welfare recipients to find work. [59] Four separate child care funding streams have been consolidated into a single Child Care and Development Fund (CCDF). At each state level, policy decisions are made with regard to eligibility, extent of the supply and availability of services, allocation of services and benefits, scope and quality of services, including health and safety standards. The states use legislation, supplemental funding and regulation to implement policy decisions. In the last decade, states have also taken the leadership role in developing and implementing pre-kindergarten services and early intervention services for young children at risk. The allocation of resources and policies vary greatly across and within the states. Some states encourage local government and community participation in the development of early childhood policies through the formation of localised planning groups, matching funding and the development of local plans as a criteria for state funding. Other states assume near complete fiscal, regulatory and policymaking responsibilities for early childhood education and care.

Developments

Public awareness campaigns, strong advocacy, and internationally-renowned research have helped to secure a place for ECEC on the political agenda in the United States. There has been a marked increase in political commitment and investment both at the federal and state levels, with concomitant expansion of funding and coverage of ECEC provision. Head Start appropriations have increased significantly in the last decade, with additional increases expected. In particular, federal money has been made available to States to expand and improve quality childcare through increased funding from the CCDF block grant. There are moves toward universal access to pre-kindergarten programmes in many states. Several multi-agency, state-wide initiatives have been developed to promote co-ordination and collaboration among state government and local government, non-profit organisations, businesses, and families. Likewise, numerous state initiatives have developed to address the question of quality, and there have been significant improvements in regulations for in-service training. Professional organisations, including the National Association for the Education of Young Children (NAEYC), have played an important role in promoting voluntary accreditation and professional development for early childhood staff.

Context

Expenditure on ISCED *Level 0 institutions as a percentage of* GDP: 0.4%. The figures provided in the US background report suggest a much smaller percentage, especially in term of public investment.

Labour force rates: in 1999, 76.4% of women aged 25-34 years participated in the labour force. 19% worked part-time. 58% of women with a child under 1 year were part of the labour force (Bureau of Labour Statistics, 2000).

---

59. The Temporary Assistance of Needy Families (TANF) Act requires that adults should participate in work activities two years after they start receiving assistance. States may exempt parents with children under one year from work requirement, and cannot penalize parents with children under 6 years if child care is not available.

Parental leave: the 1993 *Family and Medical Leave Act* (FMLA) provides for a 12 week job-protected but unpaid leave for employees in firms with 50 or more workers, at the time of pregnancy, childbirth, or their own illness or that of a family member. Employers can require that employees use their vacation and sick leave before claiming the family leave. Some paid maternity leave depending on workplace agreement.

Attention to children with special educational needs before they begin compulsory schooling: a) Children with disabilities: Federal law requires that centres catering for children should accommodate children with disabilities in "the least restrictive environment". Depending on the state, there is growing inclusion of such children. 10% of available places in Head Start are intended for children with disabilities (the actual percentage of children with disabilities in Head Start programmes is 12%); *b) Children from low-income families*: the child poverty rate in the U.S. is 22.4% after redistribution (OECD average: 11.9%). In 1997, 40% of African American, 38% of Hispanic, and 13% of white, non-Hispanic children under 6 lived in poverty (UNICEF, 2000); *c) Ethnic and bilingual children*: in the U.S., there are significant ethnic and immigrant groups: 15% African-Americans; 15% Hispanic; 4% Asia/Pacific and 1% indigenous American.

Provision

Private centre-based ECEC and family day care (90% of provision – two-thirds non-profit and one-third for-profit) is the most usual form of provision up to the age of 3 years, giving way gradually to publicly-funded kindergarten provision by the school districts from the age of 4. Rates of provision are:

0-1 year: about 20% of children are cared for by parents on a full-time basis; more than half are cared for by a relative or in-home child-minder; 22% are in private family day-care and 9% in centre-based settings, generally from the age of 3 months.

2-4 years: provision is characterised by decreasing at-home, informal care (39%) and increasing use of both centre-based settings (19% of 2-year olds and 41% of 3-year olds are in centre-based settings), and pre-primary education programmes (48% of 3-year-old children enrolled, mostly in private, part-day, nursery school programmes).

4-6 years: more than 60% of 4-year olds are enrolled in educational programmes in nursery schools (some kindergarten). Georgia and New York State have pledged to provide full and free coverage for 4-year olds in public, part-day pre-kindergarten. In 41 other States, some form of free pre-kindergarten to 4-year olds is found, sometimes extending to 3-year old children. This form of provision is expanding rapidly. Almost all (90%) 5-year olds are enrolled in kindergartens, the first year of formal schooling (85% public).

Where childcare is concerned, families pay on average about 60% of costs (rising to 70-80% of costs outside the school system), with Federal Government contributing 25%, and States and local government about 15% of costs.[60] Depending on the State, parents pay on average more than $3 000 annually per child for childcare, with low-income families paying on average 18% of income, and families earning less than $1 200 per month paying 25% of income. Some costs can be recuperated through Federal tax benefits for parents. Low-income families can benefit from fee subsidies through the Child Care and Development Fund (CCDF) block grant, but many low-income families tend to use informal, unregulated arrangements. Most school districts offer free half- or full-day kindergarten to all 5-year olds as part of formal primary schooling, and an increasing number of districts are now offering free pre-kindergarten to 4-year olds.

Child-staff ratios: different State regulations and different standards in licensing requirements; funding standards; voluntary accreditation standards and voluntary goals standards make it difficult to describe child-staff ratios for the U.S. as a whole. In general: ratios of 4-6:1 are required for infants; from 10 to 20:1 for pre-school children, with 2- and 3-year old children having ratios somewhere in the middle. However, because of the predominance of informal settings, particularly for younger children from low-income families, and the inability of many States to inspect centres and family day care homes regularly, the actual child-staff ratios can be much higher. In fact, only 14% of centres and 13% of family child care homes are rated as being of good quality.

Staffing and training

In the United States, the status and pay of early childhood staff outside the public school system are low, and staff turnover is three times higher than among school teachers. No coherent system exists to set the qualifications of early childhood workers. The characteristics of the three main provision systems are:

Head Start: to raise the level of staff training, Head Start has relied heavily on funding standards (called the Head Start Performance Standards) and from 1971, created its own professional profile, the Child Development

---

60. The above Federal and State contributions are mainly directed to programmes for low-income families and to children considered to be "at risk", *e.g.* Head Start, which covered 700 000 (36% of eligible children) three- and 4-year old children in 1998.

Associate (CDA). The CDA is equivalent (depending on the State) to half a two-year, tertiary-level, professional diploma or associate degree. It is widely recognised across the US and provides credits for a university degree in several States. The aim of Head Start (almost achieved) is to have one CDA in every classroom, while Congress recently enacted a law requiring Head Start to have 50% of its contact staff to have a two-year degree or four-year post-secondary degree by 2003.

The public school system: teachers in all (pre-)kindergarten classes are required to be certified by the State in which they work. However, a specialisation in early childhood is not required in all States. Teacher certification is based on a four-year university degree, and often a Master's degree. It is not always a requirement for working in private schools, nor, in some States, for working with young children in a public school.

The purchase-of service system: the large purchase-of service system is composed of private centres and family day care homes which are licensed by state social service agencies to provide programmes for the general population. These services are subject to licensing and funding standards, but pre-service staff requirements can be very low or non-existent. Most States, however, now require a certain number of annual hours of further training from all staff.

OECD policy issues

Among the issues for policy attention identified by the OECD Review team for the US were:

The need to create a co-ordinated and comprehensive ECEC *system*: the present patchwork of services, regulations and funding sources leads to confusion, uneven quality and inequality of access. The responsibility to provide political leadership, funding, clear policy goals and frameworks rests with government, both at Federal and the State level. An effective first step might be the nomination of a national commission to propose how government roles in ECEC could be strengthened. Stronger implication by education departments may be vital for creating a more equitable system with broad public support. Stable networks of inter-agency partnerships at the State level could also be effective.

The urgent need to address access issues: the access of children 3-5 years from ethnic and low-income backgrounds is a serious concern. Only 45% of children from 3-5 years from low-income families are enrolled in pre-school, compared to 75% among high-income families. These inequalities are often linked to contextual issues, such as housing policy, which tends to support segregation of families by income and ethnic origin. A more proactive stance toward child poverty and diversity is recommended.

The need for quality improvement: quality in childcare can be very weak, especially for the 0-3 age group, and regulations in many States may set standards far too low, even for health and safety issues. In addition, families of 4-year old children often have access only to narrowly focused, instructional type programmes. Voluntary accreditation of centres as proposed by the NAEYC can dramatically improve standards and the use of well-known methods, (*e.g.* the Project Approach) or guidelines (*e.g.* the revised *Developmentally Appropriate Practice in Early Childhood Programs*) can contribute significantly to the effectiveness of programmes.

Creating an effective staff training and professional development system: serious weaknesses occur in the initial and continued training of staff at all levels. In addition, concerns were expressed about recruitment, remuneration, status, retention and career development. Projects such as TEACH address many of these issues. The articulation of qualifications and staff licensing within and across states is also a challenge.

Appendix 2

Statistical Tables
Data for the Figures

Data for Figure 2.1. **Trends in employment rates[1] of 25-34 year-olds, 1980-99**

	Women		Men	
	1980	1999	1980	1999
Australia	49.8	63.9	91.7	85.4
Belgium	57.9 [a]	74.8	88.5 [a]	87.3
Czech Republic	66.7 [b]	60.4	94.1 [b]	90.4
Denmark	78.4 [a]	76.8	85.5 [a]	89.0
Finland	78.4	69.8	89.2	83.9
Italy	49.5 [a]	50.5	90.7 [a]	77.8
Netherlands	59.0 [c]	75.3 [d]	90.1 [c]	92.0 [d]
Norway	61.5	78.7	88.6	88.8
Portugal	57.8	75.6	91.8	89.6
Sweden	79.5	75.2	93.4	82.4
United Kingdom	64.8 [c]	71.0	89.5 [c]	87.7
United States	60.7	73.0	88.8	89.9
Austria		74.0 [d]		89.1 [d]
Canada	58.1	73.7	89.2	84.6
France	63.5	65.4	93.6	82.3
Germany	57.9	69.2	89.2	85.1
Greece	40.6 [a]	55.1 [d]	90.1 [a]	87.3 [d]
Hungary	55.0 [e]	58.1	81.7 [e]	83.1
Iceland	72.7 [f]	80.2	92.9 [f]	94.0
Ireland	34.0 [g]	71.5	85.5 [g]	88.7
Japan	47.3	59.4	95.2	91.9
Korea	35.3	47.7	90.5	82.3
Luxembourg	52.5 [a]	68.3	95.9 [a]	91.9
Mexico	37.6 [f]	43.8	94.8 [f]	94.7
New Zealand	57.1 [c]	63.7	85.6 [c]	84.9
Poland	60.6 [e]	63.3	83.3 [e]	81.9
Spain	32.4	54.1	85.7	80.8
Switzerland [h]	69.9 [f]	75.0	96.5 [f]	95.6
Turkey	32.9 [c]	30.4	90.7 [c]	88.1

1. Employment/population ratio.
a. 1983
b. 1993
c. 1990
d. 1998
e. 1992
f. 1991
g. 1981
h. 25-39 year-olds.
Sources: For all countries except Italy, OECD Labour force statistics database; data for Italy provided by EUROSTAT.

Data for Figure 2.2. **Average hours worked per week by employed women and men with a child under 3 years, selected countries, 1997**

	Women	Men
Austria	33.4	41.2
Belgium	32.6	40.9
Finland	36.8	42.1
France	34.0	41.5
Germany	30.6	41.9
Greece	37.4	45.5
Ireland	32.9	45.6
Italy	34.0	41.6
Netherlands	20.7	40.7
Portugal	38.2	44.1
Spain	36.2	42.5
United Kingdom	26.0	46.6

Source: 1997 European Labour Force Survey data reported in Moss and Deven (1999).

Data for Figure 2.3. **Trends in incidence of part-time employment rates[1] for 25-34 year-olds, 1990-99**

	Part-time			
	1990		1999	
	Men	Women	Men	Women
Australia	4.0	37.7	7.3	34.1
Belgium	1.9	27.2	4.2	31.5
Czech Republic	0.9 [a]	16.3 [a]	0.8	13.3
Denmark	5.3	27.1	6.0	24.4
Finland	3.9	11.0	5.6	14.4
Italy	2.3	9.6	3.9	17.1
Netherlands	8.2	52.5	8.7	54.2
Norway	5.1	41.6	7.5	37.3
Portugal	1.3	5.3	2.5	7.8
Sweden	5.2	39.4	7.4	32.1
United Kingdom	1.3	38.6	3.8	35.8
United States	4.9	19.5	4.9	19.0
Austria	3.1 [b]	25.8 [b]	4.1 [c]	30.2 [c]
Canada	4.1	20.5	5.6	21.4
France	2.7	20.4	5.4	27.7
Germany	3.3	30.9	5.6	30.3
Greece	1.7	6.5	3.1 [c]	10.2 [c]
Hungary	2.1 [b]	7.8 [b]	2.3	8.5
Iceland	6.0 [d]	50.3 [d]	7.9	44.5
Ireland	2.4	12.0	3.3	18.8
Japan	8.0 [e]	30.4 [e]	7.9	30.0
Luxembourg	0.5	12.6	1.1	19.6
Mexico	16.2 [d]	38.6 [d]	7.9	30.8
New Zealand	3.0	34.4	6.1	30.8
Poland	4.3 [f]	8.7 [f]	3.8	10.9
Spain	1.2	9.3	3.2	15.9
Turkey	9.2	34.6	15.2	45.2

1. Part-time employment / total employment.
a. 1993
b. 1995
c. 1998
d. 1991
e. 1997
f. 1992.
Source: OECD full-time part-time (National) employment database.

Data for Figure 2.4. **Employed men and women engaged in shift, night and Sunday work, 1997**

		Employees engaged in shift work, percentages		Employees engaged in night work, percentages		Employees engaged in work on Sunday, percentages	
		Usually	Sometimes	Usually	Sometimes	Usually	Sometimes
Austria	Females	13.6	3.5	5.8	6.5	14.5	10.6
	Males	16.1	4.8	10.8	11.6	14.2	14.5
Belgium	Females	10.5	2.1	3.0	5.5	9.5	13.7
	Males	15.4	2.6	5.9	12.2	9.2	16.9
Denmark	Females	6.4	1.2	6.6	4.1	21.8	12.3
	Males	7.9	1.5	9.0	8.6	18.5	21.1
Finland	Females	22.2	--	7.4	8.0	17.3	8.6
	Males	16.7	--	10.6	12.6	20.6	10.8
France	Females	6.0	--	2.1	5.7	8.3	17.4
	Males	9.3	--	5.2	16.3	8.8	23.2
Germany	Females	8.6	0.8	4.5	3.2	11.3	8.3
	Males	12.1	1.2	8.7	7.2	11.3	13.4
Greece	Females	6.1	3.1	2.3	6.6	11.5	16.6
	Males	8.7	3.9	4.4	13.1	15.0	20.1
Ireland	Females	9.6	3.9	5.1	8.5	12.4	16.5
	Males	9.8	3.9	6.8	18.1	20.1	19.4
Italy	Females	13.0	2.8	3.3	4.6	7.6	11.2
	Males	15.0	3.9	6.3	9.7	8.8	15.4
Luxembourg	Females	7.0	..	(1.9)	5.3	7.8	12.0
	Males	13.4	(1.0)	4.1	12.2	7.3	16.5
Netherlands	Females	6.4	0.4	1.8	7.7	15.9	7.9
	Males	8.5	0.5	2.5	9.6	14.6	10.5
Portugal	Females	4.9	(0.2)	0.4	..	13.1	1.3
	Males	7.4	0.3	1.1	..	15.2	2.3
Spain	Females	4.3	0.7	2.9	4.1	15.4	3.0
	Males	6.5	0.9	5.4	7.0	15.8	3.6
Sweden	Females	26.7	1.6	5.9	3.4	18.9	15.6
	Males	16.4	1.7	7.7	8.7	13.2	22.7
United Kingdom	Females	12.1	2.5	4.8	9.6	12.3	21.8
	Males	14.9	3.9	7.4	21.8	13.4	35.6

-- Zero or not available.
.. Not zero but extremely unreliable.
( ) Unreliable data due to small size of the sample.
Source: EUROSTAT Labour Force Survey (1997).

Data for Figure 2.5. **Employment status of women with a child aged under 6 years
by highest educational qualification, selected countries, 1997 (%)**

	High		Medium		Low	
	Part time	Full time	Part time	Full time	Part time	Full time
Austria	30	54	31	38	19	33
Belgium	29	56	28	41	18	20
Finland	5	68	9	49	5	33
France	24	52	22	35	15	21
Germany	29	35	47	24	15	12
Greece	5	69	4	40	4	27
Ireland	15	53	14	36	13	14
Italy	12	67	10	47	6	21
Netherlands	68	8	54	6	32	4
Portugal	2	92	4	73	8	54
Spain	8	57	8	35	7	20
United Kingdom	12	34	39	17	30	12

Source: 1997 European Labour Force Survey data reported in Moss and Deven (1999).

187

Data for Figure 2.6. **Relative child poverty[1] rates before and after taxes and transfers, 1990s**

		Before taxes and transfers	After taxes and transfers
Australia	1996-97	28.1	12.6
Belgium	1992	17.8	4.4
Czech Republic	1996	m	5.9
Denmark	1992	17.4	5.1
Finland	1995	16.4	4.3
Italy	1995	24.6	20.5
Netherlands	1994	16.0	7.7
Norway	1995	15.9	3.9
Sweden	1995	23.4	2.6
United Kingdom	1995	36.1	19.8
United States	1997	26.7	22.4
Canada	1994	24.6	15.5
France	1994	28.7	7.9
Germany	1994	16.8	10.7
Greece	1994	m	12.3
Hungary	1994	38.1	10.3
Ireland	1997	m	16.8
Japan	1992	m	12.2
Luxembourg	1994	22.2	4.5
Mexico	1994	m	26.2
Poland	1995	44.4	15.4
Spain	1990	21.4	12.3
Turkey	1994	m	19.7

m: missing data.
1. Includes households with income below 50% of the national median.
Source: UNICEF (2000).

Data for Figure 3.2. **Net enrolment rates by single year of age in pre-primary[1] and primary education, 1999 (%)**

	Enrolment rate in pre-primary education				Enrolment rate in primary education			
	3 year-olds	4 year-olds	5 year-olds	6 year-olds	3 year-olds	4 year-olds	5 year-olds	6 year-olds
Australia	26.3	41.1	12.9	0.8	0.0	1.6	68.8	100.4
Belgium (Flem. Com.)	98.0	98.8	97.6	4.6	0.0	0.0	1.3	94.2
Czech Republic	46.5	81.9	92.5	46.5	0.0	0.0	0.0	53.5
Denmark	66.8	90.9	94.2	96.2	0.0	0.0	0.0	4.5
Finland	32.4	40.0	47.5	70.7	0.0	0.0	0.0	0.9
Italy	95.4	100.5	97.6	0.0	0.0	0.0	0.5	100.4
Netherlands	0.1	98.0	99.1	0.1	0.0	0.0	0.9	99.8
Norway	70.0	77.3	80.5	0.8	0.0	0.0	0.0	99.7
Portugal	55.7	68.0	73.6	3.3	0.0	0.0	0.0	100.8
Sweden	64.4	69.2	74.5	104.0	0.0	0.0	0.0	5.9
United Kingdom	52.0	94.6	0.2	0.0	0.0	0.0	99.5	99.3
United States	35.2	59.0	73.8	12.2	0.0	0.0	4.9	85.6

1. The data refer to pre-primary education, which is limited to organised centre-based programmes designed to foster learning and emotional and social development in children for 3 to compulsory school age. Day care, play groups and home-based structured and developmental activities may not be included in these data.
Source: OECD Education Database (2001).

Data for Figure 3.4. **Public expenditure for pre-primary[1] education as a percentage of GDP, 1998**

	Public expenditure (excluding subsidies)
Australia	0.03
Austria	0.47
Belgium	0.45
Belgium (Flem. Com.)	0.44
Canada	0.23
Czech Republic	0.45
Denmark	0.86
Finland	0.40
France	0.66
Germany	0.36
Hungary	0.69
Iceland	0.31
Ireland	0.00
Italy	0.42
Japan	0.09
Korea	0.04
Mexico	0.32
Netherlands	0.36
New Zealand	0.21
Norway	0.58
Poland	0.52
Portugal	0.24
Spain	0.34
Sweden	0.59
Switzerland	0.20
Turkey	0.01
United Kingdom	0.42
United States	0.36

1. The data refer to pre-primary education, which is limited to organised centre-based programmes designed to foster learning and emotional and social development in children for 3 to compulsory school age. Day care, play groups and home-based structured and developmental activities may not be included in these data.
Source: OECD Education Database (2001).

189

Data for Figure 3.5. **Expenditure per child (US dollars converted using PPPs) on public and private institutions by level of education (based on full-time equivalents), 1998**

	Pre-primary[1] education	Primary education
Australia	m	3 981
Belgium[2]	1 601	2 123
Czech Republic	2 098	1 565
Denmark	5 664	6 713
Finland	3 665	4 641
Italy[3]	4 730	5 653
Netherlands	3 630	3 795
Norway[3]	7 924	5 761
Portugal[3]	1 717	3 121
Sweden	3 210	5 579
United Kingdom[2]	4 910	3 329
United States	6 347	5 913
Austria[3]	5 029	6 065
Canada	4 535	m
France	3 487	3 614
Germany	4 648	3 531
Greece[2]	x	2 368
Hungary[3]	1 985	1 951
Iceland[3]	m	m
Ireland	2 555	2 745
Japan	3 123	5 075
Korea	1 287	2 838
Mexico	865	863
Poland	2 747	1 496
Spain	2 586	3 267
Switzerland[3]	2 593	6 470

1. The data refer to pre-primary education, which is limited to organised centre-based programmes designed to foster learning and emotional and social development in children for 3 to compulsory school age. Day care, play groups and home-based structured and developmental activities may not be included in these data.
2. Public and government-dependent private institutions.
3. Public institutions.
m: missing data.
x : included in primary.
Source: OECD Education Database (2001).

Appendix 3

Questions to Guide the Preparation of the Background Report

Overview

1. The background report (BR) will be based on two types of questions: a *common core* of questions addressed to all participating countries; and *supplementary* questions tailored to the needs and circumstances of countries concerned. The following questions were prepared by the Secretariat and revised in light of comments and advice from national representatives at a meeting in June 1998.

2. The supplementary questions will be developed in consultation with the countries concerned. There may be two sources for such questions: particular issues or policy developments identified by country authorities as of high priority in the national context, and which are not fully addressed in the common core of questions; and questions prompted by other material available to the Secretariat.

3. Due to differing contexts and circumstances in the participating countries, the importance of questions to national concerns may vary. Questions may be seen as more or less relevant, or may be interpreted differently from country to country. Countries are encouraged to note such differences in emphasis in their BR, as these will be important for the review to investigate.

4. In order to collect as much comparative data and information as possible, all participating countries need to respond to a common set of questions. The questions below are grouped into five sections. It is important for the BR from all participating countries to follow this common structure. Within each section, country authorities may wish to combine, rephrase, or expand certain questions in light of the particular national circumstances. *The key requirement is that the issues underlying the questions are addressed in the* BR.

5. To be useful to country authorities and to the review, the report should aim to be an integrated document rather than a list of responses to individual questions. For some questions, brief answers may be appropriate initially; the Secretariat may ask for clarification or elaboration of responses later. There will be opportunities for country authorities to revise or expand the responses during the reviewers' visit or shortly thereafter.

6. Responses to the questions also may be complemented by material extracted from existing reports and data tables. *Wherever possible, please present responses to questions in a data table or in a figure.*

7. Terminology in ECEC can be confusing, as similar terms and labels may have very different meanings in different countries. In order to avoid misunderstandings, it is requested that all key terms referring to ECEC provision and workers/staff be provided in the original language. A glossary defining these terms in English or French should be included in the BR.

8. In the questions, the term *parents* refers to those with primary care-taking responsibility for children, regardless of biological relationship. *Families* includes those individuals whom parents and children define as being part of their families, often those who have ongoing contact and responsibility for the well-being of children.

9. The review will focus on children from birth to compulsory school age. Countries may choose to extend this age range to include children in the early years of primary school. ECEC covers a broad scope of services and options including those that are public, private, centre-based, school-based, home-based, full-time, part-time, as well as care-giving and teaching by parents, relatives, and informal carers.

Section I. Definitions, contexts, and current provision

This section will aim to provide information on the policy context for early childhood education and care. It would be helpful for any information that will help the reader contextualise ECEC policy within specific historical developments and current circumstances to be included. It will provide an overview of ECEC policies and provision currently in place.

1. What are the historical roots of early childhood education and care (ECEC) policy and provision in your country?

2. What are common understandings today of young children and the early childhood period? How does society view young children? Who is responsible for ECEC? How does ECEC policy interpret the respective responsibilities of mothers, fathers, and other members of society for caring and educating young children? Are women viewed as mothers first and foremost, or as potential workers?

3. What are the main political, economic, labour market, social, and demographic changes that have shaped ECEC policy development in recent years?

4. Is there an articulated national child or family policy? Do ECEC policies fit into a set of wider supports for children and families (*e.g.*, child and family allowances/tax credits, family leave policies, health services, etc.)?

5. What are the current objectives for and purposes of early childhood education and care? Who are the intended beneficiaries of ECEC policy? Which groups of children and families do ECEC policies target?

6. What age spans of children are generally considered to fall within the scope of ECEC policies? What is compulsory school age? Is there debate about raising or lowering this age? How many entry dates are there to primary school per year? Are children below compulsory school age attending primary school?

7. What are the available forms of ECEC provision for children from birth to compulsory school age? What is the current level of coverage for each ECEC arrangement by age of child? Where applicable, what are the typical hours/length of operation of these arrangements during the day and year? What information is available about the socio-economic and family backgrounds of the children in these different forms of ECEC? *It would be helpful for this data to be presented in a table.*

8. Are responsibilities for ECEC integrated or split across administrative auspices (*e.g.*, education, welfare, health)? If split, why does it operate this way? If not split, were services previously split? If so, when and why did this change? To what extent are responsibilities for the implementation and administration of ECEC distributed across and within different levels of government (*e.g.*, national, regional, local)? Has responsibility always been within the same administrative auspice? If not, when was responsibility transferred and why? Are there trends toward increasing centralisation or decentralisation? *Please present this information in a table.*

9. Which other government agencies or statutory bodies have significant involvement and/or interest in ECEC? What mechanisms exist to promote policy coherence and inter-agency collaboration among different ministries, levels of government, and statutory bodies?

10. To what extent are actors outside government (*e.g.*, non-governmental/non-profit organisations, community groups, staff unions, training institutions, business) involved in policy development in ECEC? Are there particularly effective institutional frameworks, networks, or programmes for promoting regular dialogue and common action among these actors?

Section II. Policy concerns

This section will focus on the main concerns related to ECEC policy. Quality and access have been identified as concerns for further investigation. Countries are invited to discuss other cross-cutting areas of concern in this section and to document them with relevant quantitative and qualitative information. It also is important to identify which particular groups of children and families are the focus of concern. The section will set the stage for the subsequent discussion of specific issues and approaches to ECEC.

A. Quality

1. How is quality conceptualised by different stakeholders (*e.g.*, government, parents, children, researchers, early childhood workers)? How do these conceptions of quality relate to overall goals of society for ECEC?

2. What specified objectives for quality exist? Do quality objectives vary in content or specificity at different levels of government? Have they changed over time? If so, how?

3. Is quality of ECEC a concern for particular groups or ages of children? Is quality variable across regions or states?

4. How are quality objectives identified and prioritised? Who is included in the process of defining quality? What is the extent of actual involvement of these various stakeholders?

5. What policy approaches have been directed explicitly toward quality improvement? What does research show about the impact of these policy approaches?

6. How is quality assessed? What inputs, outputs, or processes do evaluations of quality measure? Who is involved in the assessments? For what purposes are they conducted?

B. *Access*

1. Is access to ECEC a statutory entitlement, and if so, from what age and for whom? Has this entitlement been achieved? If not, why not? Is there a timetable for when the entitlement will be achieved and/or enforceable?

2. What are common eligibility criteria for accessing publicly-funded options (*e.g.*, universal, poor, special needs, working parents)?

3. To what extent is access to ECEC a concern for a) children of certain ages; b) families living in certain geographic areas; c) children with special educational needs (*i.e.*, children with learning difficulties and/or disabilities); d) other particular groups of children and families? What are the main barriers to equitable access to ECEC for these children and families?

4. What information is available on the supply of and demand for different forms of ECEC provision? *Please include available information in table form.* Is there a mismatch between supply and demand for certain types of ECEC arrangements?

5. In practice, to what extent do parents – including low-income parents – have a choice among a variety of ECEC options? Does policy encourage parental choice or is one model of ECEC arrangements favoured?

6. What strategies have been developed to increase access to and enrolment in quality options according to family needs and parent preferences?

7. Are there particular strategies to increase ECEC access to children with special educational needs? Is there a particular effort to include these children in mainstream ECEC provision or does provision tend to be separate? What steps (*e.g.*, staff-child ratios, staff training, curriculum, on-going assessment, etc.) have been taken to make the chosen approach a success?

8. What has been the impact of existing policies on facilitating or constraining access?

Section III. Policy approaches

This section will review and analyse approaches to executing ECEC policy. To the extent possible, particularly interesting and/or innovative examples of policy and practice should be identified. In each policy area, there should be some discussion of recent and proposed changes, and the reasons for them. It would be helpful to include a discussion of how these areas are linked. Any evidence of impact of policies on addressing quality, access, and other concerns should be included. If there are other policy issues that deserve attention in this section, they may be raised as well. In responding to each question, it is essential to consider all forms of ECEC arrangements and all age groups within the scope of the review.

A. *Regulations*

1. To what extent are ECEC arrangements regulated? Are there trends toward loosening or tightening regulations? Are there other mechanisms for ensuring that children's health, safety, and development are promoted and that a certain standard of quality is maintained in ECEC arrangements?

2. Who is responsible for ECEC regulatory policy? Is the regulatory authority an independent body? Do different agencies or levels of government handle different functions? What types of provision are regulated? What types are exempt?

3. Are regulatory standards provider-focused, child-focused, facility-focused, or a combination of these? Are regulations demand-driven? What is the justification for the chosen approach? To what extent is the content of regulations uniform or variable across regions?

4. How are regulations enforced? How often are arrangements inspected? What is the professional background and training of inspectors? What sanctions are available to inspectors? How often are they imposed? In practice, is the emphasis on technical assistance or regulatory compliance?

5. What policies are in place to facilitate information sharing on the standards attained by facilities and/or providers? Who has access to information on the regulatory track records (*e.g.*, assessments, ratings, code violations, complaints) of facilities and/or providers?

6. Do non-government sponsored guidelines, standards, or voluntary accreditation programmes play a role in promoting quality ECEC arrangements?

7. How does regulatory policy in ECEC relate to regulatory policy for other social services?

B. *Staffing*

It would be helpful to include a table that synthesises the data requested on staff roles, qualifications, and fields of work.

1. What are the different staff roles found in existing forms of ECEC (*i.e.*, including home-based provision)? What are the initial training requirements/professional qualifications (*e.g.*, level and length of training) for these positions? What age range is covered by this training/education (*e.g.*, 0-3, 3-6, 0-6, 0-18, etc.)?

2. What are the aims and expectations of early childhood work and the ECEC worker? Are staff viewed as school teachers, early childhood specialists, social network experts, etc.? Do these aims and expectations vary for staff working with children of different ages? How do these understandings impact the way training systems prepare ECEC workers?

3. Are workers trained specifically for early childhood work or for a broader professional role? How is this approach to education/training reflected in course structure and content? To what extent does training/education prepare staff to work with children with special educational needs and to respect and value diversity?

4. To what extent does the structuring of the early childhood workforce, and its education/training, reflect the structure of ECEC provision? If ECEC is (or was) split between two systems, are there efforts to promote greater coherency in staff education/training? Does the current approach encourage preparation for a variety of different types of worker, including workers with different levels of training? Is there a clear role for paraprofessionals in the current staffing scheme?

5. How much and what kind of in-service or continuous training do early childhood workers receive? What are the purposes of in-service or continuous training? What are the career prospects in ECEC work? What are the opportunities for vertical/horizontal mobility?

6. Who pays for training, basic or in-service? Are there efforts to increase the availability of and access to training?

7. How are personnel prepared to take on support, management, and other positions that involve working with early childhood workers in centre-based and home-based arrangements?

8. Are there efforts to seek a more gender-mixed workforce? What is the role of training institutions in maintaining or challenging ECEC as a gendered occupation?

9. What is the professional and public status of ECEC workers? Are ECEC job profiles, training requirements, minimum qualifications, and salaries recognised in statute? To what extent are family child care providers (*i.e.* providers caring for children in the carer's home) seen as professionals? Are family child care providers organised as publicly-funded employees or do they operate as independent, self-employed service providers?

10. How does early childhood work relate to work with school-age children in schools and in care and recreation services, with regard to training, job description, compensation, status?

11. What are the average wages of ECEC staff a) just starting work and b) with several years of experience? What are the rates of staff turnover? Are there efforts to improve status/compensation and working conditions? What are the roles of trade unions or other professional associations for the early childhood workforce?

C. *Programme content and implementation*

1. What are the main philosophies or goals guiding the different forms of ECEC programmes? Are there particular people (*e.g.*, pedagogical theorists, practitioners), disciplines, experiences, or events, which have strongly influenced ECEC practice?

2. Is there a national curriculum? If so, how is it implemented? Is it interpreted as an exact method or blueprint to be followed? To what extent can and do programmes adapt the national curriculum to local needs and circumstances?

3. What are the most common curricular/pedagogical approaches found in ECEC provision? How do these relate to the main purposes and goals of ECEC?

4. What are some innovative strategies to improve programme quality? To accommodate children with special educational needs? To respect and value all kinds of diversity (*i.e.*, cultural, ethnic, linguistic, religious, gender, and disability)? To what extent are issues of diversity explicitly recognised in curriculum, guidelines, and legislation?

5. What are some of the policies and practices in place to ease transitions in the lives of children – including transitions that occur within the family, as well as transitions from home to ECEC, from one form of ECEC to another, and from ECEC to public schooling?

6. Are there efforts to promote curricular and pedagogical continuity between ECEC and the early years of primary school?

7. What linkages and partnerships exist between and among families, ECEC programmes, schools, and community services? Are there efforts to strengthen these linkages? If so, by whom and for what purpose?

D. *Family engagement and support*

In responding to these questions, please pay attention to the roles of fathers and other male family members.

1. What is the role of parents and families in ECEC? How and to what extent are parents and families engaged in their children's ECEC? Is family involvement a policy priority, and if so, for what reason? Does family engagement vary according to the form of ECEC provision?

2. What are some of the barriers to parent involvement in organised provision? Are these barriers reinforced by income, class, educational level, ethnicity, etc.? What are some strategies to overcome these barriers? To what extent are these strategies being implemented?

3. What information is available to parents and families on cost, quality, and availability of ECEC options?

4. What do parents expect from their children's ECEC? What do they expect from ECEC workers? To what extent are these expectations met?

5. How do public and private employers support parents in reconciling work and family responsibilities (*e.g.*, through parental/family leave and flexible work schedules)? Did these policies result from enacted legislation?

6. Are there specific policies (*e.g.*, long-term, supported parental/family leave, job security, etc.) to encourage parent(s) to spend more than six months out of the labour market with their children at home?

7. What types of parent education, personal development, adult or occupational education, or family support services exist to serve the needs parents and other family members? How are these services linked to ECEC provision?

8. Are there specific programme or policy approaches to support parents and families with children with special needs?

9. What is the role of community members in supporting families and ECEC? To what extent does government support and/or fund the development of community-organised approaches to providing ECEC?

E. *Funding and financing*

1. How are the costs of providing ECEC services currently shared among the following: national government, local government or other statutory bodies, parents, non-profit/non-governmental/social organisations, and business? How has this distribution changed in recent years? What are expenditures on ECEC from these sources? *Please include this information in a table.* What are some estimates for providing ECEC services to all families who wish to enrol their children?

2. What types of ECEC are funded by government at all levels? What services or components are covered by this funding? What tax benefits are available to help parents pay for ECEC? Are fees and/or benefits determined on a sliding scale according to family income? What percentage of average family income is spent on ECEC? What is considered to be the appropriate balance between universal and targeted public funding of programmes?

3. What are some strategies to a) generate revenue; b) distribute funds to programmes/parents; and c) improve staff compensation and benefit levels?

4. What are the actual or potential effects of different kinds of financing options on improving a) quality, b) access, and c) equity? Is there evidence that increased financing for ECEC helps parents move into the labour force and obtain better paying jobs?

Section IV. Evaluation and research

This section will seek to identify the processes and information sources that are used to evaluate the impact of policies and monitor changing conditions of policies.

1. What mechanisms for policy and programme evaluation are in place? What bodies promote data collection and evaluation in ECEC? What public funds are allocated for this purpose?

2. What "indicators" are available related to ECEC, and to child well-being? To what extent are these indicators used in policy development and monitoring related to ECEC? How could existing indicators be improved for this purpose?

3. What information is routinely collected on the early childhood participants, services, workforce, and systems? How and how often is this information collected? What has been learned? For what purposes is this information used? How could this process be improved? Where are the major information gaps?

4. To what extent are regular data bases available and used in policy making and monitoring?

5. What longitudinal studies are underway to study the impact of ECEC? What does research to date show to be the relationship between costs and benefits of ECEC in your country?

Section V. Concluding comments and assessments

This final section provides the authors with the opportunity to give an overall assessment of ECEC policy in the country concerned and to comment on trends or changes in policy development. Authors may choose to include a discussion of their vision for the future of ECEC policy.

1. What have been the most significant changes in ECEC policy in recent years? How successfully have ECEC systems and practice adapted to these changes?

2. What are the most noteworthy examples of innovation in the field? To what extent have they achieved notoriety? What is their national and/or international significance for ECEC?

3. What are areas of strength and weakness in current policy and practice?

4. What are some trends or changes that might be anticipated in future policy development in this area?

5. What are some questions or issues meriting further investigation?

National Co-ordinators and Members of Review Teams

(Professional affiliations at the time of the visits)

Australia

National Co-ordinator

Mr Tony Greer
Head of Schools Division
Department of Education, Training, and Youth Affairs
Canberra

(in co-operation with the Department of Family and Community Services)

Members of the Review Team for the visit 13-24 June 2000

Mr John Bennett
Consultant, Education and Training Division
Directorate for Education, Employment, Labour and Social Affairs
OECD
Paris, France

Mr Wolfgang Dichans
Head of child day care, family day care, and childhood policy
Bundesministerium für familie,
Senioren, frauen und jugend
Geschäftszeichen (Bei allen Antworten bitte angeben)
Bonn, Germany

Professor Helen May (Rapporteur)
Institute for Early Childhood Studies
Victoria University of Wellington
Wellington, New Zealand

Ms Michelle Neuman
Administrator, Education and Training Division
Directorate for Education, Employment, Labour and Social Affairs
OECD
Paris, France

Professor Mikko Ojala
University of Joensuu
Joensuu, Finland

Belgium-Flemish Community

National Co-ordinator

Ms Sonja Van Craeymeersch
Head of Division
Afdelingshoofd
Vlaamse Gemeenschap
Departement Onderwijs
Brussels

(in co-operation with Kind en Gezin)

Members of the Review Team for the visit 18-23 October 1999

Mr Boudewijn Bekkers
Former Director of Programmes
Averroes Foundation
Amsterdam, The Netherlands

Mr John Bennett
Consultant, Education and Training Division
Directorate for Education, Employment, Labour and Social Affairs
OECD
Paris, France

Ms Tarja Kahiluoto
Senior Adviser
Ministry of Social Affairs and Health
Helsinki, Finland

Ms Michelle Neuman
Administrator, Education and Training Division
Directorate for Education, Employment, Labour and Social Affairs
OECD
Paris, France

Professor Helen Penn (Rapporteur)
Department of Education and Community Studies
University of East London
Essex, United Kingdom

Belgium-French Community

National Co-ordinator

Mr Dominique Barthélémy
Directeur de la direction des relations internationales
Ministère de la Communauté française
Bruxelles

(in co-operation with Office de la Naissance et de l'Enfance)

Members of the Review Team for the visit 25-29 October 1999

Mr John Bennett
Consultant, Education and Training Division
Directorate for Education, Employment, Labour and Social Affairs
OECD
Paris, France

Ms Sylvie Rayna (Rapporteur)
Maître de conférences
Institut National de Recherche Pédagogique – CRESAS
Paris, France

Ms Isabel Lopes da Silva
Researcher
Institute of Educational Innovation
Ministry of Education
Lisbon, Portugal

Ms Michelle Neuman
Administrator, Education and Training Division
Directorate for Education, Employment, Labour and Social Affairs
OECD
Paris, France

Czech Republic

National Co-ordinators

Mr Petr Roupec
Deputy Minister for Regional Education
Ministry of Education, Youth and Sports
Prague

Dr. Jaroslav Sekot
Director
Higher School of Education and Social Care
Prague

Members of the Review Team for the visit 1-10 March 2000

Ms Josette Combes
Lecturer and Researcher
University of Toulouse le Mirail
Laboratory of Social and Cultural Ecology
Toulouse, France

Professor Lars Gunnarsson (Rapporteur)
Department of Education
University of Göteborg
Göteborg, Sweden

Dr. Márta Korintus
Head of Department and Psychologist
National Institute for Family and Social Policy
Budapest, Hungary

Ms Michelle Neuman
Administrator, Education and Training Division
Directorate for Education, Employment, Labour and Social Affairs
OECD
Paris, France

Denmark

National Co-ordinators

Ms Helle Beknes
Educational Adviser
Ministry of Education
Department of Primary and Lower Secondary Education
Division of Educational Content
Copenhagen

Ms Lisbeth Denkov
Head of Section
Ministry of Social Affairs
Copenhagen

Members of the Review Team for the visit 5-14 April 2000

Mr John Bennett
Consultant, Education and Training Division
Directorate for Education, Employment, Labour and Social Affairs
OECD
Paris, France

Ms Patrizia Orsola Ghedini
Assessorato Politiche Sociali, educative e familiari, qualita urbana, immigrazione, aiuti internazionali
Regione Emilia Romagna
Bologna, Italy

Dr. Perrine Humblet
Assistant Professor
Director, Research Unit on Children's Policy and Services
Université Libre de Bruxelles
Brussels, Belgium

Ms Michelle Neuman
Administrator, Education and Training Division
Directorate for Education, Employment, Labour and Social Affairs
OECD
Paris, France

Professor Bridie Raban (Rapporteur)
Mooroolbeek Chair of Early Childhood Education
Research Fellow
Department for Education, Training and Youth Affairs (DETYA)
Canberra, Australia

Finland

National Co-ordinators

Ms Sirkku Grierson (until June 2000)
STAKES (National Centre for Welfare, Health, Research and Development)
Helsinki

Ms Barbro Högström (from June 2000)
Senior Adviser
National Board of Education
Helsinki

Members of the Review Team for the visit 17-26 May 2000

Mr John Bennett
Consultant, Education and Training Division
Directorate for Education, Employment, Labour and Social Affairs
OECD
Paris, France

Professor Philip Gammage (Rapporteur)
de Lissa Chair in Early Childhood
University of South Australia and
Department of Education, Training and Employment
Adelaide, Australia

Ms Michelle Neuman
Administrator, Education and Training Division
Directorate for Education, Employment, Labour and Social Affairs
OECD
Paris, France

Ms Ulla Nordenstam
Director of Education
National Agency for Education
Stockholm, Sweden

Dr. Milada Rabušicová
Associate Professor
Department of Educational Studies
Faculty of Arts, Masaryk University
Brno, Czech Republic

Italy

National Co-ordinator

Mr Mario Giacomo Dutto
Director General
Ministry of Education

Members of the Review Team for the visit 8-17 March 1999

Mr Abrar Hasan
Head of Education and Training Division
Directorate for Education, Employment, Labour and Social Affairs
OECD
Paris, France

Ms Barbara Martin Korpi
Deputy Assistant Under-Secretary
Ministry of Education and Science
Stockholm, Sweden

Ms Michelle Neuman
Administrator, Education and Training Division
Directorate for Education, Employment, Labour and Social Affairs
OECD
Paris, France

Dr. Rebecca New (Rapporteur)
Associate Professor and Program Co-ordinator Early Childhood Education
Department of Education
University of New Hampshire
Durham, New Hampshire, United States

Dr. Martin Woodhead
Senior Lecturer
Milton Keynes Centre for Human Development and Learning
School of Education
The Open University
Milton Keynes, United Kingdom

Netherlands

National Co-ordinators

Mr Mark Weekenborg
Co-ordinator Youth Policy
Ministry of Education, Culture and Science
Zoetermeer

Ms Anke Vedder
Senior Policy Adviser
Ministry of Health, Welfare and Sport
The Hague

Members of the Review Team for the visit 26 October to 4 November 1998

Mr John Bennett
Consultant, Education and Training Division
Directorate for Education, Employment, Labour and Social Affairs
OECD
Paris, France

Professor Tricia David (Rapporteur)
Centre for International Studies in Early Childhood
Canterbury Christ Church College
Canterbury, United Kingdom

Mr Abrar Hasan
Head of Education and Training Division
Directorate for Education, Employment, Labour and Social Affairs
OECD
Paris, France

Mr Pino Kosiander
Assistant Professor
HiNT (Nord-Tröndelag College)
Department of Education
Early Childhood Programme
Levanger, Norway

Ms Michelle Neuman
Administrator, Education and Training Division
Directorate for Education, Employment, Labour and Social Affairs
OECD
Paris, France

Professor Teresa Vasconcelos
Director General for Basic Education
Ministry of Education
Lisbon, Portugal

Norway

National Co-ordinators

Ms Kristin Bruusgaard Arneberg (until September 2000)
Deputy Director General
Ministry of Children and Family Affairs
Oslo

Ms Eli Sundby (from September 2000)
Deputy Director General
Ministry of Children and Family Affairs
Oslo

Ms Kari Jacobsen
Adviser
Ministry of Children and Family Affairs
Oslo

Members of the Review Team for the visit 30 November to 9 December 1998

Professor Peter Moss (Rapporteur)
Thomas Coram Research Unit
Institute of Education
University of London
London, United Kingdom

Ms Michelle Neuman
Administrator, Education and Training Division
Directorate for Education, Employment, Labour and Social Affairs
OECD
Paris, France

Ms Rosemary Renwick
Senior Policy Analyst
Learning and Evaluation Policy
Ministry of Education
Wellington, New Zealand

Professor Albert Tuijnman
Institute of International Education
Stockholm University
Stockholm, Sweden

Ms Anke Vedder
Senior Policy Adviser
Ministry of Health, Welfare and Sport
The Hague, The Netherlands

Portugal

National Co-ordinator

Professor Teresa Vasconcelos
Escola Superior de Educação de Lisboa
Lisbon

Members of the Review Team for the visit 26 April to 5 May 1999

Dr. Anthony Bertram (Rapporteur)
Director
Centre for Research in Early Childhood (CREC)
University College Worcester
Worcester, United Kingdom

Dr. Jo Hermanns
Senior Advisor
Co Act Consult
Maastricht, The Netherlands

Ms Kari Jacobsen
Senior Adviser
Ministry of Children and Family Affairs
Oslo, Norway

Ms Michelle Neuman
Administrator, Education and Training Division
Directorate for Education, Employment, Labour and Social Affairs
OECD
Paris, France

Mr Patrick Werquin
Principal Administrator, Education and Training Division
Directorate for Education, Employment, Labour and Social Affairs
OECD
Paris, France

Sweden

National Co-ordinator

Ms Barbara Martin Korpi
Deputy Assistant Under-Secretary
Ministry of Education and Science
Stockholm

Members of the Review Team for the visit 9-18 June 1999

Mr John Bennett
Consultant, Education and Training Division
Directorate for Education, Employment, Labour and Social Affairs
OECD
Paris, France

Professor Sharon Lynn Kagan (Rapporteur)
Senior Associate
Yale University Bush Center in Child Development and Social Policy
New Haven, Connecticut, United States

Professor Susanna Mantovani
Presidente Corso di Laurea in Scienza della Formazione Primaria
II Università degli Studi di Milano
Milan, Italy

Ms Michelle Neuman
Administrator, Education and Training Division
Directorate for Education, Employment, Labour and Social Affairs
OECD
Paris, France

Ms Tine Rostgaard
Social Science Researcher
The Danish National Institute of Social Research
Copenhagen, Denmark

United Kingdom

National Co-ordinators

Mr Nick Blake (from March 2000)
Team Leader of Early Excellence Centres
Department of Education and Employment (DfEE)
Early Years Division
London

Mr Patrick Curran (until March 2000)
Team Leader of Early Excellence Centres
Department of Education and Employment (DfEE)
London

Members of the Review Team for the visit 1-10 December 1999

Ms Kristin Bruusgaard Arneberg
Deputy Director General
The Norwegian National Board of Education
Oslo, Norway

Professor Ferre Laevers
Catholic University of Louvain
Faculty of Pedagogic Sciences
Louvain, Belgium

Dr. Sally Lubeck (Rapporteur)
Associate Professor of Educational Studies
School of Education
University of Michigan – Ann Arbor
Ann Arbor, Michigan, United States

Ms Michelle Neuman
Administrator, Education and Training Division
Directorate for Education, Employment, Labour and Social Affairs
OECD
Paris, France

United States

National Co-ordinator

Dr. Naomi Karp
Director
National Institute on Early Childhood
Development and Education
Office of Educational Research and Improvement
US Department of Education
Washington, DC

(in co-operation with the US Department of Health and Human Services)

Members of the Review Team for the visit 27 September to 8 October 1999

Ms Jytte Juul Jensen
Senior Lecturer and International Co-ordinator
Jydsk Paedagog-Seminarium
Risskov, Denmark

Ms Michelle Neuman
Administrator, Education and Training Division
Directorate for Education, Employment, Labour and Social Affairs
OECD
Paris, France

Dr. Pamela Oberhuemer (Rapporteur)
Senior Educational Researcher
State Institute of Early Childhood Education and Research (IFP)
Munich, Germany

Mr Mark Weekenborg
Co-ordinator Youth Policy
Ministry of Education, Culture and Science
Zoetermeer, The Netherlands

Appendix 5

Commissioned Papers

GORMLEY, W. T, Jr. (July 1998),
Early Childhood Education and Care Regulation: A Comparative Perspective, Background paper prepared for the OECD Thematic Review of Early Childhood Education and Care Policy.

GROOT, W., MAASSEN VAN DEN BRINK, H. and DOBBLESTEEN, S. (June 2000),
The Economics of Early Childhood Education, Background paper prepared for the OECD Thematic Review of Early Childhood Education and Care Policy.

KAMERMAN, S. B. (May 1998),
Early Childhood Education and Care (ECEC): An Overview of Developments in the OECD Countries, Background paper prepared for the OECD Thematic Review of Early Childhood Education and Care Policy.

MOSS, P. (May 1998),
Training and Education of Early Childhood Education and Care Staff, Background paper prepared for the OECD Thematic Review of Early Childhood Education and Care Policy.

MYERS, R. G. (June 1998),
Financing Early Childhood Care and Education Services, Background paper prepared for the OECD Thematic Review of Early Childhood Education and Care Policy.

ROSTGAARD, T. (March 2000),
Developing Comparable Indicators in Early Childhood Education and Care, Background paper prepared for the OECD Thematic Review of Early Childhood Education and Care Policy.

ROSTGAARD, T. (October 2000),
Recommendations for data and indicator development for ECEC systems, Background paper prepared for the OECD Thematic Review of Early Childhood Education and Care Policy.

VERRY, D. (July 1998),
Some Economic Aspects of Early Childhood Education and Care, Background paper prepared for the OECD Thematic Review of Early Childhood Education and Care Policy.

Appendix 6

Country Codes Used in Tables and Charts

Thematic Review Countries	Code
Australia	AUS
Belgium	BEL
Czech Republic	CZE
Denmark	DNK
Finland	FIN
Italy	ITA
Netherlands	NLD
Norway	NOR
Portugal	PRT
Sweden	SWE
United Kingdom	UKM
United States	USA

OECD PUBLICATIONS, 2, rue André-Pascal, 75775 PARIS CEDEX 16
PRINTED IN FRANCE
(91 2001 01 1 P) ISBN 92-64-18675-1 – No. 51815 2001